Ethnography for the Internet

Ethnography for the Internet:

Embedded, Embodied and Everyday

Christine Hine

Routledge
Taylor & Francis Group

LONDON AND NEW YORK

First published 2015 by Bloomsbury Academic

Published 2020 by Routledge
2 Park Square, Milton Park, Abingdon, Oxon OX14 4RN
605 Third Avenue, New York, NY 10017

Routledge is an imprint of the Taylor & Francis Group, an informa business

A catalogue record for this book is available from the British Library.

ISBN 13: 978-0-85785-504-6 (hbk)
ISBN 13: 978-0-85785-570-1 (pbk)

Library of Congress Cataloging-in-Publication Data
Hine, Christine.
Ethnography for the Internet : embedded, embodied
and everyday / Christine Hine.
pages cm
ISBN 978-0-85785-504-6 (hardback) – ISBN 978-0-85785-570-1 (paperback)
1. Internet–Social aspects. 2. Internet users.
3. Ethnology–Research–Methodology. I. Title.
HM851.H558 2015
302.23'1–dc23
2014036734

Typeset by Fakenham Prepress Solutions, Fakenham, Norfolk, NR21 8NN

Contents

List of Illustrations

Acknowledgments

The thoughts presented in this book have developed over many years, and it is therefore impossible to note all of the people who have helped along the way with useful comments and insights on ways to study the Internet. I apologize, therefore, for not thanking many people individually. I am conscious that I owe a huge debt both to the many colleagues in academic circles that I have interacted with and discussed these ideas with over the years, and also to the many participants in the field sites I describe in Chapters 4, 5, and 6, many of whom gave generously of their insights and were willing to give up substantial time and effort in order to help me to understand what was going on from their point of view. I am particularly conscious of a debt owed to Nicola Green for an introduction to Freecycle and for many enlightening conversations about it along the way, to Vince Smith for sharing his vision of the possibilities and perils of cybertaxonomy, and to Thordis Sveinsdottir for fascinating insights into what immersive online fieldwork could be. The fieldwork described in Chapter 5 was funded by the Economic and Social Research Council grant R000271262-A.

Although I cannot list here all of the academic conferences and workshops that made a difference to my thinking about ethnography for the Internet, I'd like to mention three events in particular that stand out in my mind. Nanna Schneidermann and Elizabeth Williams Ørberg with Steffen Dalsgaard organized a workshop on Facebook: Fieldwork at Aarhus University, and I gained an enormous amount of insight from hearing about the experiences of participants at that meeting. Janet Vertesi brought together a fascinating array of scholars for a meeting on the Ethnographer in the Network at Princeton University, and again, discussions with participants at this meeting were hugely stimulating. Finally, the series of workshops on Digital Methods as Mainstream Methodology (http://digitalmethodsnmi.com/) funded as a Network for Methodological Innovation by the ESRC National Centre for Research Methods and organized by Steve Roberts, Yvette Morey, Helene Snee and Hayley Watson provided a series of really useful occasions for meeting with like-minded scholars and hearing about some fascinating examples of digital research.

As ever, I owe a debt of gratitude to my family: to Simon for forbearance and support in the face of another *&*!%! **%!^! book, and to Esther and Isaac for accepting me being boring at weekends and for allowing me to hog the computer when it should really be being used for watching videos of pandas falling out of trees or for playing Club Penguin.

Christine Hine

−1−

Introduction

From one point of view, that of the textbook, doing ethnography is establishing rapport, selecting informants, transcribing texts, taking genealogies, mapping fields, keeping a diary, and so on. But it is not these things, techniques and received procedures that define the enterprise. What defines it is the kind of intellectual effort it is: an elaborate venture in, to borrow a notion from Gilbert Ryle, "thick description."

(Geertz 1973: 6)

Doing ethnography is like trying to read (in the sense of "construct a reading of") a manuscript—foreign, faded, full of ellipses, incoherencies, suspicious emendations, and tendentious commentaries, but written not in conventionalized graphs of sound but in transient examples of shaped behaviour.

(Geertz 1973: 10)

ETHNOGRAPHY FOR THE CONTEMPORARY INTERNET

This book is an exploration of some steps we can take to adapt the already complex and tricky process of conducting ethnography in pursuit of "thick descriptions" to suit the conditions of contemporary society, in particular the conditions created by the increasing saturation of everyday life with various forms of computer-mediated communication. Ethnography is prized as a method for getting to the heart of meaning and enabling us to understand, in the round and in depth, how people make sense of their lives. It certainly promises, then, to give us a way to get to grips with some recurrent and topical questions. Has the Internet changed our lives? Has it, fundamentally, changed us? Has it levelled the playing field of social inequality, or have new forms of privilege emerged? Are we conforming more, or less, to social norms in the age of the Internet? Has the Internet strengthened, enriched, or challenged our sense of community? Has the Internet engendered new forms of identity or enabled us to better be ourselves? The ethnographic focus on holistic understanding seems well suited to giving us answers to these questions and helping us to avoid glib simplification. It is also very well suited to giving us a critical stance on over-generalized assumptions about the impact of new technologies. Taking a multi-faceted view, as ethnographers do, and focusing on how lives are lived, how technologies are adopted and adapted to our lives, and how social structures are made seems a promising way to capture what is distinctive about our contemporary way of life, and what is enduring about the challenges we face, and our means of coping with them.

However, what seems at first sight obvious—that ethnographers can usefully give accounts of the modes of life that emerge around computer-mediated communications—becomes more problematic when we start to think about where we are going to send our ethnographers, and what they will do when they get there. The feeling that things might have changed, which prompts the ethnographic interest, at the same time raises challenges for the formulation of ethnographic projects that will truly deliver on the promise to provide the depth of understanding that ethnography allows. It is the core proposition of this book that solving these challenges and delivering on that promise requires some creative adaptations of the ethnographic method. Making these adaptations may take us a long way from a conventional form of ethnography, but I would argue that even though we may change our strategies, it is still possible, in the process, to retain a commitment to some fundamental principles of ethnography as a distinctive mode of knowledge production. In the rest of this book I will be outlining why these strategies are required, demonstrating where they are novel and how they relate to fundamental methodological principles, and illustrating through case studies how these adaptive strategies can help us to illuminate the contemporary social arrangements that arise in and around the Internet. The remainder of this introduction will outline the structure of the book, and describe the contemporary Internet, which provides the stimulus and the challenge for finding new ways of being ethnographic. This Internet is very different, in many ways, from the Internet that I wrote about in *Virtual Ethnography* in 2000 (Hine 2000), and yet it is also recognizably the same: I will therefore highlight along the way some key points where the approach developed here builds on and deviates from that earlier text, written for a previous Internet age.

It should be said at the outset that I would reject any notion that mediated communication is in some way not appropriate or sufficient as a medium for conducting an ethnographic study. Ethnography, to be sure, was originally founded on the premise that it was important to go and spend time with people, to interact with them and live amongst them, and to develop a first-hand understanding of their way of life. Ethnographic understanding was developed in close proximity, and the early ethnographers shunned the notion that one could rely solely on hearsay and secondary accounts. This foundational commitment to participation and development of first-hand knowledge may render the prospect of conducting an ethnographic study through mediated communications somewhat troubling. Indeed, to rely on only one medium when the participants involved have many different ways of communicating and representing themselves to each other could be problematic, and could jeopardize that holistic, rounded understanding that ethnographers aim to develop. But this does not, in itself, mean that ethnographers should not take part in mediated communications when that is what the people that they are studying do. Where mediated communications are a significant part of what people do, I feel it should be self-evident that the ethnographer needs to take part in those mediated communications alongside whatever face-to-face interactions may occur, as well as taking note of any other forms of document and recording that circulate amongst participants. In subsequent chapters I will be exploring the different kinds of contribution that an ethnographer's participation in mediated communications can make to his or her understanding, and how different forms of understanding gained from different media can be reconciled, or maintained in a productive tension.

It is important, then, for ethnographers to take part in the diverse forms of communication and interaction that those they study use and not to write off any of these forms of communication as inherently less informative or as un-ethnographic. Acceptance of this point does, however, cause some problems for an ethnographic project, because it challenges the ethnographer's ability to make sense of situations as a unified whole. Mediated communications are troubling for ethnographers because they often seem to leave us unable to comprehend a situation as a singular entity with all of its ramifications and to find out what it means for its participants. We cannot be simultaneously with both of the participants in a telephone conversation and thus we will only see the changing facial expressions, the multi-tasking activities and the post-conversation response from one perspective. When one of our informants updates his status on Facebook, he may tell us what he meant by it, but we cannot be quite sure what his friends make of what he writes, nor indeed which of his friends may even have seen the status update any more than, as Geertz (1973) reminds us, we can understand from observation of the action alone what is meant when we see someone close one eye to wink. When we watch a fight break out on Twitter we cannot be sure whether any of the followers of those involved are seeing the same fight, at the same time, and understanding it in the same way that we do. The very notion of a singular "situation" as a pre-existing object breaks down when we look closely. The Internet has brought us together in myriad new ways, but still much of the interpretive work that goes on to embed it into people's lives is not apparent on the Internet itself, as its users weave together highly individualized and complex patterns of meaning out of these publicly observable threads of interaction. An ethnographer in such circumstances must get used to a perpetual feeling of uncertainty, of wondering what has been missed, and attempting to build interpretations of events based on sketchy evidence.

Of course, it has always been true that ethnographers are limited in their ability to see and participate in events. Even in a village, conducting a conventional study based on face-to-face interactions over a prolonged period of time, an ethnographer will be making close connections with one family whilst wondering what is going on in the house next door. Even without bringing mediated communication into the mix, ethnographers were limited in their ability to encompass the whole of the situation: ethnography is conducted on a scale determined by the human perceptual capacity. However much an ethnographer tries, she cannot be omniscient, and some aspects of the situation she studies will always escape her understanding. The concern, then, is an old-established one that predates the advent of mediated communication. However, the turn to mediated communication on such a dominant scale does bring a new complexity to ethnographic proceedings, and raises a very real concern that the limitations on perception within a mediated landscape might threaten the contribution made by ethnographic enquiry or limit the ethnographer's ability to draw robust conclusions. Ethnographers cannot help but be affected by the general cultural current of concern that mediated communications might not be quite as good as the real thing, and hence develop an uneasiness about the robustness of the forms of knowledge that might be acquired by these means.

It appears, then, that contemporary ethnographers are stuck in a very awkward situation. Some very significant things, culturally speaking, are happening, and ethnographers should be well placed to develop insightful, detailed, and complex accounts of exactly what is going on and what it means. Mediated communication is a highly significant part of many contemporary phenomena of interest, and while ethnography has conventionally favored face-to-face communication, ethnographers exploring these contemporary phenomena would generally wish to embrace mediated communication and understand how these diverse modes of interaction contribute to the cultural milieu. Whatever it is that people do, an ethnographer would generally want to be observing them doing it, and wherever possible doing it with them. Embracing mediated communication means, however, accepting the limits to perception that various forms of mediation confer, and accommodating some consequent loss of ability to develop a holistic and detailed understanding. Doing ethnography through mediated interactions can mean the loss of a secure sense of a geographically based object of study, or involve abandoning the notion that one studies a defined social group or community, depending on how the patterns of communication cross geographic spaces and social boundaries. Ethnography is highly necessary for understanding the Internet in all its depth and detail, and yet it can be challenging to develop ways of conducting ethnographic studies which both embrace all that mediated communication offers and still provide us with robust, reliable insights into something in particular.

Ethnography of mediated communications thus seems to be both necessary and doomed, simultaneously. We need ethnography in order to help us understand what is going on, but the very nature of the change taking place seems to evade ethnographic understanding. There is hope, however, because ethnography is at its heart a highly adaptive approach that suits itself to the conditions that it finds. An ethnographic study cannot be wholly designed in advance, for the methods of inquiry that an ethnographer develops are uniquely suited to the specific situation being studied. It is a boot-strapping method, which builds itself afresh in each location, based upon the ethnographer's emerging understanding of the situation. If we accept, therefore, that in some circumstances living with a lack of certainty and an enduring ambiguity about what things mean is an inherent part of the conditions in which participants find themselves, then experiencing and embracing that uncertainty becomes an ethnographer's job, and pursuing some form of absolute robust certainty about a singular research object becomes a distraction, and even a threat, to the more significant goal of working out just how life is lived under these conditions in which such stability is at best a very temporary achievement. The paradox then slips away—an ethnographer can focus best on understanding modes of life through immersion in them, learning their values and practices from the inside, and focusing on making active and strategic choices about what to study and how to study it.

This book is focused on ethnography *for* the Internet, rather than ethnography *of* the Internet, because the Internet cannot be grasped as a complete entity that one could study in its entirety. One cannot do an ethnography *of* the Internet as a meaningful research object in itself, although many potential research objects can be made from it, and are either contained within it or connected to it in some way. This book is also not focused solely on ethnography *through* the Internet, because in order to understand mediated communications one is also often led to study face-to-face settings in which they are produced and consumed, and to comprehend the settings in which they become embedded. The book focuses instead on ethnography *for* the Internet because ethnography is an adaptive approach that is different for each circumstance in which it finds itself, and I am discussing the strategies that may be useful in an ethnography adapted for the circumstances that the contemporary Internet provides. In the next section I will briefly describe some significant aspects of that contemporary Internet, before moving to a more detailed account of the distinctive forms of knowledge that an ethnographic approach to the contemporary Internet can provide.

THE CONTEMPORARY INTERNET

As the twenty-first century moves into its teens, the Internet has become a mass phenomenon. According to the biennial Oxford Internet Survey, which draws on a representative sample of the UK population, the proportion of UK individuals with Internet access reached 78 percent of the population over 14 in 2013 (Dutton et al. 2013). This figure has steadily risen since the Oxford Internet Surveys began in 2003, when 59 percent of the population claimed to be Internet users. There remain, however, a small percentage who have never used the Internet and cannot see themselves doing so, and there is also a small but significant number of ex-users of the Internet. In 2003 there was also a significant gender gap, with 64 percent of men and 55 percent of women claiming to be Internet users. By 2013 this gender gap was no longer statistically discernible, with 79 percent of women and 78 percent of men in the survey using the Internet, a difference within the error margin of the data. There are, however, some more enduring inequalities, with likelihood of being an Internet user correlating to age, level of formal education, and income. In the UK the Internet demographic, as captured by the Oxford Internet Survey (Dutton et al. 2013), reflects a national population for whom various kinds of opportunity are structured by education and access to resources. The Internet is a mass phenomenon, but it is not universally available, and there are still some underlying inequalities that structure access.

A similar picture of a steadily growing Internet population plays out across the globe, although the proportion of users in different countries does differ widely, depending on such factors as economic resources, technological infrastructure, and literacy levels. The International Telecommunications Union estimated that in 2011 Internet penetration globally was 32.5 percent of the population, but that this overall statistic broke down into Internet penetration of 70.2 percent across the developed countries and 24.4

percent in the developing world (International Telecommunications Union 2012). The differences can be very stark indeed. Data from the International Telecommunications Union for 2012 had levels of Internet penetration across Scandinavia at over 90 percent of the population, whilst many nations in Africa and Asia were listed as having less than 20 percent of their population online. This International Telecommunications Union report also estimated that less than 2 percent of individuals in Somalia, Ethiopia, Sierra Leone, and Guinea had access to the Internet (International Telecommunications Union 2012). The Internet is indeed a mass phenomenon in North America, Europe, and Australia, but much less so in Africa and much of Asia, and in many areas of the globe is still completely out of reach as a practical proposition for much of the population.

In much of the world, then, the Internet is a mass phenomenon, but this is still very much dependent on national context. There are places in the world where one may be able comfortably to assume Internet access among almost everyone one meets, whilst there are other countries where one would struggle, outside of major cities, to find anyone who had access to the Internet. For an ethnographer it is important to note that the Internet is not always seen as an accessible phenomenon, and to be aware that there will be an accompanying diversity in the cultural connotations of Internet access and lack of access. In some areas *not* to have Internet access is a norm, whilst elsewhere is might be seen as a marker of extreme poverty, or as a marked act of rejection of the modern age.

Even in those areas where the Internet is a mass phenomenon, this need not imply that everyone has the same experience of the Internet, nor expects the same things from it. In their report on the 2011 Oxford Internet Survey, Dutton and Blank (2011) identified the emergence of the "next generation Internet users" as a group of people who have a markedly different relationship to the technology from the first-generation users (who continue to co-exist with the next generation). Next-generation Internet users made up 44 percent of UK Internet users in the 2011 Oxford Internet Survey and 67 percent of users in the 2013 survey (Dutton et al. 2013), this group being defined as those who access the Internet from multiple locations and on multiple devices. This group of users are distinctive in what they do with the Internet: they upload more content than the first generation users who are more tied to single locations and devices, and they have integrated the Internet more thoroughly into their leisure and entertainment, downloading music and watching videos online more often. Whilst there are many similarities between first-generation and next-generation Internet users, with both groups increasingly seeing the Internet as their first port of call for information-seeking, there are also indications that there are some fundamental differences between their expectations of the Internet and their experiences of it.

The Internet is, therefore, scarce in some parts of the world, but in many places it is becoming a mass phenomenon that is taken for granted. Even within those places where it is available to the majority, it is also potentially a fragmented phenomenon, with different sectors of the population accessing it on different devices, doing different things with it, and expecting different things of it. Alongside the trend of massification that has occurred in many countries and is underway in others, there is therefore also a trend of fragmentation into different kinds of experience. Ethnography for the Internet therefore has to proceed quite cautiously in finding out what the phenomenon "Internet" represents for the particular group of people who are the site of interest in any given study. It is important to think particularly carefully about the extent to which Internet use is standard within a population, what its cultural connotations are, and how the devices that are available to access it shape what it means to people. No single solution to doing ethnography for the Internet will be found, because what the Internet is can vary so dramatically.

In areas where the Internet has become a mass phenomenon it has also, to some extent, become banal. It can be difficult to find people talking about the Internet, as such, in everyday settings because it has become a part of everyday life, a taken-for-granted means of being and doing, socializing, shopping, and passing time, rather than a marked activity of "going on to the Internet." The Internet has often become an infrastructure that underpins the things that people do, rather than a foregrounded activity that they do in its own right. People often talk much more naturally about individual applications, like Facebook, Twitter, or email, than they do the Internet, as such. As we have generally become more accepting of the things that people do on the Internet as being real, socially meaningful activities, the fact that those things happen on the Internet has in itself become less notable. In the early days of the Internet it was often common to talk of the Internet as a "cyberspace," remote from everyday experience. It was at that point still a matter of debate and commentary whether activities that people carried out there were legitimate forms of social activity. It would, in those early days of the Internet, still often be thought a matter for concern if someone talked about "online friends," and it would at that point certainly occasion significant comment if two people announced that they had met and fallen in love on the Internet. Such stigmatization of online intimacy can still occur, but it happens alongside an matter-of-fact acceptance of buying a book online, downloading a song, checking insurance quotes, or joining a dating site as fairly ordinary things that anyone might do without needing to highlight that they had done them online.

The Internet is thus often banal in everyday life to the extent that in contexts where its use is commonplace we do not often foreground it as we go about using it in our everyday activities. The underlying technology which enables the diverse forms of data circulation, accumulation, and communication that go on becomes very remote from everyday experience. Some scholars make it their business to re-foreground the Internet and the various technologies that enable it, highlighting the extent to which it provides a form of social ordering and social differentiation. They argue that there is a risk that this process of banalization (Graham 2004) may blind us to undesirable elements of the new infrastructure, or involve us acquiescing involuntarily with unwelcome aspects of these new forms of data circulation (Beer 2013), or lead us into accepting without due question particular notions of how social relations should be organized, which become embedded in software (Mackenzie 2006). These scholars highlight aspects of new technological infrastructures which may do invisible work on a social level, shaping behaviors and embedding inequalities.

The Internet is now frequently taken for granted and overlooked in everyday existence, and these scholarly activities take responsibility for foregrounding potentially significant aspects. Another, more widely accessible, form of topicalization goes on in news stories. Contemporary news media, on television and in print, tend to assume that the Internet is familiar and available to their audience. They reinforce a notion of a banal Internet which is a taken-for-granted way of accessing information and entertainment. At the same time, the Internet remains a fruitful source of stories for the mass media, which often highlight the remarkable qualities of the Internet as a site for social activities. Figure 1.1 shows a small and unsystematic sample of headlines covering a range of such different circumstances in which newspapers topicalized the Internet, in the summer of 2013. These news headlines focusing on the Internet highlight concerns about the extent of Internet access and the potential for social exclusion, alongside worries about dangers of online pedophilia and Internet pornography, the possibility of control and the prevalence of censorship in other parts of the world, and the role of the Internet in sustaining, or potentially threatening, intimate relationships.

Politicians want to control the Internet *The Evening Standard* (London), July 23, 2013
Public ban on Internet porn *The Independent* (London), July 1, 2013
Paedophile who posed as pop star on Internet to target girls is jailed *Yorkshire Post*, September 17, 2013
Millions shun the Internet *The Express*, August 9, 2013
China renews fight to control the Internet *The Daily Telegraph* (London), August 26, 2013
Iran: Filtering Internet futile, says president-elect *The Guardian* (London) – Final Edition, July 3, 2013
Facebook founder's mission to bring Internet to the whole world *Yorkshire Post*, August 22, 2013
Man groomed schoolgirls on Internet sites *The Northern Echo*, July 20, 2013
Terry Gilliam blames Internet for the breakdown in "real relationships" guardian.co.uk, September 2, 2013
Internet "vital" for care homes *The Herald* (Glasgow), August 19, 2013
Jurors warned over research; Internet contempt *The Daily Telegraph* (London), July 31, 2013

Figure 1.1   A selection of headlines from UK newspapers in the summer of 2013

In these headlines the Internet is topicalized as a site of both opportunity and risk, and as a significant agent in various social situations. The precise form the issues take is specific to the Internet in 2013, as a mass phenomenon with significant persistent inequalities, and an increasingly global technology. The issues are not, however, dramatically different from those which were raised in relation to the Internet of 2000, at a time when only 28 percent of U.K. adults claimed to have access to the Internet at home, according to an Oftel survey (Oftel 2000). Figure 1.2 shows an unsystematic sample of newspaper headlines from the summer of 2000. An air of novelty pervades the coverage, as denoted by a focus on developing trust and learning skills, and a concern with whether the Internet is reaching its full potential or peaking in significance. The headlines tend to focus on the U.K., in contrast to the global significance of the Internet as depicted in 2013. The notions of risk and of opportunity are, however, familiar. The Internet of 2000 and the Internet of 2013, on the basis of this very crude comparison, are not radically different. Similar themes persist in the association of the Internet with various forms of economic and social opportunity, and with diverse risks and dangers, accompanied by persistent concerns regarding who has access, and who is or should be in control of what happens online.

Bid to build trust in the Internet *Express & Echo* (Exeter), July 18, 2000
Father of Internet defends e-commerce *Aberdeen Press and Journal,* September 18, 2000
Learn to surf the Internet *Evening Herald* (Plymouth), September 12, 2000
Internet take-up slowing down *Evening Times* (Glasgow), August 11, 2000
Suspected Internet bank hackers released on police bail *Evening News* (Edinburgh), August 23, 2000
Corrs lead pop stars into war on the Internet's cyber shoplifters *The Express,* July 14, 2000
Sold to the quicker clicker; buying and selling over the internet has never been easier or more cost-effective. David Emery looks at the world of the online auction *The Evening Standard* (London), July 7, 2000
Judges log on for first Internet cases *The Independent* (London), June 28, 2000
Pervert banker caught in trap; lured by child porn on net *Daily Record,* September 20, 2000

Figure 1.2   A selection of headlines from UK newspapers in the summer of 2000

Whilst we have a banal Internet that many of us use to go about our daily business, we thus also have a topicalized Internet, which becomes a focus for expressions of hope and anxiety and a site for making moral judgments about the kind of world we ought to live in. Some of our expectations of what the Internet may mean for us come from very localized experiences, as we learn how to use it from friends, workmates, and family, and learn from them not just what to do, but what it is deemed acceptable, normal, and desirable to do. Beyond our own individualized experiences, however, the mass media do a lot to reflect the Internet back to us, building a cultural object, "the Internet," invested with hopes, fears, and expectations.

The Internet thus exists as much as a cultural object as it is a practical way of doing things we want to do. This cultural object is somewhat recognizable as a stable object over the course of the last decade and more, even though the individual things one can do with it have changed. One significant regard in which the expectations of the Internet may have changed more radically, however, is the notion of the Internet as a place where ordinary people can "have their say." In recent years it has become increasingly easy for people to upload their own content and be an active part of the web environment, with the proliferation of social networking sites, discussion forums, rating and review sites, and blogs. Captured in the popular phrase "Web 2.0" (O'Reilly 2005), the idea of a second wave of Internet development focused on participation has been influential in characterizing a changing set of expectations about the relationship between ordinary users and the Internet. Sociologically speaking, this development is particularly interesting because it offers the potential to radically reshape relations of expertise, positioning ordinary people as experts (Eysenbach 2008a, 2008b), and sidelining traditional sites of authority.

The term Web 2.0 may not stand up to close scrutiny as delineating the original uses of the Internet from those we have now. Many of the strands of the current participatory Internet can be seen in the discussion forums that developed very early on in the Internet's history, and, conversely, there are still plenty of static web pages around. A strict delineation of the Internet then and now is difficult to sustain. However, the term does have some usefulness, largely because it has been so resonant for so many people. This lauding of the development of a participatory web (Blank and Reisdorf 2012) is significant as much for the reshaping of our expectations around the relationship between the Internet and ordinary users as it is because it might describe the actual, specific uses we may make of the Internet. I may not, personally, contribute much to the participatory web: I have a tiny social networking presence, I don't tweet much, and I rarely provide online reviews about products I've bought or places that I've been. The idea that the Internet is a participatory space is, however, very significant to me in that I think of the Internet as a place where someone like me might contribute, and that expectation shapes the way that I read Internet content. Even though I might not myself be participating very actively, as a passive reader, my reading is shaped by the expectation that this is a participatory space. Thinking of the Internet as a participatory space enables me to see myself mirrored in it, and encourages me to calibrate myself against it. Shifts in the Internet as a cultural object thus have the capacity to influence not just the active things that we do online, but also a wider set of expectations about what we might do and what that would mean. These expectations shape our interpretation of the world that we encounter online.

The ethnographer of the Internet is thus confronted with a very complex and confusing domain. People make many different things of the Internet, and they suffuse it with diverse cultural meanings depending on their direct experiences of it; the tales they tell of it with their friends, family, and workmates, and the stories they receive about it from mass media. They use it to sustain social interactions across expanses of space and time, and in real-time with people in the next room. The Internet is multi-spatial, in the various new forms of space that emerge online, the connections that it enables across geographic spaces, and the forms of mobility that its users engage in as they encounter it on multiple devices. The experience of the Internet spans different forms of temporality, as we engage in interactions that are sometimes persistent and archived for the long term, and at other points as fleeting, immediate, and ephemeral as a chat on a street corner.

All of these aspects of the Internet are very interesting cultural phenomena to document, crying out for a detailed ethnographic engagement to work out what they mean and how they shape our contemporary notions of subjectivity, personhood, and sociality. The Internet needs ethnography, but those very factors that make it fascinating are also challenging for ethnographers, as they seek to find coherent ways to carve out a researchable object from the mass of temporal and spatial complexity and the interweaving social and cultural processes that create the Internet and embed it in everyday life. The Internet is inherently diverse, flexible, and heterogeneous, and thus demands an adaptive, situated, methodological response. Some inventive methodological strategies are required to enable us to explore the textures of social life which result as people combine online and offline experiences in complex, and unpredictable fashion.

DOING ETHNOGRAPHY FOR THE INTERNET

In the next chapter I begin making a case for understanding the Internet as an embedded, embodied, everyday phenomenon (for shorthand, the E^3 Internet), which we can illuminate by giving it serious ethnographic examination. These qualities of the contemporary Internet make it a particularly intriguing object to study, but at the same time they make demands of our methodological agility. Chapter 2 begins with a review of the potential contribution of ethnography to understanding the Internet, and then deals with each of the three aspects of the contemporary Internet in turn, reviewing recent literature and highlighting consequent methodological challenges. First, I outline the grounds for thinking of the Internet as an embedded phenomenon. The Internet is often not experienced as a transcendent "cyberspace" in contemporary society, but has become something which is embedded into people's lives in ways which are meaningful within specific contexts (Bakardjieva 2005). This embedded Internet poses a methodological challenge in that the frames of meaning-making which the ethnographer is required to pursue are initially unpredictable, often diverse, and can require considerable agility of method and mobility of focus. Second, I turn to the embodied Internet. Again, rather than being a transcendent cyberspatial site of experience, the Internet has increasingly become a part of us. Often we do not think of "going online" as a discrete form of experience, but we find ourselves being online in an extension of other embodied ways of being and acting in the world. This section will explore the extent to which experience of the online environment has become seamlessly integrated with other embodied experiences. I also reflect on the tensions between the public portrayal of a universal "Internet" and the very personalized experiences we may have, using Tsing's work on the friction between the universal and the specific (Tsing 2005).The methodological challenge is to recognize the consequent diversity and highly personal nature of the online experience, suggesting a shift towards recognition of the ontological diversity of the Internet and an embrace of reflexive and autoethnographic methods as a valuable component of a virtual ethnography.

The third methodologically challenging aspect of the contemporary Internet for consideration is the everydayness of our experiences of the online. It follows from the literature reviewed thus far that much Internet usage can be portrayed as mundane and unremarkable, as increasingly we simply deploy it as a way of doing what makes sense to us rather than marking it as an exceptional way of doing things. The Internet can, in fact, disappear as a remarkable facet of everyday life, as it becomes simply an infrastructure which offers a means to do other things. This section reviews work on the sociology of infrastructure (Bowker and Star 1999; Star 1999) and fluid technologies (De Laet and Mol 2000) to argue that the everyday Internet remains a highly significant technology and cultural site worthy of serious anthropological and sociological attention. The resulting methodological challenge is to capture and make visible such aspects of the Internet as have become unremarkable, and to examine the specificity of circumstances in which the Internet comes back into the cultural foreground, often as a notable phenomenon for political or media attention.

Following on from this outline of the particularly challenging qualities of the contemporary Internet for an ethnographer, Chapter 3 then moves on to outline some strategies for dealing with these challenges. The chapter draws on examples derived from a range of ethnographic studies focused around the Internet, in order to cover situations ranging from wholly online ethnographic studies in virtual worlds to cross-platform approaches and studies of mobile Internet experiences mediated by smartphone apps. The first section of the chapter focuses on the question of field sites, exploring in practical detail how the ethnographer decides where to go. Part of the challenge of exploring the everyday Internet is that we cannot readily conceive of the Internet as a singular object contained within one site. Drawing on multi-sited ethnography (Marcus 1995), mobile methods (Buscher and Urry 2009), and literature from science and technology studies focusing on the ontological multiplicity of objects (De Laet and Mol 2000; Mol 2002), this section formulates a strategy for exploring the emergence of Internet use as a meaningful practice across online and offline sites. This approach dwells on the importance of the ethnographer's developing sensitivity to the various possibilities of connection that different modes of presence and interaction offer, and argues for the importance of attention to the varying texture of social existence which comes from some forms of connection presenting themselves as obvious and easy, whilst others are hidden from us or difficult to make. Mobile strategies benefit from a reflexive attention to where the ethnographer is able to move and which avenues appear to be blocked off.

This discussion of the process of identifying field sites leads into an exploration of the activities the ethnographer carries out when he gets there. A standard ethnographic repertoire of learning-by-doing, observation, recording activities and archiving documents, and interviewing key informants still applies within ethnographic studies of diffuse, multi-sited, and multi-modal activities, but some creative adaptations may be required. Following on from the understanding of the contemporary world as connected in diverse ways, comprised of multiple modes of presence and interaction, it is also useful to have some creative ways of understanding where we stand and what territory we inhabit. The everyday Internet offers a wide diversity of experiences and an overwhelming array of information and interaction, which is an issue for the everyday Internet user as well as a methodological challenge for the ethnographer. Social research has in recent years developed inventive ways of sorting through the wealth of data that online interactions make available, deploying a range of methods of aggregation and visualization which might not in themselves be ethnographic, but are yet compatible with an ethnographic urge to understand the object of inquiry from multiple perspectives.

In particular, the work of Thelwall (2004, 2009) and Rogers (2013) is provocative for strategies to orient an ethnographic engagement with the Internet. In addition to these dedicated tools for social research, the various ready-to-hand tools that any Internet user could use for navigating and visualizing the online world are particularly interesting in this regard. It is proposed that the tools provided to help the everyday Internet user cope with this vast and diverse information ecology, offering various forms of visualization, summary, search, and analysis, provide ready-to-hand tools for the virtual ethnographer, provided due attention is given to the extent to which these technologies shape experiences through hidden assumptions. This section also explores the role of archives in ethnography, and the extent to which ethnographic engagement can usefully extend beyond real-time interactions.

The next section discusses recent developments in reflexive ethnography and autoethnography as a response to the challenge offered by the embodied nature of the Internet and its tendency to embed itself as an everyday part of other institutions and activities. The very individualized experience of the Internet suggests that we can usefully draw on reflexive ethnography (Davies 2012) and developments in autoethnographic research (Ellis 2004) to explore the researcher's own embodied and embedded experience as a source of methodological insight. This section builds on and develops arguments advanced in *Virtual Ethnography* (Hine 2000), which suggested that the ethnographer can usefully draw on her own experiences as a source of insight into the unresolvable uncertainties and tensions that can be a part of the Internet experience. Autoethnography has, however, also been a somewhat controversial development, and in discussing the application of this strategy to Internet ethnography I will also be discussing potential concerns such as overindulgence in the ethnographer's own insights and the potential lack of corroborative evidence. In a final section of the chapter I then look back to the "principles of virtual ethnography" outlined in Hine (2000) and ask to what extent the strategies outlined here are in line with those principles. This final section of the chapter presents a set of methodological principles, attending to the opportunities and challenges offered both by contemporary methodological developments and by the contemporary E^3 Internet.

Chapter 4 forms the first of three that bring the methodological principles to life with specific examples from the author's primary research. Discussing a specific substantive focus enables me to demonstrate in detail the ongoing adaptation of ethnographic strategies to emerging circumstances that characterizes ethnography. Each of these chapters ends with some points for reflection, highlighting the choices made and encouraging the reader to explore how he or she might translate them to other substantive domains.

This first substantive chapter discusses research based on Freecyle, Freegle, and other related mailing lists that enable the free exchange of unwanted goods which would otherwise be destined for landfill. The chapter evaluates a range of ethnographic strategies I have used to contribute to understanding the phenomenon, including autoethnography, email interviews, face-to-face interviews, and observation of online discussions about Freecycle and Freegle in various contexts, including both the lists themselves and parallel conversations on Mumsnet, and on Facebook and Twitter. The chapter will demonstrate that autoethnography is a powerful tool for exploring the ambiguities and uncertainties inherent in Internet usage, but that reliance on autoethnography alone limits insights into the embedding of Internet use in diverse sites of meaning-making.

Chapter 5, the second example-based chapter, makes the case for a connective and multi-faceted ethnographic strategy to explore a phenomenon enacted in diverse sites connected in multiple and complex ways. The approach includes use of ready-to-hand tools for Internet exploration, supplemented by pursuit of emergent connections between different sites and sources of interpretation. It particularly stresses the significance of understanding institutional structures, regulatory frameworks, and disciplinary cultures as they are enacted in and form a backdrop to everyday practices. The examples are drawn from ethnographic research on the development of e-science in biology (Hine 2007, 2008).

Chapter 6 explores the potential of use of the Internet as a form of unobtrusive method (Lee 2000; Hine 2011a) for exploring mundane aspects of everyday life. In particular, it focuses on the novel potential that the Internet offers to an ethnographer interested in understanding how people interpret television and embed it into their everyday lives. The Internet, it is argued, offers a significant methodological advantage for these purposes, allowing the researcher to observe both sites of intense fan engagement and myriad more casual, passing mentions and references to television people make as they go about their everyday online activities. An observational study of these traces, whilst it may be immersive and exploratory, is not, however, necessarily in itself ethnographic without an additional attempt to develop understanding of what each of the practices observed in this way mean to participants. The chapter highlights the different frames of meaning-making that an ethnographer might go on to access in order to make sense of the traces of television consumption found on the Internet, and stresses, as with previous chapters, the choices that are open to the ethnographer to take a study in different directions. The examples are drawn from research looking at the television series *The Antiques Roadshow* as it is manifested online

(Hine 2011b), entailing cross-platform explorations of television as mediated via various forms of audience response, including Twitter, producer-owned forums, and opportunistic use of existing discussion forums to discuss programs.

The concluding chapter pulls together threads from the three example-based chapters to consider the case for a flexible approach to methods for exploring the Internet, which will be agile in the face of ongoing developments both in the technology and its cultural embedding and strategic in their orientation to different forms of research question. The ethical and practical challenges faced by the ethnographer and the tools and skills that support ethnography for the Internet are explored. One of the key difficulties that the contemporary Internet offers the ethnographer is its unpredictability: events can develop and blow over very quickly, move from minor insignificant incidents to mass events without warning, and involve unanticipated combinations of different forms of interaction (placing corresponding stress on the ethnographer's ability to move fast and to recognize and capture different forms of data on the fly). This chapter asks what the ethnographer's response should be in the face of fast-moving, unpredictable events that can arise rapidly on the Internet and threaten straightforward notions of field site or community, finally asking whether a "pop-up" version of ethnography that responds rapidly to emerging events is ever justified.

2

The E³ Internet: Embedded, Embodied, Everyday Internet

WHAT DOES ETHNOGRAPHY OFFER FOR UNDERSTANDING THE INTERNET?

As a research method, ethnography is distinctive in its use of the embodied experiences of the researcher as one of its primary means of discovery. Unlike other research methods, which aspire to develop depersonalized and standardized instruments of data collection, ethnography celebrates the involvement of the researcher in the whole process of engaging with the field, gathering data and interpreting results. An ethnographer is required to immerse herself in the setting, and to try to see life from the point of view of those who habitually populate that setting. By doing this, she can bring back a distinctive insight into how the way of life that she studies makes sense to those involved in it. The ethnographer's immersion may involve taking part in the same activities that people living in the setting carry out, enabling the ethnographer to develop an understanding from the inside, which takes seriously how activities feel as much as what they achieve. Even where the practicalities of the setting preclude full participation, an ethnographer's immersion in the setting allows her to learn by observing in very close proximity, and enables her constantly to test her emerging interpretations with the people involved. "Being there" is the most significant aspect of the ethnographer's methodological orientation, since it allows for a direct, embodied experience of the field, and guards against a reliance on over-simplified second-hand accounts.

Ethnographers often feel the need to reflect this daily proximity and the sense of mutual commitment between participants and ethnographer in the written outcomes of the research. Rather than developing a disengaged or detached style of reporting, which might make an artificial separation between an all-seeing researcher and a stereotypically unreflexive or insight-deficient "native," the ethnographer is often very present in the text alongside participants, who are also presented as complex and impossible to know in their totality. An ethnographer will often write reports in a style which makes clear her own involvement in the production of knowledge, discussing the active steps that she took to generate the insights into the culture that is described, and openly examining her doubts about the robustness of conclusions, the contingencies of the decisions that she made, and the difficulties and frustrations that were encountered. This style of writing also recognizes an important epistemic observation: each ethnographer's insights are in large part unique to him or her, and we would not necessarily expect another ethnographer in the same setting to produce the same outcomes. Current ethnographic convention accepts that the ethnographer will feature prominently in the story, and the ethnographic author will draw attention to the very personal and contingent nature of the account. Ethnography derives its claims to authenticity from the directness of the experience that the ethnographer had of the setting and from the intensity of immersion within it, rather than aspiring to the production of objective facts, and this commitment is visible within the final ethnographic text. Ethnography does not make a claim to developing an objective account independent of the specificities of a particular ethnographer's engagement with the setting.

The co-presence of the researcher with the setting can lead to the ethnographer developing a solidarity with participants in the setting: close contact involves getting on day-to-day, and makes it difficult to maintain an aloof stance. The ethnographer has to develop her insights as she goes along, and will often be called upon to respond and give opinions on what is happening before she feels ready to do so. Because she is there, visible to informants and moving amongst them, an ethnographer develops a form of commitment to those in the setting. The ethnographer's pronouncements on the setting happen on a moment-by-moment basis, and are not confined only to a pristinely packaged end-of-project report. Marcus (1998) describes the "circumstantial activism" that an ethnographer develops to respond to the situation that she finds herself in, particularly when moving between different sites. In each interaction, the ethnographer makes such interventions as seem suitable for the moment, rather than waiting only to make a singular, detached statement about the setting once at a safe distance from it. Far from being concerned about somehow influencing or altering the object of study, the ethnographer accepts the responsibilities and challenges of being present within it.

In what follows I will be pursuing the notion of a bodily-located, circumstantially active and experientially focused ethnography and exploring how this form of understanding can be fostered and sustained in a world suffused by mediated communications. This is a model of ethnography based upon a desire to develop understanding derived from a direct and authentic experience of phenomena, whatever and wherever they might be, however diffuse or hard to define. In order to do so, we need to move away from thinking of the "being there" that characterizes ethnography as requiring a located form of presence (Beaulieu 2010), in order to focus more clearly on experiential aspects of the methodology, where "experience" may be construed in multiple ways, including within its remit various mediated forms of experience. An ethnographer, even in the Internet age, continues to develop a distinctive form of knowledge by being, doing, learning, and practicing, and by a close association with those who do so in the course of their everyday lives. In a media-suffused world, close association may come to mean proximity through mediated interaction, and ethnography needs to be ready to adapt itself to that form of proximity as much as physical closeness—but without losing sight of the original principles which motivate ethnographic engagement and make ethnography such a distinctive and insightful form of knowledge.

Schatzman and Strauss (1973) talk about the field researcher as a strategist and a methodological pragmatist. This broad approach frames the discussion in this book of various strategies for pursuing authentic, reportable experience of phenomena that involve the Internet in some way. In this model of ethnography, being in the field is about working out how best to go about understanding it:

> The field researcher is a methodological pragmatist. He sees any method of inquiry as a system of strategies and operations designed—at any time—for getting answers to certain questions about events which interest him. He understands that every method has built-in capabilities and limitations that are revealed in practice (through the techniques used, for given purposes and with various results), evaluated in part against what could have been gained or learned by any other method or set of techniques. (Schatzman and Strauss 1973: 7)

A crucial aspect of this quotation is the notion that the capabilities and limitations of methods are revealed in practice, and thus is it not possible, for example, to know in advance what interviews might be needed, what questions should be asked, what form of presence is appropriate, or whether a particular line of enquiry will be "enough" to understand what is going on. Decisions about method are tentative, and their effectiveness evaluated in retrospect.

Ethnography is therefore always adaptive in its choice of methods, and we might expect it to be so again in the face of the conditions presented by the Internet. Indeed, much of the discussion of ethnography in online settings that has taken place across the social sciences in recent years has suggested that ethnographers in these new circumstances are required to be particularly agile in their methods and adaptive in their strategies. Proponents of ethnography conducted in purely online settings have argued strongly for the relevance of ethnography as a mode of understanding in online settings, but also stressed that this kind of setting demands changes in the way that studies are conducted and the forms that data take. Williams (2007), for example, suggests that the fast-changing nature of online settings and the diverse forms which data can take are particularly challenging, while Robinson and Schulz (2009) argue that ethnographic practice has perforce to evolve and adapt in the face of the constantly changing nature of computer-mediated communication and of the populations who use it. Boellstorff et al. (2012) present their experiences of ethnography in diverse online environments in a handbook, conscious that they cannot prescribe strategies for all online settings, but proposing instead that they can instead usefully outline strategies that have worked for them, which build on, but are distinct from, those used in offline settings.

As much as the methods used by ethnographers have adapted to different online circumstances over time, the relationship between ethnographic methodology and the Internet and the aspirations of ethnographers have also evolved. Robinson and Schulz (2009) separate the development of ethnographic practice in relation to mediated communication (and particularly the Internet) into three phases. According to their chronology, a first phase of pioneering cyberethnography focused on online sites that appeared particularly interesting for the degree of identity play and separation from offline identities that participants practiced. The pioneering cyberethnographers studied field sites on the Internet because they appeared to offer different conditions from the offline world. Subsequently, "legitimizing ethnographers" explored the transfer of offline ethnographic practice and concepts such as field site and participant observations into the online domain (and in this category the authors include my own previous discussion of ethnographic approaches to the Internet [Hine 2000]). This wave of cyberethnography was less committed to a principled difference between the online and offline. Following on from this claiming of the Internet as legitimate territory for ethnographic insight, Robinson and Schulz (2009) describe how subsequent ethnographic approaches to the Internet increasingly became multi-modal, exploring the use by participants of combinations of face-to-face and mediated interaction.

Like all chronologies, the one developed by Robinson and Schulz (2009) simplifies history and glosses over many significant differences. Nonetheless, it provides a useful framework for evaluating where I see the aspirations of the current book. I remain committed to a project of "legitimizing cybereth-nography," which for me involves an ongoing commitment to examination of methodological principles as applied to the Internet, and a close consideration of the grounds for formulating the knowledge generated about the Internet by various ethnographic approaches as robust, authentic, and useful. For me, this is an ongoing question not resolved once and for all in the early days of the Internet, but still alive as we continue to adapt our methods in the face of new circumstances. This book is also, however, situated within the third, multi-modal phase of cyberethnography identified by Robinson and Schulz (2009), because my focus is not on a field site located purely online. Because I focus on an ethnography that is *for*, and not *in*, the Internet, and because I focus on what I will argue in the rest of this chapter is an embedded, embodied, everyday Internet, I view co-presence with the field as a matter which may involve either mediated interaction, or face-to-face engagement, or both, and I propose many different strategies for engagement with the field. I focus in the current book on describing strategies that *may* prove useful, rather than taking a prescriptive approach to outlining what ethnographers should do. The useful qualities of these various approaches will only be revealed in practice, as Schatzman and Strauss (1973) remind us.

One of the aspects of my focus that differs from a purely online approach to ethnography is that I wish to sustain some doubt about the best place to go to study the Internet and the most useful things to study when one gets there. It might now seem obvious, thanks to the success of such seminal online ethnographies as Baym's (1995, 2000) study of the rec.arts.tv.soaps newsgroup, that ethnographers can go online and find field sites there. Similarly, Kozinets (2009) makes a persuasive case for studies of "online cultures and communities," as if such things are coherently bounded and pre-exist the interests of the ethnographer. Boellstorff et al. (2012) develop guidance on ethnographic strategies based upon several quite diverse settings, which are united by the fact that they are largely contained in an online realm. It is perfectly possibly, and widely accepted, that ethnographers can find field sites online. Such studies are, however, a very small subset of the full complement of ethnographic studies we might wish to carry out, which will in some way incorporate or touch upon the Internet, but will not find themselves thoroughly subsumed within it. As Boellstorff (2010) argues, a single virtual world can be studied ethnographically in itself, but it is also possible for ethnographic studies to focus on the ways in which different virtual worlds interact, or on the interactions between the virtual world and the real world. It is to this latter group of ethnographic studies that I direct my attention, although, like Miller and Slater (2000), I would reject the notion that there is a pre-existing distinction between virtual world and real world. Rather, I would aim to remain agnostic in advance about the extent to which anybody making use of the Internet to go about their business might see this as participating in a "virtual world." In what follows I will be exploring in more detail how one can constitute a field site involving the Internet without making an assumption that the Internet acts as a discrete virtual domain. The approach that I explore will build on the idea that ethnography can be focused on following connections, rather than being focused on a specific place. Such an approach is, I would suggest, in line with the enduring ethnographic commitment to a focus on holistic understanding, albeit a holism understood in terms of openness to connections.

Ethnography conventionally aspires to develop holistic accounts of the settings it studies, but the meanings of this aspiration to holism have changed over time. The idea that ethnography could give a comprehensive account of a bounded, discrete cultural entity has been subject to comprehensive critique. Marcus (1989), in a paper called "Imagining the Whole," points out that the notion that an ethnography offers a comprehensive account of a specific local culture tends to present the local culture as a knowable whole, which incorporates some features of a wider world system of politics, economics, and so on, that wider system being outside the ethnographer's remit and not knowable through ethnographic approaches. This model, he argues, tends to reify aspects of the wider system which are instead arguably only ever present as they are materialized within specific local circumstances, and thus embeds a micro/macro distinction which does not stand up to close scrutiny. Marcus (1989) argues for a reimagining of the project of holistic ethnography that does away with the distinction between the micro-level of local cultures and the macro-level of world systems, and with it the idea that ethnographers should be building comprehensive accounts of local cultures. Instead, he proposes a notion of ethnography that accepts that no account of a culture can be fully comprehensive, but proceeds on the basis that wider systems are meaningfully present on a local scale, and can be effectively studied as such through ethnographic approaches. The new form of holism Marcus (1989) imagines focuses on the ethnographers' ability to visualize and pursue connections and to see activities on a micro level as manifestations of macro-level phenomena. This is a version of ethnographic holism that is characterized by a focus on contextualization and embedding, rather than a claim to comprehensiveness (Falzon 2009a).

Taking this open approach to ethnographic holism, rather than selecting in advance those aspects of the situation that we will record, in the way that a pre-determined interview schedule or survey questionnaire might do, the ethnographer remains open to diverse aspects of the setting being interconnected. For an ethnographer, a study of food within a particular population would not start and end with looking at what people ate. Rather, an ethnography focused upon food would remain open to being surprised at what food meant to the people in question, and would be interested in any aspect of their living arrangements, their routines and rituals, their relationships, and their identities that influenced or was influenced by their practices around food and the meaning invested in them. We would not simply assume that external influences such as "government policy" or "gender structures" shaped practices in relation to food, but would be alert to situations in which such structures were brought into being by participants as motivations or explanations. The connections which the ethnographer would follow could only really be derived by being a part of the setting over a prolonged period of time and finding out what went on there. An ethnographer sets out to study something with the expectation that other, unanticipated aspects of the setting will become relevant, and thus suitable research instruments cannot be designed in advance. Ethnography is thus very much an adaptive method, in that it begins from the premise that it will not be immediately apparent what the relevant dimensions of contextualization will be, and so the full research question cannot be anticipated in advance and nor can the appropriate field in which to study this question be fully defined at the outset.

The adaptive nature of ethnography means that it is "boot-strapped," built up piece by piece as the ethnographer develops understanding in incremental steps and works out what it is that he wants to know about. It is difficult therefore to generalize an ethnographic toolkit in advance, and frustratingly challenging to specify before beginning the study exactly what the ethnographer might do. In general, however, the ethnographer's toolkit contains many of the standard components of social science research methods. Ethnographers do carry out interviews, conduct surveys, quantify behavior, and draw maps. The differences from other approaches relate as much to the lack of advance specification of method as they do to the actual methods used. By refusing to decide in advance what will be most interesting to explore in the setting, the ethnographer remains open to novel discoveries about the unique ways that a particular way of life might be organized and to the prospect that activities may make sense in surprising ways.

If the methods of inquiry cannot be predicted in advance in an ethnographic study, nor can the appropriate place to study be readily identified. In conventional terms an ethnographer might have been thought of as providing a comprehensive account of the culture in some identifiable bounded locale such as a village, but this was often largely a pragmatic starting point rather than a principled object of study. In practice, ethnographers often began with a pragmatically identified focus, but remained open to finding out that this boundary did not reflect how those involved saw the relevant connections and boundaries. Ethnographers study cultural connections and meaning-making practices that may not be co-incident with specific geographically based boundaries. Marcus (1995) proposes that ethnographers can usefully study aspects of the world system by following objects of inquiry around, rather than staying in one place. Indeed, the notion of multi-sited ethnography has become particularly prominent within anthropology in recent years, as the constructed nature of the field as object of research has been recognized (Gupta and Feguson 1997a; Amit 1999) and as different models for conceptualizing the object of ethnographic inquiry have come to the fore (Falzon 2009b). The notion of multi-sitedness should not, however, be taken to imply that by simply running around more ethnographers can, after all, produce comprehensive accounts of definable cultural objects, nor that ethnographers always have to move (Falzon 2009a). As Candea (2007) argues, it can still be useful for an ethnographer to focus on a somewhat arbitrary location, and set some boundaries to the study, and to take overt responsibility for whatever limits those boundaries set upon the conceptual explorations that can be carried out. Cook et al. (2009) argue for an "unsited" field, which detaches the conceptualization of field sites from notions of space and place, avoiding the implicit understanding of a multi-sited ethnography as a piecing together of different components and focusing instead on theoretically driven decisions about research priorities. Varied notions of the field therefore abound, and ultimately the decision about where the ethnographer should go needs to be taken on a combination of pragmatic and theoretically sensitive grounds, being conscious both of what one can realistically do and of the explanatory limits that stopping in particular places might impose upon the study.

These discussions about the arbitrary yet highly consequential nature of the choice of field site have much to say to the central issue of how we are to do ethnography for the Internet. Whilst it is clearly possible to take an arbitrary cut and define a field site encompassed by a particular online forum, or a particular group of people, such spatially constrained choices will often be theoretically limiting. Ethnography for the Internet can benefit from being more open and more inventive about the choice of field site, enabling different kinds of connection to be pursued. It will never be possible, of course, to grasp the whole of the Internet ethnographically (it is, after all, famously "too big to know" [Weinberger 2011]). An ethnographer can, however, creatively explore what it means to people to have the Internet in their lives. The ethnographer's participation becomes a way of getting close to that lived experience of the Internet, developing an understanding of how it feels to navigate the social textures of everyday life. By being a part of using the Internet, the ethnographer is sensing what is easy and difficult, what is sanctioned, and what is taboo. The Internet may be too big for us to know, but the ethnographer can usefully develop a sense of how it feels to live with that vastness, finding out how sense is made out of the ineffable. We will carve out arbitrary field sites—we will choose to focus on one object rather than another, to pursue one possible line of contextualization rather than another, and to stay in particular places or move away from them on theoretically informed whims. There is no holistic ethnography of the Internet, in the sense of offering a comprehensive account of what it means. There is, however, an ambition to understand the Internet as a contextual and contextualizing phenomenon. We want to understand what people think they are up to when they are using the Internet. But how do we do that?

Geertz (1993) explains that the ethnographer is often attempting to bridge between the "experience-near" forms of description that people use to talk about their world and the "experience-distant" concepts that inhabit academic texts, abstracting from the specify of situations and allowing for comparisons to be drawn between them. Carrying out that bridging work requires a very close connection with the life-world that one studies, but does not necessarily mean that one has to become a fully immersed member of that life-world:

> To grasp concepts that, for another people, are experience-near, and to do so well enough to place them in illuminating connection with experience-distant concepts theorists have fashioned to capture the general features of social life, is clearly a task at least as delicate, if a bit less magical, as putting oneself in someone else's skin. The trick is not to get yourself into some inner correspondence of spirit with your informants. Preferring, like the rest of us, to call their souls their own, they are not going to be altogether keen about such an effort anyhow. The trick is to figure out what the devil they think they are up to. (Geertz 1993: 58)

Geertz goes on to explain that, for him, working out what people think they are up to involves a close scrutiny of the means they have available for expressing and understanding themselves and their world. He illustrates with some provocative examples, including a discussion of the systems of naming children in Bali, and the very particular way in which this system of naming by birth order positions individuals on a social stage.

Geertz, here, homes in on a very specific anthropological project in which he is engaged, focused on the varying notions of selfhood current among different groups of people. However, his caution that we cannot get inside the skin of the people we study and must think more pragmatically about what it is we hope to gain by our proximity to them is useful even if we do not share that anthropological focus on selfhood. For instance, I find this insight into ethnography's concerns and limitations useful even though my own theoretical interests tend towards issues of concern within sociology and science and technology studies rather than anthropology. Geertz's methodological insights become particularly provocative when we consider Internet-mediated ethnographic encounters, in which the proximity we develop may be a question of sharing a Facebook newsfeed, or participating in an email exchange, rather than a prolonged physical co-presence. In Internet ethnography, the terms "experience-near" and "experience-distant" could usefully be rendered as "technology-specific" forms of engagement and "technology-neutral" forms of engagement. The ethnographer's task as a participant in a Facebook group is to bridge between the technology-specific status update, and the technology-neutral social act that the status update performs. Just as in Geertz's examples, a close attention needs to be given to the means of expression that the Facebook status update makes available. Just as with the system of naming children in Bali, the Facebook status could be seen as making available a particular way of understanding oneself and one's relationship to the world.

For Geertz, ethnography is certainly not a matter of simply collecting systems of representation, or symbolic forms, and reading off the culture from that abstracted collection of signs. It takes concerted work and prolonged engagement to see these signs in action and work out how their meanings are negotiated in use. Neither is ethnography in Facebook simply a matter of reading off the culture that is created by the distinctive forms of communication that it makes available. For one thing, Facebook is used in very diverse ways. It takes close scrutiny, and some prolonged and immersive engagement, to pick up the nuances of how any particular group of people who may come together on Facebook may make use of its features. For another, not everything we want to know about Facebook, as an ethnographer, is apparent publicly on Facebook itself. To find out how some particular group of people understand themselves through Facebook it may well be necessary to look at how those Facebook activities are produced and consumed, how they travel beyond the online location and are embedded in other forms of activity.

As an ethnographer, one can usefully remain agnostic about whether the Internet really does, in any comprehensive sense, transform society. It is not helpful to assume in advance that there is something special about the digital. Indeed, the Internet, and the "digital" are not available to us in any transcendent sense, but are emergent in practice as they are realized through particular combinations of devices, people, and circumstances (Ruppert et al. 2013). If the Internet is emergent in practice, it is then also potentially multiple (De Laet and Mol 2000; Mol 2002) and not resolvable to a singular set of implications. Ethnography for the Internet need not assume that there is a single knowable Internet out there—rather, it seeks to understand the particularity and specificity of engagements with the Internet, as a component of everyday life.

CHALLENGES FOR ETHNOGRAPHY AND THE INTERNET

Thus far I have argued that ethnography provides a distinctive and very useful way of examining the Internet, which allows us to develop an in-depth understanding of the textures of social experience that arise as people engage with the various technologies that comprise the contemporary Internet. We can formulate field sites which touch on and encompass the Internet in multiple ways, some of which involve a concerted focus on a specific site contained within the Internet, others of which move around, and pursue connections between online and offline sites. We make decisions about how to shape our field sites on a combination of pragmatic and theoretical grounds, in order to allow us to pursue interesting questions. By becoming immersed in settings and in forms of mobility we can develop in-depth understanding of the sense which people make of their various forms of engagement with this set of technologies. Although the Internet, in itself, is too big to know, we can usefully explore what it is that people in particular situations make of it.

For many years I have been attempting to carry out ethnographic studies of what people think they are up to when using the Internet, trying out various modes of engagement and definitions of the field, and formulating strategies adapted to each of the circumstances that I encounter. Along the way I have studied some quite diverse settings. I started out with online ethnography looking at what the people producing websites and participating in online discussions in response to a high-profile media event thought they were up to (Hine 2000). In that study I examined emergent online social structures and looked at the way that various media portrayals of the Internet shaped expectations of what the Internet could and should do for people. I carried out documentary analysis on websites themselves and on media coverage of the Internet, employed discourse analysis to investigate online forums, participated in and observed online events, and carried out interviews with the creators of websites and participants in online forums. I argued that the Internet could be construed simultaneously as a cultural site, where people did things, and a cultural artefact which was made meaningful within other contexts, and that ethnographic strategies could usefully encompass both aspects, and explore how they were mutually entangled.

Following on from the high-profile media case explored in *Virtual Ethnography* (Hine 2000), I went on then to examine a more specialized group, studying how scientists, in particular, were using the Internet. In the mid-1990s I was engaged in an ethnographic study of the deployment of information technology in human genome research, and undertook more conventional, location-based fieldwork both in a genetics laboratory and amongst the software developers and support team, using as an inspiration the model of laboratory ethnography pioneered in sociology of scientific knowledge (Lynch 1985; Latour and Woolgar 1986). Ethnography is used within the sociology of scientific knowledge to examine in close detail what scientists do in their day to day work in the laboratory, with the goal of understanding the process of constructing scientific facts (Latour and Woolgar 1986). As I participated and observed in the genetics laboratory and the software development offices, the Internet was emerging as a significant location which the participants in the offline settings that I studied were orienting to in their work. It thus became harder and harder to ignore the online forums or to separate them out as a distinct field site on their own. In attempting an ethnography of scientific practice I thus gradually began to feel obliged to encompass online spaces, and to explore how they influenced and were entwined with the offline spaces of the laboratory and software development offices. As a part of this work I examined a specific online discussion group where laboratory techniques were discussed (Hine 2002), looking at the ways in which the social and physical boundaries of the laboratory in real life were re-enacted in online space through discursive practices.

Subsequently, my interest in the role of the Internet within scientific research was expanded via an exploration of the development of publicly available distributed databases of biodiversity information (Hine 2007, 2008). This study took the scientific discipline of biological systematics as its focus of inquiry, involving engagement in natural history museums and botanic gardens, and their online counterparts, across software development projects and online forums. Archival material was used to explore the genesis and transformation of hopes for the rejuvenation of the discipline through embrace of information technology, and to investigate the circulations and translations between policy and practice in various domains. The study was ethnographic in spirit, but expanded its scope to embrace the historical and the autobiographical in an eclectic mix of methodological strategies intended to work out why, and for whom, particular technological solutions made sense at particular times. Again, the Internet featured as a cultural site, in that it was a significant place where scientists met and discussed and where new spaces of knowledge production emerged. It was also a significant cultural object, in that it carried some powerful connotations for users and commentators. Using the Internet was seen as an important way of being up to date, and of reaching out to potential users of scientific knowledge.

My interest in the role that the Internet plays in the very specific concerns of scientific research has been accompanied by an enduring interest in the role of the Internet in more mundane, everyday settings. I have been interested in the entwining of mass media with the Internet, exploring the extent to which the Internet both provides an outlet for new forms of audiencehood to emerge and at the same time makes it feasible for audience researchers to develop a new sense of everyday engagement with media (Hine 2011b). Finally, I have more recently been exploring the use of online locally based gifting networks such as Freecycle and Freegle, finding out how these computer-mediated connections interact with people's sense of their locality and those who inhabit the locality alongside them. In each of these cases I am concerned to understand the Internet not as some free-floating sphere of social interaction apart from everyday life, but as an embedded part of the everyday lives of the people who use it. Taking a holistic ethnographic stance as inspiration, I have tried to work out what the Internet uniquely means in each of these settings, not expecting that it will have some transcendent set of effects that it exerts on each of the domains in which it is used.

I have eclectic research interests, which has the advantage, for current purposes, that I have been developing ethnographic strategies for some very diverse research settings. They are tied together, however, by a commitment to ethnography as an experiential form of knowledge, and a belief that engagement with the field should be driven by a pursuit of the ways in which a setting uniquely makes sense, rather than the application of a particular model of what a field should be. Each methodological solution is therefore unique. There are, however, strategies that remain useful across many different sites, and, as ever, an ethnographer in one setting can always usefully take inspiration from approaches that have worked elsewhere. The situations that I have been engaged in are very diverse, but looking back across these studies, and reflecting on challenges faced and adaptations made, some common issues have arisen. Three particular aspects of the contemporary Internet experience have repeatedly struck me as especially challenging to development of ethnographic strategies. For development of an ethnographic strategy for the Internet, it has seemed particularly significant that it is *embedded* in various contextualizing frameworks, institutions, and devices, that the experience of using it is *embodied* and hence highly personal and that it is *everyday*, often treated as an unremarkable and mundane infrastructure rather than something that people talk about in itself unless something significant goes wrong. These three "Es"—for shorthand purposes, the E^3 Internet—provided a backdrop for thinking about why it is difficult to apply ethnographic principles to the contemporary Internet, and how we might do so successfully.

I do not intend to say that these three "Es" uniquely and comprehensively capture the contemporary Internet, or are in some way completely novel, or distinguish the Internet now from that in earlier time periods. They are instead a device for articulating some generic challenges that the contemporary Internet offers for ethnographers, as a route towards formulating transportable strategies. Ethnography is an adaptive methodology, always created afresh for the circumstances in which it finds itself, but ethnographers can usefully learn from one another and can draw on a repertoire of approaches. The E^3 framework offers a means to think systematically about why some strategies are likely to work for illuminating specific things we might be interested in knowing about the Internet. In the following sections I will articulate in turn what I mean by each of the "Es," discussing some of the ethnographic orientations and strategies which arise.

EMBEDDED INTERNET

In technical circles, the term "embedded Internet" refers to the increasing trend for an ability to connect to the Internet to be built into everyday objects (Intel 2009). This "Internet of things" (Gershenfeld et al. 2004) allows for objects to sense and respond to their environments, and send messages to monitoring devices. We are promised that a world containing such an embedded Internet will be smarter, allowing for the objects around us to take appropriate actions on our behalf, adapting themselves to needs we may not even know that we have as yet. The embedded Internet of this vision promises computing power and predictive capacity seamlessly built into the world around us. In referring to an embedded Internet I am not specifically referencing this scenario, although the embedding of Internet capacity into everyday devices is undoubtedly a topic of ethnographic concern. The way that such smart devices will become actors in our domestic and working landscapes, and the extent to which we will take account of them, recognize their agency and transform our other human–human and human–machine relationships to accommodate them are crying out for ethnographic attention. The exploration of this form of embedded Internet is a very specific form of ethnographic challenge that may be on the horizon. It is not, however, this relatively technologically esoteric form of embedded Internet that I intend to reference here: rather, it is the more general sense in which the Internet becomes entwined in use with multiple forms of context and frames of meaning-making.

It might nowadays seem obvious that the Internet is embedded in everyday life, but this was not always so. In the early days of the mainstream Internet, it was common to talk about the Internet as offering up access to a new form of space: cyberspace (as popularized by William Gibson in the science-fiction novel *Neuromancer* [1984]). The Internet was conceived as a new frontier, which could be colonized by whatever new structures and identities people wished to build. Cyberspace was construed as a domain apart from everyday life, imagined as offering up new possibilities for pioneering developments, separate from prevailing modes of governance and potentially free from enduring structures and inequalities experienced in "real life" settings, as famously captured in John Perry Barlow's *Declaration of the Independence of Cyberspace* (1996). This transcendent model of cyberspace was a dominant metaphor for understanding the possibilities of the newly emerging Internet (Arora 2012) and proved hugely productive for creating a sense of wonder and expectation around the socially transformative possibilities of the Internet. This model of the Internet emphasized the role of the technology in opening up possibilities for social interaction to be re-organized across time and space and for identities to be fluid and multiple. The Internet was also envisaged as a manifestation of post-modern ideas about the breakdown of enduring structures of power and knowledge and identity (for example Poster 1995; Turkle 1995; Stone 1996).

The notion that the Internet was a sphere of social innovation, within which whatever structures had gone before could potentially be re-made, proved very stimulating in academic circles. On the one hand, framing the Internet as an esoteric domain separate from the concerns of everyday life could be seen to position it as frivolous and lacking in the weighty concerns that might be deemed the proper work of academic researchers. Those who focused on the Internet found themselves the target of a certain amount of derision from their more "serious" colleagues. On the other hand, however, the air of novelty around the Internet, and the conception of cyberspace as a new and separate domain, suggested a new frontier for academic understanding and motivated close attention to what the emergent online culture might be like, attracting researchers from a wide range of disciplines (Baym 2005; Hine 2005). The Internet seemed to offer a laboratory in which social scientists could watch society being made from scratch. As uses of the Internet for a wide array of purposes flourished, the new social formations and activities that took place on the Internet began to be taken seriously, both by journalists (Rheingold 1993; Dibbell 1999) and academic social scientists (for example, the pioneering collections edited by Jones 1995, 1997, 1998).

The notion that the Internet can act as a significant cultural domain in its own right has subsequently been both the motivation for, and the upshot of, concerted efforts by ethnographers over subsequent years to experience and document the social structures that emerge in online spaces. Ethnographers have studied various forms of online interaction, including discussion groups, real-time chat rooms, multi-player online games, and virtual-reality environments (particularly notable examples include Baym 2000; Kendall 2002; Schaap 2002; Taylor 2006; Williams 2007; Boellstorff 2008; Nardi 2010). Such studies have often involved the researchers in observation and interaction beyond the bounds of the online site itself. Where participants meet up in real life, or use other channels of communication such as chat rooms alongside a gaming environment, then the ethnographer would usually want to take part too, in order to experience the full spectrum of interactions with one another that participants enjoy. Nonetheless, the field site tends to be construed as centering on a group of people who are defined by their connection with a specific online space. In this conception of ethnography for the Internet, the field is conceptually largely contained within the Internet, and the ethnographer seeks to understand how the activities within that field are structured by and make sense to the participants.

The notion of a field contained within the Internet certainly offers a powerful lens for finding out what it is that people do online, and in particular for understanding how online spaces emerge as orderly social settings. It is the route towards understanding a quite specific set of theoretically oriented questions. Ethnography within online spaces can look in close detail at how a distinctive culture may emerge in such a space, with its own sets of norms and values, with common understandings of humor, reciprocity, and a sense of its own identity as a social formation distinct from others. Online spaces can form cohesive social entities that are readily describable in terms such as community, or they can offer more diffuse social formations that still offer their participants a sense that they are in a distinctive space which carries certain expectations of their behavior and still have characteristics amenable to ethnographic exploration. It is, as Boellstorff (2010) argues, perfectly legitimate to conduct an ethnographic study in such a site, provided that the over-arching research question is defined suitably. Legitimate and often illuminating though it may be, however, a model of ethnography organized around a self-contained cyberspatial Internet is not appropriate for all research questions that ethnographers might wish to ask of the Internet. In particular, this model of ethnography is ill-suited to answer questions about the ways in which the Internet makes sense as one way of interacting among others, one mode of existence alongside the many alternatives which people may experience on a daily basis. Other research strategies, and different models of the field site may be needed to explore this embedded Internet.

Whilst the cyberspatial model of the Internet was highly influential in shaping the first wave of academic studies of the Internet, it did indeed soon become apparent that many social interactions that went on in and around the Internet were not comfortably encompassed by this model. According to Silver (2000), if the first wave of Internet studies was framed around the "twin pillars" of virtual communities and online identities, a second wave soon emerged, which took a more critical stance on the potential transformative properties of the Internet. This new generation of studies still paid close attention to what people did online, but also looked at the contexts from which these activities emerged, and paid attention to the stories told about these online activities and the structures and processes that made it much easier for some people than others to participate (Silver 2000). Researchers were prompted to ask what difference the Internet made to people in context (Howard 2004) and were looking at the processes through which it became embedded into people's lives in ways that made sense to them (Bakardjieva 2005). A shift also occurred in popular discourse, positioning the Internet as a mundane artefact entangled with the immediacies of other aspects of life, as Sterne (2006: 17) describes:

> Claims for the revolutionary promise of digital technologies are dissipating [...]: advertisers have moved to "digital lifestyle" campaigns that represent digital technologies as commodities to be integrated into everyday life rather than as epochal forces that will transform it.

As popular discourse increasingly stressed what one could do with the Internet, as it became clear that the Internet did not necessarily float free from the rest of people's experience, as it emerged that there was a significant prospect of a digital divide with real social consequences, and as the notion of an Internet free from prevailing forms of social inequality receded, an urgency to ask kinds of research question that could not be answered by studies solely contained within an Internet-enabled cyberspace gathered pace.

It had already been apparent to some, including ethnographers, that the Internet need not be thought of as inevitably a space apart from everyday life. Miller and Slater (2000) had taken an approach to the ethnography of the Internet, radical for its time, which started from a physical place, Trinidad. They set out with the goal of working out what the Internet meant in Trinidad in particular, rather than assuming that there was some separate, transcendent and uniquely definable cyberspace that people inhabited. Miller and Slater's (2000) approach demonstrated that the Internet could mean quite different things to different groups of people, and it could be used in very specific ways as a means of realizing particular cultural interests and biases. Miller and Slater did not assume the existence of the "virtual," but proposed that it would exist only in so far as it was brought into being by particular sets of cultural practices. There could be quite different ways of experiencing the Internet which might not view the online domain as a form of cyberspace. "The Internet" was not in fact a single cultural artefact, but many different cultural artefacts depending on the people who were using it (Hine 2000). It would thus be unnecessarily limiting to design ethnographic studies of the Internet as if it always existed as a cyberspatial experience. It could not be assumed that we could work out how a particular set of online practices made sense to participants only by observing those participants online. An ethnographer should rather, according to Miller and Slater (2000), follow a specific group of people using the Internet and follow them online in whatever sense they turned out to conceive of this practice. More recently Miller (2011) has taken a similar approach to the ethnography of Facebook, starting not with fieldwork within Facebook, but exploring how its meaning is constructed by a range of Trinidadian users that he spends time with, both interviewing them and exploring Facebook through their eyes.

An "embedded" approach to Internet ethnography, as proposed by Miller and Slater (2000), provides for different sets of research questions to be asked, as compared to the cyberspatial approach to Internet ethnography. Specifically, an embedded approach helps us to ask how the Internet comes to mean different things in different settings. In other words, it embraces the multiplicity of the Internet. Such an approach is resonant with recent work in the sociology of science and technology, which has stressed that technologies can usefully be thought of as possessing multiple identities. According to this perspective, rather than being an external agent that impacts upon society, a technology can be construed as a component of dynamic cultural circumstances which give meaning and identity to the technology (De Laet and Mol

2000; Mol 2002). The identity of a technology thus does not pre-exist any given setting of use, but is established through the practices that bring it into being in that setting (Law and Lien 2013). Different practices can produce multiple and divergent enactments of a technology (or a disease, or an organism, or an organization—in fact, any of the artefacts that we think of as stable entities can, according to this framework, be thought of as potentially multiple and only locally stabilized through our practices). Whilst we may in an everyday sense talk about technologies as stable artefacts, as a methodological heuristic this perspective from sociology of science and technology suggests that we should expect, and prepare for, technologies to be multiple. Taking this methodological heuristic of multiplicity to the Internet suggests that it may indeed be a mistake to assume that if the Internet is around then cyberspace always exists. More generally, a multiplicity heuristic suggests that it will be useful to play close attention to the circumstances in which we enact the Internet: how do we bring it into being as a component of our everyday life, what identities do we ascribe to it, and how do we experience it in diverse ways?

This anticipation that there will be multiple understanding of the Internet resonates with Markham's (1998) observations that the Internet may not always be experienced as a place to go, but could also be seen as a tool or as a way of being—although, according to the expectations sown by the sociology of science and technology, we should not expect even this list to be exhaustive. A technology as fluid, dispersed, and flexible (De Laet and Mol 2000) as the Internet should be expected to be experienced in many different and unpredictable ways, difficult to capture in straightforward pre-determined taxonomies of usage. We therefore need to be agnostic in advance about the spatial organization of connections, and what they will mean to people. Contemporary Internet research needs to be alert to novel spatial formations, beyond the previously dominant metaphors of network and community, and question the separation of online and offline space (Postill 2008).

This multiple understanding of technology has resonance with frameworks developed for studying the embedding of media in diverse circumstances, and the role of media in identity formation. Courtois et al. (2012: 402) discuss a multi-dimensional understanding of media consumption, which extends upon previous conceptualizations of media as meaningful in a dual sense as both material artefacts and as texts:

> ... we subscribe to the concept of a triple articulation that dissects media consumption as the symbolic interplay of media as an object (*first articulation: e.g., television, computer*), as a text (*second articulation: e.g., lyric, game, video*

clip), and as a context (*third articulation; alone in the bedroom, together with family in the living room*).

The study of Flemish teenagers conducted by Courtois et al. (2012) explored the use of multiple media technologies, including phones, games consoles, MP3 players, televisions, and computers. The researchers in this case conducted a survey and interview-based study to explore how teenagers used these technologies and to identify the interactions between objects, texts, and spaces. An ethnographer of the Internet could usefully use this notion of triple articulation as object, text, and context as a sensitizing device, keeping in mind the potential need for attention to any of these multiple aspects in order to understand the embedded Internet experience, albeit without expecting each to be experienced as separate entities in practice.

To re-cap, then, the cyberspace metaphor was highly influential in developing a sense that online communications were to be taken seriously as a way that people came together and developed new identities and new social formations. Ethnographic studies of online spaces were key in establishing the nature of the new social formations that occurred online. Many Internet researchers, however, subsequently rejected this notion of an Internet studies contained within the Internet, and sought to study diverse ways in which the Internet was contextualized. When this approach is taken, it rapidly becomes apparent that the Internet means quite different things to different people, and takes on multiple identities. The cyberspatial metaphor, and with it the notion of an ethnographic field site contained within the Internet, proves to be just one way to understand what the Internet means. Viewed in this way, the contextual, embedded approach to understanding the Internet is not inherently superior to the cyberspatial understanding. Each is the product of a particular cultural moment, serves to answer specific kinds of question about the Internet, and has its own local validity. Nor does the embedded model sweep aside the cyberspatial model and render it irrelevant. There are still online spaces which develop distinctive and well-ordered cultures. It is still relevant and interesting to find out what people do when they are online, and what forms of identity, structure, and inequality emerge when people come together in online space. However, there are now also many ethnographers who want to study the embedding of the Internet in various dimensions of everyday life. As researchers, we are neither above the current cultural trends nor wholly the victims of them, but are active participants within them. As the current cultural trend moves away from cyberspace it is important to be able to engage with the questions of our day, which tend to focus on the role of the Internet in our organizations and institutions, in our families and our schools, and in our aims to live sustainable, fulfilling, and equitable lives. Contemporary ethnographers may re-cast these questions and take a critical approach to the values that they embed, but they will often want and need to engage with the over-arching interest in an embedded Internet.

The Internet can be viewed as embedded according to many different dimensions of embedding. Miller and Slater (2000) took an anthropological approach to embedding, focusing on the role of the Internet in Trinidadian culture, but there are many other potential ways to frame the context in which the Internet is viewed as embedded beyond the spatial and the cultural. We could, for example, look at the role played by the Internet in the development of particular modes of family life in contemporary society or the embedding of the Internet in local communities, or we could explore how specific organizations and institutions make the Internet their own (Rainie et al. 2012). We can look at the extent to which the Internet both embeds and is embedded within other media forms (Bolter and Grusin 2000). We can look at the embedding of social networks into the Internet, and the Internet into social networks (Garton et al. 1997). Each of these forms of embedding suggests a direction in which an ethnographer might pursue connections, offering up a frame of meaning-making within which particular Internet activities make sense.

In addition to these social dimensions of the embedded Internet, we can also look at the embedding of our Internet experience into specific devices. Emerging data from successive waves of the Oxford Internet Survey (Dutton and Blank 2011; Dutton et al. 2013) suggests that the experience of using the Internet on multiple devices and whilst on the move is very different from that of the user bound to a single point of Internet access on the desktop. There are now many different ways in which apparently the same Internet functionality can be viewed, and so many different ways in which people might experience it. The ethnographer thus has a major challenge to address when deciding which device to use for her own Internet activity, and how to compare that experience with the experience that any of the participants might be having. Choosing one device over another might entail becoming more aligned with the experience of one set of participants over another, and it may be important to have insight into what difference this may make.

Internet content can also be viewed as a multiply embedded phenomenon. Content from the Internet continuously circulates and is extracted and re-embedded, featuring in word-of-mouth conversations, in printed reports, and mass media, shaping and being shaped by the myriad activities of everyday life and public existence. One of the defining characteristics of the digital, after all, is the ease with which it can be moved, recombined, revisualized, recalculated, and repurposed. We therefore cannot know in advance how other people will view what we are viewing and where the data might end up. We are not asked to be omniscient or psychic—ethnographers always have been limited by their own perceptual abilities and embodied capacities for observation. We cannot expect to address all aspects of the re-embedding of the Internet content we examine, nor produce an exhaustive account of where exactly it travels and what it does there. This is not what ethnography is good at, and not what it aspires to achieve. Instead, we acknowledge the dynamics of embedding, remain alert to the possibilities of unexpected travel of data and of new forms of connection, and try to remain focused on how situations emerge and make sense to some people of interest. And we make conscious choices, mindful of the research questions that drive us and the issues that we wish our findings to speak to.

The embedded Internet poses many methodological challenges for an ethnographer, in that the frames of meaning-making that the ethnographer could potentially pursue are initially unpredictable, often diverse, and can require considerable agility of method and mobility of focus to explore. The precise solutions will depend on individual circumstances, and on the specific aspirations of the ethnographic study in question. In future chapters I will be exploring some strategies which may help ethnographers in coping with the embedded Internet and could be adaptable to other circumstances. The next chapter explores some over-arching strategies for making field sites for the embedded Internet, focusing on openness to field sites not arbitrarily confined to online domains, taking a connective approach and being open to unexpected ways in which the Internet makes sense to its users, and being open to the way that expectations about what the Internet is for are transmitted and cemented. In the subsequent chapters that focus on specific examples, various dimensions of embedding will be explored. Chapter 4 explores the embedding of the online gift-giving network Freecycle within local communities, within households, and within specific devices. Chapter 5 considers the development of distributed databases in biology, and explores the sense in which contemporary developments are embedded within a specific material culture and contemporary political climate as well as within the history of the discipline. Chapter 6 looks at the embedding of television within the Internet, and asks how the Internet makes available new modes of ethnographic inquiry for the understanding of mass media in everyday life. These chapters also, however, manifest strategies which cope with the embodied and the everyday Internet, and these concepts in turn require explanation before we turn to discussion of concrete ethnographic strategies to cope with them.

EMBODIED INTERNET

As described above, cyberpunk fiction, and particularly its notion of cyber-space, was highly influential in shaping early expectations of the Internet. We were encouraged to think of going online as stepping into an alternative space. As a corollary, we were also led to think of the Internet as a space where one could potentially become someone else, developing an alternative identity to the one held in the physical world, or indeed, leaving the physical world identity behind altogether. The process of constructing virtual identities became a significant focus of research efforts. However, it has increasingly become apparent as Internet use has become embedded in everyday life that, rather than being a transcendent cyberspatial site of experience, the Internet has often become a part of us, and that virtual identities are not necessarily separate from physical bodies. We do not necessarily think of "going online" as a discrete form of experience, but we instead often experience being online as an extension of other embodied ways of being and acting in the world. There is in contemporary Internet usage often a considerable degree of recognizable continuity between one's online and offline experiences and identities and, in fact, one's performance on social networking sites may often be judged according to whether it is authentic rather than "fake," comparing the online self directly with its offline counterpart. In this section I will discuss the extent to which experience of the online environment has become seamlessly integrated with other embodied experiences, and explore the implications of this integration for the ethnographer's orientation to the field. It becomes apparent that online and offline are not related in some predictable fashion in terms of embodiment, and the ethnographer's embodied interactions with the field are thus both highly individualized and highly consequential for shaping understanding of the field. Properly recog-nizing the diverse and highly personal nature of the online experience poses a considerable methodological challenge. Some strategies for addressing this challenge will be outlined at the end of the section.

The idea of "leaving the meat behind" was, as Bell (2001) describes, one of the prevalent early myths around cyberspaces, founded in a cyberpunk literature which focused on leaving the body behind and "jacking in" to a discrete online domain of existence. The body was represented as an encum-brance to be abandoned as soon as possible, since it tied one to a bodily identity which constrained self-expression and to a set of physical constraints which, once in cyberspace, need no longer be acknowledged. Cyberspace appeared to offer a pure existence of the mind. Many commentators, however, stepped up to the mark to explore the over-simplifications which this position represented. Stone (1992: 113) explored the diverse and changing relationships between bodies, identities, and virtual spaces, but stressed in conclusion that "even in the age of the technosocial subject, life is lived through bodies." Lupton (1995) focused on the emotional and embodied relationship that users have with their computers, exploring multiple senses in which the body was present in the relationship with a computer. Whatever went on in cyberspace the user would have at some time to return to a body with physical needs. Events in cyberspace would also evoke emotional and physical reactions in an inescapably embodied user. Argyle and Shields (1996: 68) described the embodied experiences of a user who could simultaneously be present in cyberspace and a physical body seated on a chair at a keyboard, looking at a screen:

> If we believe that the body must be present in a physical sense to be a factor amongst individuals, that there is separation, and that we can communicate from one level without other levels being present, then it will be very difficult to find physicality on a computer net. The body is not there. The screen, keyboard and monitor are physically in contact with the user, with the flesh up against barrier after barrier. But if we argue for a multiplicity, multiple layers of being, a way to be in the body at all times, to express the whole of the person so there can be no separations, and we view the human as an extremely creative entity wishing to touch its fellows, then how can we eliminate the physical at all?

This notion of multiple ways of being, and multiple notions of physicality, offers a useful way of understanding the complexities of online experience. To some extent the online world can be an immersive one. It is possible to feel as though you are co-present with other virtual beings in an online world, and at that moment to forget your physical body and offline location. This effect is, however, only temporary. You will, at some point, be recalled to physical needs, because the body cannot live online and eventually requires attention. The complexity of multiple ways of being is not just about an alternation between online immersion and physical presences, however. The choice to allow the online world to be immersive is a loaded one, because during that immersed online experience we are absenting ourselves from other forms of engagement, and making, implicitly or explicitly, a statement about what is important to us. A family member sitting in a living room engaged in an online gaming session may be immersed in the online world, but their continued physical presences in the room coupled with an overt lack of engagement with other family members speaks to their priorities, and may be read as such. Being immersed in an online world does not necessarily replace responsibilities as parent, sibling, or friend to co-present others, nor does it, in that sense, absent one from various forms of accountability due to a socially engaged body in the physical world.

Even if it may sometimes be immersive, then, the online world does not necessarily substitute for or replace bodily experience. The Internet user is an embodied user. Bodies, however, do not simply exist in the world in a singular form, but are brought into being in a complex and multiple fashion (Turner 1991). It is therefore not sufficient to say simply that one is here or there, embodied or not, online or offline. Both online and offline are complex modes of being, which often need to be disaggregated (not lumped together as if all online experiences or all offline experiences were somehow the same) in order to tease out what each might mean to people under specific circum-stances and how each might relate to a physical body. As Markham (1998) stressed in her reflexive online ethnography, the Internet is not always experi-enced as something to immerse oneself in, as depicted by the cyberpunk fiction. Rather, she outlined, the Internet could be experienced in multiple ways, including acting as a place, as a tool, and as a way of being. Working out how the Internet is experienced in any particular instance becomes a matter for ethnographic insight, combining reflection on how the experience feels to the ethnographer with a close engagement with the experiences and interpretations of participants in the situation.

The Internet is potentially experienced by embodied users in different ways depending on the circumstances. More starkly apparent, possibly, is the extent to which the Internet has changed over time, and our relationship to the experience of using the Internet has adapted to its growing familiarity and to the extended array of social situations which being online offers. Latterly, the advent of social media and broadband Internet have, in a very pragmatic sense, recast our relationship with the Internet. As Gies (2008) describes, Internet users now often expect to transmit and receive a broad array of information about one another, utilizing the increasingly audio-visual nature of Internet communication and grounding their use of the Internet in a much wider array of performances of a bodily reality. Internet use was always in some senses an embodied experience, but the contem-porary reality of social networking sites focuses popular attention on that embodiment in new ways. As we routinely caution young people against contacting strangers on the Internet, and as we set our privacy settings on social networking sites according to how well we know people, we reassert the significance of the Internet as a means to interact with known, embodied others whom we have knowledge of across more than one medium. In popular discourse and everyday experience the Internet has become much more routinely a place to express an embodied self rather than a place to leave the body behind.

The bodies that use the Internet are socially situated bodies, and various aspects of social positioning and material circumstances shape the Internet experience, leading to the emergence of a digital divide with potentially far-reaching consequences for social inclusion and opportunity (Hargittai 2008). In addition to large-scale social segmentation, individual biographies determine how accessible and meaningful the Internet might be and shape what we use it for. The Internet has, for example, become a valued source of information on many aspects of contemporary existence, but is not necessarily experienced in the same way across the life course. People turn to the Internet not as an escape from everyday existence, but in order to inform and enrich their understanding of events happening in their lives. Parents, for example, turn to the Internet at particular times of crisis, transition, and uncertainty (Plantin and Daneback 2009). As Gies (2008) describes, the body itself can provide a significant motivation to go online, whether this be to find health related information, seek support from fellow suffers, or pursue sexual gratification. The Internet thus can be seen to sit alongside, depend upon, and reinforce a sensual and emotional physical body, rather than necessarily substituting for that body. How the Internet is embedded into our lives is in part a product of an embodied engagement with the Internet, and in turn, of course, the Internet can shape our experience of embodiment as the information and insights we find online help us to understand ourselves in new ways.

Such concerns have been the focus of an emergent branch of anthropology, cyborg anthropology, which takes the relationship between the human body, human subjectivity, and agency and various forms of technological prosthesis as the topic of investigation (Downey et al. 1995; Downey and Dumit 1997). This field of study influenced by perspectives from science and technology studies takes it that the consequences of new technologies for the human condition are not to be assumed as outcomes of some objective qualities of the technologies themselves, but emerge in more complex and dynamic fashion as technologies are employed in specific circumstances and become part of the human experience (Haraway 1991). Within cyborg anthropology, the technology/human relationship becomes the focus of attention, with the goal of exploring the distinctive and enduring qualities of the contemporary human condition. Similarly, a field of digital anthropology has more recently emerged, with the goal of documenting the human condition as shaped by and expressed through engagement with digital technologies:

The intention is not simply to study and reflect on new developments but to use these to further our understanding of what we are and have always been. The digital should and can be a highly effective means for reflecting on what it means to be human, the ultimate task of anthropology as a discipline. (Miller and Horst 2012: 3)

This direct focus of cyborg and digital anthropology on the technology/human relationship will not be shared by many ethnographic studies that involve the Internet. Ethnography for the Internet does not have to share anthropology's project of examining the human condition, and an ethnographic engagement with the Internet need not become primarily an ethnography of a cyborg relationship with the Internet. It will, however, be useful for any form of ethnography involving Internet usage to acknowledge that we access the Internet as embodied social beings, and that the ethnographer's experience of that embodiment is just one among many possible experiences. To be in the field as an ethnographer engaged with a field that encompasses the Internet we have, at some point, to *be* online, and it is important to reflect on what that "being" entails—how is it made possible, how does it feel, how does it compare with other ways of being? This sensitivity builds on the established focus on the participatory aspect of ethnography, which values learning by doing and by reflecting on how far experience is and is not accessible on the basis of volition alone, and documenting how particular forms of engagement feel. This focus on embodied, sensual, and emotional engagement with the field has been an enduring feature of the distinctive claims of ethnography as a form of knowledge production, and it is no less significant for an ethnography involving the Internet than it is for any other form of ethnography.

In future chapters I will be documenting in more detail some research strategies that ensue directly from this recognition of the importance of the embodied Internet for ethnographic understanding. In Chapter 3, the role of autoethnographic and reflexive ethnography is explored, highlighting the contribution made by the ethnographer's developing sense of the structures of feeling developing around various forms of interaction. An ethnographer can, I argue, usefully focus in on autoethnographic experiences to reflect on embodied experiences of the Internet and to explore the texture of everyday lived experience as it moves between online and offline domains. Ethnographers can learn from their own experiences of moving around, finding out which moves are easy and which difficult, what kinds of contact are sanctioned and which are taboo. Accounts of such insights are, however, not to be taken as somehow necessarily more "authentic" than those of the activities of other participants, and they do not replace the necessity in most projects to explore the diversity of experiences including, but not confined to, those of the ethnographer.

Focusing on the idea of an embodied Internet encourages a shift towards recognition of the diversity of the Internet experience and as a corollary encourages a recognition of reflexive and autoethnographic methods as a valuable component of ethnography for the Internet.

EVERYDAY INTERNET

It follows from the discussion thus far that much Internet usage has become mundane and unremarkable, as we very often simply deploy it as a way of doing what makes sense to us as embedded and embodied social beings. The Internet can, in fact, disappear as a remarkable facet of everyday life, becoming simply an infrastructure that offers a means to do other things. Despite often being viewed as mundane, however, infrastructures are not necessarily undeserving of critical attention. Work in the sociology of infrastructure has argued that it is important to look at the invisible structuring work that infrastructures do. By taking an infrastructure for granted we may be accepting certain choices and priorities that are built into that infrastructure. Even if the Internet does appear to have become mundane, then, it may be important to examine closely the work which we are allowing the various Internet applications that we rely upon to do for us, and the decisions which we are implicitly allowing these infrastructures to make on our behalf. In the rest of this section I will explore in more detail this perspective on infrastructures, and consider the potential that it offers to suggest ethnographic strategies for the Internet.

The everyday, mundane Internet poses a methodological challenge for ethnographers in that we may need to develop strategies to capture and make visible such aspects of the Internet as have become unremarkable, moving against the cultural tide to talk about issues that are not topics for everyday discussion. At the same time, it is important to recognize that the Internet does sometimes come back into the cultural foreground, as a notable phenomenon for political or media attention, as a matter of more local concern for organizations and individuals, or as a problem when it fails to work as we have come to expect. As discussed in Chapter 1, the Internet features in popular culture as both banal and topicalized. Portrayals of the Internet are situated phenomena, and the ethnographer needs to look carefully at the conditions under which they arise, and to explore the role of the topicalized Internet in shaping our relationship with the Internet and our expectations about what to do with it, on an everyday basis, as it becomes mundane. The ethnographic challenge of the everyday Internet (and its counterpart, the exceptional Internet) is to treat both with equal skepticism, looking both at the invisible work done by the Internet when we treat it as mundane, and the expectations shaped by our attention to an exceptional Internet, which popular accounts endow with the potential to drive social change for good or bad.

Work in the sociology and anthropology of infrastructure provides some useful precedents for thinking about infrastructural technologies as a site of invisible work, in that the design of the technology and the way in which we interact with it has the effect of making some actions easier and others more difficult, carving out social roles and responsibilities and defining possible actions. Bowker and Star (1999), for example, discuss classificatory systems such as the International Classification of Diseases and a scheme for defining nursing interventions to show how these systems carve out priorities and embed values and choices. With different classifications, different groups of people find their experiences valued or negated. An infrastructure could be a classificatory system or standard protocol, or it could be a more tangible artifact such as the electrical plugs that allow us to access power systems (Star 1999). Different groups may relate to a given infrastructure in different ways: a standard can seem perfectly acceptable and indeed invisible if one's preferences are catered for, but if not, its inflexibility can require one to do extra work to fit in or adapt. To illustrate, Star discusses the problems of a customer who has specific allergies in the face of the efficiency of the fast-food restaurant's mass-production systems (Star 1991). Various forms of resistance and adaptation are possible, but all require additional work from a customer who steps outside the mainstream.

Infrastructures can thus be important sites of social and political ordering: they position some people as "normal" and marginalize others. Anthropologist Anand (2011) describes the interweaving of complex sets of technological and political factors involved in working with the infrastructure that shapes access to water for the population of Mumbai. I quote at length here, to preserve the impact of a description which is both complex and elegant in its portrayal of the different factors at play:

Through manipulations of pressure, water is made available to diverse social groups. Not only do these practices enable settlers to live in the city but also effect what I call hydraulic citizenship: a form of belonging to the city enabled by social and material claims made to the city's water infrastructure. Produced in a field that is social and physical, hydraulic citizenship is born out of diverse articulations between the technology of politics (enabled by laws, politicians, and patrons) and the politics of technology (enabled by plumbing, pipes, and pumps). It depends on the fickle and changing flows of water, the social relations through which everyday political claims are recognized, and the materials that enable urban residents to connect to and receive reliable water from the urban system. As settlers and other residents constantly evaluate and respond to the dynamic flow of water in the city, these connections both elucidate and differentiate the ways in which settlers are able to claim and live in the city. (Anand 2011: 545)

Anand captures here the complexity of infrastructuring, showing that the form that infrastructures take can be highly consequential in the demarcations of inclusion and exclusion that result, such that access to water constitutes a form of citizenship. Developing and embedding an infrastructure can be a social and political act as much as technological development.

It is clear that access to water can be consequential for the ability to live in a particular place or not. When we turn the same framework to the Internet, however, we are no longer talking about provision of the conditions for life itself. We are, though, considering a technology that is potentially hugely consequential for shaping access to other social and political resources. The Internet has also become hugely significant as a cultural phenomenon, increasingly used to conduct friendships and family relations, to provide education and entertainment, and to conduct politics, business, and pleasure. From this perspective, studies of how key Internet technologies are developed become important as sites of critique and intervention, as it becomes consequential to know how technologies arise and become embedded in circumstances of use, whose perspectives and priorities are favored, and who becomes marginalized. In this vein, Graham (2004) warns against a potential for quietism stemming from unquestioning acceptance of networked technologies, and counsels a vigilance towards the particular forms of sociotechnical power that become invisible when we accept such technologies as a taken-for-granted part of everyday life.

There have been some detailed accounts of the development of Internet-related technologies and the building-in of specific priorities and values. Abbate's (2000) history of the early development of the Internet traces the complex inter-weaving of academic and military concerns and user-led innovation that produced the Internet's underlying infrastructure. Looking at more specific technologies that depend upon that infrastructure, Taylor (2003) explored the assumptions about identity and embodiment built into the possibilities for avatar design provided by computer game designers, and

Bowker (2000) discusses the development of biodiversity databases as a process which progressively embeds values into an emergent infrastructure. Mackenzie (2005) explores the development of that often taken-for-granted and invisible component of Internet connection, Wi-Fi, and explores the different ideas about connectivity, identity, security, and mobility that go into the underlying protocols and various projects to enact them in practice. Mackenzie (2005) chooses in his account to foreground the development and operation of an infrastructure which is usually placed in the background, and to stress the social and political dimensions of the decisions which it embeds. In this work he develops a position which he subsequently describes in relation to software more generally as a process of excavating social, cultural, and political dimension of this form of work:

> Despite appearing "merely" technical, technical knowledge-practices overlap and enmesh with imaginings of sociality, individual identity, community, collectivity, organization, and enterprise. Technical practices of programming interlace with cultural practices. (Mackenzie 2006: 4)

These studies exemplify an important strand of ethnographic and historical work which specializes in making infrastructure visible, in looking at how these infrastructures develop, and exploring the extent to which this form of work solidifies choices and values that impact upon subsequent users. This perspective seeks to take the everyday Internet and expose the extent to which it invisibly shapes actions. Ethnographic strategies for this kind of work draw on conventional forms of ethnographic observation, involving immersion within the everyday work of technology development, focused on coming to know the culture of developers and understanding the decisions which they make, the constraints placed upon them, and the values that they work with. Some such workplaces are single geographically located organizational sites. Often, however, researchers studying the development of digital technologies are themselves studying distributed sites that require mobility and agility from the ethnographer to acquire a grasp of work undertaken in networked physical and virtual sites (Star 1999; Takhteyev 2012). Even in such complex and fragmented situations, the guiding ethnographic principle of coming to know in depth and in detail how actions make sense to participants sustains the inquiry, and provides for the fundamental insight that specific technologies could always have been otherwise, and that choices embed social values and provide for social consequences.

A standard set of sensibilities from science and technology studies (using Latour's [1987] exhortation to researchers to open the black boxes of technologies) is therefore of great help in bringing to the fore the sense in which the everyday Internet we take for granted could have been otherwise. As an ethnographer working on users, rather than producers of the Internet, these concerns should be in the back of one's mind as one looks at how a specific set of people, in particular circumstances, accept what the infrastructure of the Internet offers and make it their own. Often, however, ethnography for the Internet will not actually involve studying the circumstances in which Internet technologies are developed, and will focus solely on situations of use where the technology has achieved a relatively stable identity: people understand that it has a certain set of functions, which are appropriated and made meaningful in their own specific circumstances, but to a large extent black-boxing of the technology will already have occurred or, to use another set of ideas from science and technology studies, the technology has achieved closure (Bijker and Pinch 1987).

As the technology becomes an unremarkable component of everyday life, another important issue that confronts ethnographers is the extent to which the Internet might have become something that people rarely talk about explicitly and find difficult to treat as a topic for conversation. The ethnographer may find himself investigating something many people around him treat as mundane, unremarkable, and irrelevant. To a certain extent this is the standard challenge faced by any ethnographer. As we attempt to explore how a particular cultural setting works on its own terms, we find ourselves attempting to develop the "stranger perspective," foregrounding that which for participants is wholly normal, and highlighting that it could have been otherwise. As Hirschauer (2006) describes, the ethnographer is always confronted by the "silence of the social," attempting to put into words something that is otherwise unspoken in its descriptions of how the social works. In Bloch's (2008) terms, the ethnographer is seeking to explain "what goes without saying," an activity that builds on experiential knowledge of the setting as much as the retrospective verbalized accounts that participants can give us about what is going on.

When dealing with this everyday Internet, an unremarkable aspect of getting some other, more remarkable activity done, the ethnographer's immersion in the setting, coupled with a determination to notice and question the taken-for-granted, is a key strategy. Informants' accounts are of course important to take the ethnographer outside a self-obsessed set of interpretations of what is going on from his own limited perspective. Ethnographers need to triangulate their own perceptions with those of other participants. However, the ethnographer's immersion in the setting (which in the case of ethnography for the Internet almost inevitably implies settings, as a plural which includes both online and offline engagement) is key in developing an understanding of the strangeness of the everyday Internet as a means of getting things done. The ethnographer actively questions the implications of various forms of engagement and reflects upon why particular choices of medium make sense and what their consequences might be. Ethnography for the Internet involves developing an acute awareness of the social texture of lived experience as it moves between media and across situations. A sensitivity needs to be developed for changes in emotional mood, in feelings of presence and connectivity, for moves that are sanctioned and easy, and those that are difficult or taboo. Ethnographers for the Internet move around, and learn much about the everyday Internet by constantly reflecting on the properties of their movement. This is a sensory ethnography (Pink 2009), in which much can be learned by reflecting on the differential sensory engagement of the various media in use. Star's (2002) focus on studying the connection between lived experiences and technologies is a useful guide for the study of the everyday Internet, as we look at materialities of interaction with infrastructures, explore the work being done, and look for emergent social ordering.

As the Internet becomes everyday it will, of course, become harder to separate out the Internet as such from the general flow of existence. Whatever the domain we examine, changes will be apparent, and will be the subject of commentary, but it will be unclear to what extent such changes are attributable to Internet, in themselves. As Beer (2013) describes, in the domain of popular culture, it has become almost meaningless to try and separate new media and popular culture, such is the degree of enmeshing between them. According to Beer we need to become attuned to the ways in which popular culture and notions of taste no longer circulate according simply to conventionally understood social segmentations and membership of specific social groups. Increasingly, data circulates according to algorithms, which shape what we see, and past activities are archived and become active agents in shaping our ongoing exposure to popular culture. For Beer, the study of popular culture must, perforce, attend to the role of these dynamics, as "the study of contemporary culture requires an understanding of these circulations, the folding back of data into culture and the material infrastructures that make them possible" (Beer 2013: 4). As an ethnographer, the Internet becomes a landscape we and the people that we study inhabit, but this is a landscape that is actively shaped and brought into being by our actions. Ethnography for the everyday Internet involves studying the way that people move through, bring into being, attend to, and ignore that landscape as they go about their daily activities.

Even as a technology becomes everyday, there will be circumstances in which it is topicalized. A loss of Wi-Fi connection, hard drive breakdown, or mobile phone dropped down the toilet are the occasion for a significant attention to what the technology means in our lives. A university that I worked at once had a catastrophic failure of email servers, which disabled all email accounts for a period of days. We had never talked so much about the way we used email as we did in those few days, as we reflected on the practices we had to change, and the activities it had become difficult to do. Taking away a technology is a good way to stimulate talk about what it means. Reflection on everyday technologies does not always have to involve such catastrophes, however. Even where a technology has become routine, we will often preserve a repertoire of talk that can foreground the technology in a narrative, casting it as an active agent instead of an unspoken element of the background (Hine 1995a, 1995b). Thus, even while we take the Internet for granted, we will often still preserve a way of talking that gives it agency, that reflects on it as a grand phenomenon that potentially changes lives and impacts society. In much of our everyday lives we disaggregate the Internet, emailing people, updating Facebook statuses, checking in with our friends, and Googling facts. In other narratives we unify the Internet, attributing it a single identity that brings benefits and risks. Media portrayals contain both aspects of the Internet too, rendering it at the same time an everyday way to keep in touch (tweet your responses to the program, check us out on Facebook) and a grand phenomenon that offers up commercial opportunities, endangers our children, and transforms societies, as depicted in the newspaper headlines shown in Figures 1.1 and 1.2.

An ethnographer can usefully pay symmetrical attention to both aspects of the everyday Internet, seeking to explore the consequences of the silence of the Internet as a component of everyday life and to understand how, and when, we identify it as a grand phenomenon with significant, large-scale consequences. A corollary of taking the "stranger perspective" cherished within ethnography is to seek to explore how positions make sense without taking it for granted that they do so. Both the remarkable and the unnoticed everyday Internet are therefore of ethnographic interest, and amenable to ethnographic exploration. Ethnography for the everyday Internet needs to ask how the Internet is characterized, and under what circumstances. What connections are forged between the Internet and other phenomena, and what comparisons drawn? What frameworks do participants draw on for understanding what the Internet means, and what categories and distinctions do they draw on when depicting the technologies involved and the people affected? Inspired by Tsing's (2005) work on the friction between the universal and the specific, what tensions arise between the public portrayal of a universal "Internet" and the very personalized experiences we may have of it?

Ethnographic strategies for the everyday Internet therefore focus on being sensitive to the variable topicalization of the Internet, paying careful attention to the specific circumstances in which accounts of its significance are produced. An awareness of the structuring potential of technological infrastructures can be built by careful observation of participants, by interacting with participants to generate their accounts of the choices, constraints and silences following on from its use, and by reflecting on the ethnographer's own immersion within the setting in order to build a sensitivity to the resulting social textures. To the extent that Internet cultures are often somewhat familiar to the ethnographers who study them, the ethnographic strategies that are used are often biased towards making the familiar strange, rather than the opposing ethnographic strategy of making strange and exotic cultures seem familiar by demonstrating their internal logic and connection with recognizable conceptual frameworks (Ybema and Kamsteeg 2009). Seeking to take a stranger perspective on the Internet involves remembering that its use is both shaped by and shaping of local circumstances, and that what appears routine and natural there would not necessarily appear so from another location.

CONCLUSION

In this chapter I have been arguing for a multi-modal approach to ethnography for the Internet, which does not treat an online/offline boundary as a principled limit for ethnographic field sites, but accepts that the themes and issues we study will perforce very often cross that boundary (or be agnostic about the existence of such a boundary as an organizing principle for social experience). The E³ framework of sensitivity towards an embedded, embodied, everyday Internet is an encouragement to look both inward and outward in search of ethnographic holism. We are encouraged to look outward from the Internet in itself towards myriad potential connections and frames of meaning-making. We are encouraged to look inward in search of the embodied experience of using the Internet as a component of an everyday life that does not necessarily attend to whether or not something happens online as a primary matter for concern. An ethnographer can usefully take a symmetrically skeptical stance both towards claims that the Internet occasions radical innovation and social change, and that it continues the values of the past or becomes altogether unremarkable. Inspired by the sociology of infrastructure, ethnographers may wish to look especially carefully at situations where technical decisions are being made, for those decisions can be highly consequential for social ordering, and can also bring into visibility sets of values otherwise unarticulated.

At this stage, these pieces of advice to a potential ethnographer are somewhat bland generalizations, as suggestions to be sensitive to this and look closely for that which do not tell an ethnographer, faced with an actual situation and a set of foreshadowed problems, in any useful degree, what she should actually do. This situation is, of course, to some extent compatible with the stance that approaches to ethnography are always adaptive, and generalized advice is formulated in an expectation that there is no correct model of ethnography for the Internet. In being adaptive to circumstances, choice and strategy are particularly significant for the ethnographer. The moves we make need to be carefully considered, since they are highly consequential for the constitution of the object that we study. Ethnography is purposive rather than passive: however, it is not "adaptive" in the sense that we just do what the field tells us to, but rather, we actively adapt our strategies in order to explore something in particular. There is thus no single model of ethnography for the Internet: however, in the expectation that some more concrete advice on engaging with the Internet in various ways will be useful, in the next chapter I go on to explore strategies for formulating the field and engaging with it that are particularly relevant for an E^3 Internet.

3

Ethnographic Strategies for the Embedded, Embodied, Everyday Internet

INTRODUCTION

Ethnography is an immersive method, using the ethnographer's participation to build a multi-faceted portrayal of the research setting. Participation by the ethnographer is an important aspect of the ethnographic knowledge generation process, because it allows the ethnographer to observe in minute detail exactly how activities happen, rather than relying only on selective retrospective accounts from participants. Where practical and ethical considerations allow the ethnographer actually to learn to do what participants are doing, this deeper level of participation offers the ethnographer an emotional and embodied understanding of how activities feel, beyond the verbal accounts that participants can give. It is also important for ethnographers to be immersed within research settings because this places them in direct contact with the participants in the setting, as much visible to them as they are to the ethnographer. This prolonged exposure makes the ethnographer publicly accountable to participants for their actions: "getting it wrong" becomes a public event, and the ethnographer learns from the experience of fitting in, or not, as events unfold. Overt participation also allows for emerging themes and interpretations to be discussed with participants and for hunches and predictions to be tested out. An extended timeframe is significant in ethnography, because it allows for the ethnographer to do serious thinking about what the observations he is making might mean whilst he is still in the field. The extended period of fieldwork which the ethnographer carries out both means that he has some security that he has been exposed to a wide range issues of significance in participants' lives and that he has had the opportunity whilst still in the field to revise assumptions, revisit categories that do not quite work, and refine frames of analysis. The reflection that happens after having left the field is important in crafting a theoretically sophisticated and robust argument, but it does not substitute for this opportunity to reflect and revise whilst in the field.

These qualities of ethnography as a process of knowledge generation are, I would argue, as relevant to an ethnography of an embedded, embodied, everyday Internet as they are to any other setting. However, in order to realize the process of ethnographic knowledge generation in such a setting, some unusual strategies may be needed. Ethnographies conducted in diffuse, unpredictable field settings, which move between face-to-face and mediated forms of interaction may look, on the face of it, quite different from ethnographies in more conventional bounded field sites. In order to work out what strategies might be useful and appropriate, some revision of what we mean by key terms may be helpful. For example, the notion of prolonged immersion that features so heavily in the description above may need to be revisited, for it is difficult, when a field site is multi-sited and diffuse, to be sure what immersion means, and how to achieve it for prolonged periods of time. It might seem that an ethnographer studying activities in and around the Internet as embedded in everyday life will have difficulty living in their field site for a long period of time. However, rather than saying that we therefore cannot do ethnography of this kind of phenomenon, it may instead be useful to remember what the epistemic gain from prolonged immersion was intended to be. If we do so, we may be able to find ways of achieving that aspect of the method through alternative means, rather than rejecting certain kinds of setting as inappropriate for ethnographic study altogether. If the epistemic gain from prolonged immersion is about having the time to formulate and reject emergent theories in the face of ongoing engagement with the field, and about having a clear sense of the normal and the unusual for this setting, then this can be achieved even where a setting is not one in which one can plausibly "live" for a long period of time. The notion of prolonged immersion simply needs to be rearticulated to encompass the experience of mediated forms of engagement and to involve following connections rather than assuming physical co-presence in geographic space.

Other aspects of the ethnographic tradition translate relatively well to mediated settings. In field sites which involve both online and offline modes of communication, an ethnographer can usefully aim to participate in whatever activities the participants in question carry out, being led by them, and engaging in interactions according to whatever medium participants deem appropriate. A part of the learning that the ethnographer engages in focuses precisely on this question of working out which medium is deemed appropriate for different activities, with the goal of being able to make choices as participants would make them, and to be able to articulate the grounds and consequences of those choices. In some of these media the ethnographer and participants will be mutually visible to one another, and the ethnographer will benefit from the same epistemic gains as a conventional ethnographer in a face-to-face setting, being held accountable by participants for their actions, and being able to ask participants for accounts of their actions in turn.

Some media readily lend themselves to a sense of awareness of co-presence, and in fact many social networking sites demand it, in that privacy settings are under the direct control of participants who must actively accept friends' requests. In such settings it is difficult for an ethnographer to lurk unnoticed. In other settings it may not be as easy for the ethnographer to sustain mutual visibility with participants. In an online discussion group, for example, it may be quite normal to lurk without posting, and thus to remain invisible to other participants. As an ethnographer one can choose to post messages to the group, but to do so repeatedly without offering contributions to the group themes or goals would usually be a breach of group etiquette and could make the ethnographer unpopular. In this circumstance, it is important to remember that the group itself need not necessarily be treated as a bounded field site in its own right: group members may well have other means of communicating and other settings where they meet, and the ethnographer could engage with these instead and as well. Mutual visibility for ethnographic purposes may not, therefore, have to happen solely through the medium of the online discussion group itself, and can be achieved through direct email contact, through participation in face-to-face meetings, through blogging, or in whatever additional means are deemed sensible and appropriate by that group. Ethnographers need to be active participants in order to build up a robust, well-rounded account, and this will probably involve being visible in some form to participants but not necessarily all the time, in every medium that participants use. It will be important to reflect on the conventions of co-presence and reciprocity within each medium as deployed by participants, and to keep account of when and where members become visible to one another (and how they themselves deal with lack of mutual visibility in certain media).

The rest of this chapter focuses on developing a set of strategies that may be helpful in carrying out ethnography for the embedded, embodied, everyday Internet, based upon this notion of finding new ways to achieve the fundamental principles of the ethnographic knowledge generation process. The chapter draws on examples derived from a wide range of ethnographic studies focused around the Internet, including some of my own studies, but also extending beyond, in order to cover examples ranging from wholly online ethnographic studies in virtual worlds to cross-platform approaches and studies of mobile Internet experiences mediated by smartphone apps. The first section of the chapter explores the forms of field site that emerge through exploration of various frames of meaning-making that ethnographers might explore in and around the Internet. Following on from this discussion of field sites, the next section explores the application of a standard ethnographic repertoire of participation, reflective and descriptive field notes, interviews, and questionnaires as they apply in this kind of field site and also considers the use of various means of mapping and visualizing digital data as aids to fieldwork. The section after this turns to the question of reflexive and autoethnographic insight as particularly useful in exploring the embodied experience of Internet use. Finally, the chapter draws to a close with a summary of some core ethnographic principles for the embedded, embodied, everyday Internet.

FIELD SITES FOR THE EMBEDDED INTERNET

Thus far I have referred in general terms to "the setting" or "the field" without specifying very clearly how we might define these concepts in practice. It is certainly important to have some conception of what the field of interest might be, since a clear corollary of conceiving of ethnography as immersive and participatory is that we must have a sense of a location in which to immerse ourselves and an understanding of the nature of the activities in which we are to participate. As already discussed in Chapter 2, however, thinking of the Internet as embedded, embodied, and everyday complicates our sense of place, and puts in question where the appropriate activities in which the ethnographer will participate may be found. In this section I will therefore explore some guiding principles for identifying an appropriate focus for ethnographic engagement and for specifying what, exactly the object of study might be. I will discuss some relevant debates in anthropology and in sociology in turn, before turning to the specific issue of Internet-focused studies, and examining some strategies for identifying appropriate field sites for the embedded Internet.

Although we routinely speak of "the field site" in the singular, the object of study in ethnographic tradition has, in practice, rarely been a tightly bounded geographic space or cultural unit. Even where the original guiding focus might be specified as a particular place, for purposes of convenient shorthand, this is in practice only a provisional specification. As the ethnographer works with participants to find out how their practices make sense, new locations and connections with other groups of people come into view as relevant to understanding the original focus of inquiry. A conception of group boundaries as fluid and situated, brought into being for specific purposes or symboli- cally constructed (Cohen 1985: 209) rather than existing in an objective, transcendental sense, is often the upshot of this form of inquiry. Because ethnography is an exploratory and adaptive method that sets out to find out how things make sense, and because boundaries themselves may not objec- tively pre-exist the particular circumstances in which they are referenced, it is generally not thought possible to specify in advance exactly what the boundaries of the study will be.

The focus of the ethnography, provisional though it may be, is often chosen because it appears on the face of it to offer the chance to explore a theoretically interesting point or significant issue for the ethnographer's home discipline. Ethnography is not simply empirically descriptive, but develops instead a theoretically enriched form of description through which ethnographers hope to make an intervention in the ongoing debates within the academic field, or policy domain, to which they orient themselves. The choice of field, and the decisions about where to go, are often therefore made with a conception of what may be interesting to the discipline in mind. As Schatzman and Strauss describe it, this urge to find interesting things to discuss and theoretical contributions to make can in fact override the urge to produce a definitive and comprehensive description:

> More important to him than "nailing it down" is "linking it up" logically, theoreti- cally, and empirically to other findings or discoveries of his own and others." (Schatzman and Strauss 1973: 8)

This understanding of any individual ethnography as a contribution to a corpus, and of ethnographic writing as more than the sum of multiple individual descriptions, frames the ethnographer's understanding of some directions as particularly interesting to pursue. Anthropological ethnography is often overtly comparative, deploying common concepts across field sites in order to illuminate differences in cultural formations. In other fields, a pressing policy question, or a need to explore a specific theoretical question focused on the implications of particular practices, may motivate the ethnographer's interest. A field site may therefore be strategically chosen, and once in the field, the ethnographer may choose particular aspects to explore over others because of this set of interests that transcend the specific study in question.

In recent years a strand of anthropological debate has focused specifically on the question of how a field site should be conceptualized, and what form it should take. According to Gupta and Ferguson (1997b) discussion of the definition of the field site was, for many years, neglected within anthropology:

> But what of "the field" itself, the place where the distinctive work of "fieldwork" may be done, that taken-for-granted space in which an "Other" culture or society lies waiting to be observed and written? This mysterious space—not the "what" of anthropology by the "where"—has been left to common sense, beyond and below the threshold of reflexivity. (Gupta and Ferguson 1997b: 2)

Gupta and Ferguson then open up for critical discussion the means by which ethnographers define the places where they do their work, and in particular they explore the question of whether different notions of field are required for a contemporary world that seems more mobile and more connected than has been the case previously. They do, however, note that stretching the notion of the field introduces some tensions for anthropology in particular, as the discipline has often defined itself around the distinctive nature of the immersive fieldwork that it holds dear. Gupta and Ferguson (1997b) advocate a close examination of the epistemic purchase that the notion of the field has offered, alongside a more pragmatic recognition of the role of the linked notions of fieldwork and field site in sustaining both the identity of the discipline, and the identity of individual anthropologists. The role of the field in constructing the identity of the anthropologist arises since careers in anthropology are often defined around a specialism in ethnography of a particular, often geographically defined, region. Not having a regional specialism potentially makes it harder for an anthropologist to pinpoint what distinctive form of expertise they offer in situations such as job applications where such issues matter. An understanding of definitions of the field as consequential for individual and disciplinary identity needs to be kept in mind in all that follows: some ethnographers, depending on disciplinary affiliation, may be freer to explore alternative conceptualizations of the field than others. All, however, need to keep in mind the question of the specific epistemic purchase offered by the notion of immersive fieldwork, and the potential threat to the ethnographic knowledge generation process if new formulations of the field do not allow for this aspect of ethnographic engagement.

Despite the tensions attendant on redefining the field, it has increasingly been recognized that the field site is an artful construction rather than something one simply "finds" (Amit 1999). This recognition opens up a space for discussion of the extent to which the ethnographer exerts agency over the nature of the field she chooses to explore. Constructions of the field, as the papers collected in the volume edited by Amit (1999) exemplify, are not necessarily focused on a specific place in which the ethnographer becomes immersed for a long period of time separated from the ethnographer's usual way of life. Ethnography sometimes takes place much closer to home, and sometimes uncomfortably entwines the ethnographer's personal and professional identities (Dyck 2000). Ethnographers have also increasingly explored field sites that are defined in non-spatial terms, for example crossing national boundaries (Hannerz 2003) or exploring the experiences of migrants (Olwig 2003). The object of the ethnography for Olwig (2003) is a group of people, defined as a group in so far as they conceive of themselves as an interconnected entity, and thus neither focused in advance on a particular place nor on a pre-defined set of people whom the ethnographer determines in advance as a bounded group. The object of the ethnography emerges through fieldwork, as the significant identities and locations unfold.

The idea of artfully constructed, non-spatially defined field sites received a particular boost from Marcus's (1995, 1998) discussions of multi-sited fieldwork. Marcus (1995) explored different defining concepts for a form of ethnographic fieldwork that took as its focus objects of study not confined to geographic space. He suggested that for some strategic purposes it would be useful for ethnographers to move around, using as their organizing principle for movement a non-spatial or transgeographic concept such as a conflict, a circulation of objects, or even a metaphor. The idea of multi-sited ethnography in Marcus's formulation is that sometimes the strategically interesting aspect of contemporary life to be explored is characterized by connection and mobility rather than static location, and that in such circumstances the ethnographer should be willing to move.

Subsequently there has been considerable discussion of the extent to which ethnography can usefully be construed as a multi-sited practice, highlighting the benefits and drawbacks of such an approach in terms of epistemology and disciplinary identity. A volume of papers collected by Falzon (2009b) captures many different aspects of the discussion which ensued from Marcus's (1995) original intervention, including Candea's (2007) defense of the strategic choice to focus on an arbitrarily chosen bounded site even in the face of an inter-connected world, and Cook et al.'s (2009) discussion of the purchase offered by conceiving of field sites as unsited, rejecting even the notion of a network of interconnected discrete sites which some have taken from the term "multi-sited." Marcus himself has revisited the debate, to clarify and extend the extent to which multi-sited fieldwork practice should be seen as distinct from more conventional single-sited studies. He suggests that there is a potential for a radical departure from conventional notions of the field site:

The past habit of Malinowskian ethnography has been to take subjects as you find them in natural units of difference—cultures, communities; the habit or impulse of multi-sited research is to see subjects as differently constituted, as not products of essential unity of difference only, but to see them in development—displaced, recombined, hybrid in the once popular idiom, alternatively imagined. Such research pushes beyond the situated subject of ethnography towards the system of relations which define them. (Marcus 2012: 19)

In this work Marcus (2012) suggests that while we could think of a multi-sited field as merely a mapping out of already understood processes, it would also be possible to think of a multi-sited field as an alternative, more radical reconstruction of the field, in which the multi-sited field only emerges through the process of ethnographic engagement. The shape of the field is the upshot rather than the starting point, and is the product of an active ethnographer strategically engaging with the field, rather than a passive mapping of a pre-existing territory or cultural unit.

Such debates are very timely, and very productive, for informing development of ethnographic strategies for the embedded, embodied, everyday Internet. When the object of interest is an embedded Internet, which connects with and finds meaning within diverse and unpredictable aspects of contemporary existence, it can help to have an open and imaginative approach to where the field might be found, as long as we do not present the upshot as a definitive description of an objectively existing entity. Part of the challenge of exploring the embedded, embodied, everyday Internet is that it is often not most useful, analytically, theoretically, or practically, to conceive of the Internet as a singular object contained within one site. Internet content may circulate far beyond the initial online setting in which it was generated, and the Internet, as a technology, may acquire quite different meanings and identities in different settings of use (De Laet and Mol 2000; Mol 2002). Even if we choose to follow the Internet (or rather, some aspect of the Internet) as the object of study across different sites, it would be a mistake to expect it to be a stable and identifiable object in different settings. Some judgments will always be required about what constitutes a relevant connection, which connections to follow, and which aspects of the Internet are going to be productive and interesting to study in depth. We will often be unsure about which aspects to follow, and there will be many uncertainties that the ethnographer needs to address by making overt choices, exerting agency over the shape of the field. This, then, looks more like the radical reconstruction of the field as the product of the ethnographer's agency as described by Marcus (2012), rather than a straightforward mapping of pre-existing interconnected sites.

Whilst anthropological debates have focused on the notion of the field and the possibility of multi-sited objects of study, developments in sociology have focused on the notion of mobility, and the extent to which new methods could allow for objects of inquiry that are not assumed to have a static existence in a single location. Buscher and Urry (2009) suggest that mobile methods are important to allow sociologists to move away from a spatially located notion of society, and to enable them to explore the extent to which movement and immobility, between them, constitute society. Under the banner of mobile methods (Buscher and Urry 2009) a call is made for studies that specialize in understanding the movement of people, things, and ideas, encompassing forms of mobility that include: the bodily travel of people; the physical movement of objects; imaginative travel conjured up as we anticipate actions in distant places; virtual travel across networks of mediated communications; and communicative travel as people are connected in interactions face-to-face and via mediated communications. Each form of mobility is underpinned by its own infrastructures, and the various forms of mobility mutually reinforce and entwine with one another to produce complex structures of meaning-making. Mobility is as much a sensory experience as it is a practical effect of taking a thing elsewhere, and as such, a multi-faceted ethnographic approach is among the methods proposed as suitable to grasp these entwined aspects of mobility. In particular, Buscher and Urry (2009) suggest that traveling with participants, and participating in the various patterns of movement and experience that emerge, is a powerful means to explore the sensory and constitutive nature of mobility. Alongside the embodied engagement of the ethnographer, Buscher and Urry (2009) also suggest creative use of a variety of approaches to observing and recording mobility, including video records, time-use diaries, tagging and tracking objects, engaging with creative writing and works of imagination, and studying key transit points. They also suggest various strategic devices that the ethnographer can use in order to move with participants:

> Inquiries on the move—like the shadowing, stalking, walk alongs, ride alongs, participatory interventions and cultural biographies we have described—enable questions about sensory experience, embodiment, emplacement, about what changes and what stays the same, and about the configuration and re-configuration of assemblies of objects, spaces, people, ideas and information. (Buscher and Urry 2009: 110)

The authors recognize that this form of mobile study demands that the ethnographer focus very carefully on co-ordinating her own moves in appropriate fashion in order to accompany and learn from participants. There is thus a strong focus on developing a reflexive insight into the experience of mobility and developing expertise at making moves in ways sanctioned by participants. As with the multi-sited ethnography described by Marcus (2012), the field as an object of study is emergent, impossible to specify in advance, and the product of a creative engagement between ethnographer and participants.

This set of sociological developments in mobile methods has some direct application to ethnography for the Internet. One of the forms of mobility that Buscher and Urry (2009) discuss involves virtual travel via the Internet, and as such they find it appropriate for ethnographers to engage with participants as they use the Internet, to explore the constitution of sites on the Internet, and to contemplate use of the Internet as an imaginative and sensory experience as much as a practical exchange of information. The usefulness of the mobile methods that they describe for the purposes of ethnography for the Internet is not, however, confined to a recognition that ethnographers can usefully travel on to the Internet with participants. Instead, the mobilities approach can be inspirational in a broader sense for Internet ethnographers wanting to find appropriate ways to cast the field. By focusing on the mobility of the analyst alongside that of participants, the proponents of mobile methods allow for the emergence of objects of study that are not confined to single sites, whether those be online or offline, but allow for exploration of diverse forms of connection and circulation between them. The mobilities approach allows for non-spatially located objects of study that are focused on patterns of connection and circulation, and this is particularly appropriate for an embedded, embodied Internet.

Mobile and multi-sited conceptualizations of the field translate particularly well to study of the Internet, as an embedded, embodied, everyday phenomenon. As discussed in Chapter 2, ethnographic studies of discrete online settings were highly influential in establishing that there was something culturally significant to take seriously on the Internet, when the Internet first began to become a mainstream phenomenon. Subsequently, however, in parallel with, if not always directly influenced by, ongoing debates in anthropology and sociology, many Internet ethnographers have taken on the challenge of exploring more spatially complex field sites. Leander and McKim (2003), for example, explored the online practices of teenagers, by conceptualizing online and offline as mutually elaborative, and moving their focus back and forth between online and offline modes of engagement. Similarly, Aouragh (2011) traversed online and offline spaces in an ethnographic study of Palestinian mobility as realized through Internet spaces. Aouragh explored

the meanings that Internet activities acquired for differently located participants, and critically examined the extent to which Internet mobility overcomes
other forms of immobility imposed upon participants.

Ethnographers have, therefore, found it fruitful to move between online
and offline, and this mobility makes it difficult to conceptualize of the field
as a bounded entity. Ethnographers may start out with a specified focus of
interest that potentially spans both online and offline, but remain agnostic
about how, precisely, online and offline activities will turn out to matter to one
another. Taking this approach, one alternative way of conceptualizing the field
that can seem quite natural to ethnographers studying connections between
online and offline spaces is the notion of the field as network. Burrell (2009),
for example, studied the social appropriation of the Internet in Accra, Ghana,
and found that conceptualizing the field as a network, rather than a bounded
location, proved to offer a suitable organizing principle:

> The impossibility of drawing a boundary around such a social phenomenon arose
> from two conditions. First, the subject matter was the Internet, a global network
> of machines, information, and people; yet the Internet is too vast be studied as
> a whole. Second, it was also a study of everyday life in Accra that, beyond the
> Internet, is lived in the broader context of daily interaction with a material and
> media culture that has ambiguous and/or multiple origins. (Burrell 2009: 187)

Burrell (2009) carved out a networked field of enquiry by following heterogeneous forms of connection between Internet cafés in Accra, specific
online sites and the broader notions of the Internet as a technology and a
system. Connections to explain arose from following the movements of interviewees from those cafés across the city and online, and yet this was not a
passive following, but arose from some strategic choices that Burrell (2009)
made, according to theoretical interests in the localization of the Internet
in a specific geographical place. Her Internet was embedded in place, and
she considered connections between the mundane details of the everyday
Internet in this place, and the prevailing rhetoric of a topicalized, globalized
Internet. The resulting ethnographic account was highly dependent upon
the specific entry points that Burrell (2009) chose and the moves that were
considered both practical and interesting to make: it also, however, aspired
to describe something of a more transcendent significance in documenting
a certain kind of connection that characterizes a contemporary way of life.

The starting point for a connective, or networked ethnography need not be
a geographic place, as it was for Burrell (2009). Fields and Kafai (2009), for
example, develop a connective ethnography that explores the practices of a

group of children using an online gaming environment. They start from the classroom, and set out to understand learning practices through a combination of video recording, interviews, log files of activity on the site and observational field notes. Farnsworth and Austrin (2010) also take a networked approach to ethnographic study of the Internet, but again, unlike Burrell (2009) they do not begin from a notion of geographic place to orient their focus. Nor do they focus on a discrete group as Fields and Kafai (2009) did. Instead they concentrate on a spatially distributed phenomenon, global poker, and explore poker's changing nature and significance as it is manifested in new televised and online spaces. Farnsworth and Austrin (2010) understand their field as constituted through actor-networks comprised of technological and human mediators. They engage with poker as manifested in diverse sites and different technological platforms, and consider how different actors and locations are brought into play as the technology which mediates poker for players and observers changes. The resulting ethnographic field is conceived as an actor-network that they explore through various forms of participation and observation. The field encompasses both the everyday mundanities of poker as practiced in various sites, and the various structures of regulation and governance that seek to control it. Farnsworth and Austrin (2010) experience an overwhelming amount of potential sites and aspects to explore, and they note that their field is inherently unstable, and potentially proliferating and extending all of the time. Their organizing principle of the actor-network allows for this kind of indeterminacy in the field. The field, as such, is bounded by their own strategic choice to explore a strand of questions that they develop around the difference which various mediators make to the practices of poker.

Another example of a networked field of exploration is offered by Larsen (2008) in a study of digital photography. Whilst it is possible, and more conventional, to study photographs as a representational form, Larsen chooses to understand photography as a practice, and in particular to explore the networked circulation of photographs that becomes feasible through virtual space. This approach suggests a selection of different sites to explore, including the tourist sites where many photographs are taken, the online sites where they are accumulated, juxtaposed, tagged, and categorized, and the home locations where photographs develop what Larsen (2008) calls an "afterlife" as they are viewed and displayed in new settings. Ethnographic practices thus focus on observing and interviewing participants in the various locations, highlighting their understandings of what is going on, and exploring the resulting patterns of mobility of photographs as they move sites and change meanings in different circumstances. Larsen's (2008) approach suggests the importance of taking account of photographs as they travel through time, developing a sensitivity to the different meanings that they acquire: since photographs prove to be mobile, the ethnographer can learn from accompanying them on their journeys.

An alternative approach to defining the field is taken by Lin (2011) in her study of OpenStreetMap making. She draws on her own embodied experiences of participating in mapping, together with attendance at local community mapping events and an international conference. This conference provided both an opportunity to participate in a key event for the international mapping community, and the chance to recruit interviewees who could talk about their involvement from a variety of perspectives. Lin was able to focus on the "various emotional, cognitive and social repertoires involved in open source mapping" (2011: 67), and rather than conceiving of her field as a network she considered it a system of connecting and overlapping social worlds. This social worlds framework enabled her to focus on a single object of inquiry, in OpenStreetMap, but to conceptualize it as a socio-technically complex system that acquires diverse meanings in the different social worlds in which it is embedded. Lin (2011) combines a deep embodied knowledge of the phenomenon from her own participation with an appreciation of diversity derived from participation in public events and engagement with interviewees.

Ethnographers who explore phenomena that are not bounded by single sites, whether their organizing principle be tracing networks, identifying social worlds, or following phenomena across multiple sites, need some way of identifying the connections they will follow. A wide variety of techniques is available to ethnographers looking to find relevant connections to pursue. In some cases, the ethnographer will be led to specific online spaces by the practices of participants as explained in interviews: participants may talk about the discussion groups that they frequent, the Facebook groups they belong to, or the sites to which they upload their photographs. In other cases, the technologies of the Internet themselves suggest connections to pursue. For example, Beaulieu (2005) discusses how following hyperlinks can be an ethnographic strategy, and Beaulieu and Simakova (2006) developed a complex understanding of hyperlinks as located in time and in the space of websites, and as both bearing practical significance in linking sites together and carrying a symbolic meaning. For Beaulieu and Simakova (2006), following hyperlinks is an ethnographic practice in its own right, but the ethnographer does far more than simply click and go: this ethnographic use of hyperlinks involves a much more contemplative practice.

This approach to ethnographic understanding of hyperlinks as a form of cultural connection can be broadened out to other forms of document. Geiger and Ribes (2011) focus on techniques for following connections through documentary practices in their discussion of trace ethnography. They are motivated by an interest in ethnography of distributed organizations, spanning wide geographic distance, in which various forms of document are generated by participants and used by them to co-ordinate and understand collective activity. The traces of activity preserved in log files, such as records of edits made to a document, make participants in distributed systems visible to one another. It is thus very important for the ethnographer to engage with these traces and explore both what they might mean to participants and how they constitute participants as visible actors to one another. The traces left in a log file might be frustratingly thin or incomplete, and seem thus not amenable to ethnographic insight. However, by engaging with them, the ethnographer is able to gain valuable experiential insight precisely into how it feels to operate in a distributed organization where this is the kind of information on other participants that is available to one. Each software platform will have its own conventions about which log files are kept and for how long, what they record and to whom they are made available. These "memory practices" (Bowker 2005) provide a resource for participants to develop a sense of identity and relationship to the group. They also provide a resource for the ethnographer to follow in mapping out the group, although as before, not as a passive form of following, but rather as an active process of interpretation and reflection on the meaning of various forms of trace for identity and practice. The embodied experience of the ethnographer in attempting to make sense of these traces can be an important source of insight into the opportunities and constraints that participants encounter and the emotions that accompany them.

Unlike the documents used by Geiger and Ribes, the traces for ethnographers to follow are not always readily observable without some more direct intervention. Traces may, instead, need to be captured by use of recording devices introduced by the ethnographer. Voilmy et al. (2008), for example, take a very fine-grained approach to observation of the mobile communication practices of just one commuter, combining different forms of observation to build a multi-faceted understanding. They deploy a combination of direct observation by an accompanying researcher, geo-location to track movements through space, and video-recording of use of mobile devices via video glasses worn by the participant. This approach loses something in the conventional ethnographic terms of immersion and participation, and restricts the frames of meaning-making to be pursued quite arbitrarily. Nonetheless, it contains some stimulating ideas for development of ethnographic approaches to engage with the challenges of keeping up with mobile participants. Here the connections followed are those forged by one participant kept under observation by the ethnographer. The connections are made available for exploration through creative use of recording technologies which allow the ethnographer, to a limited extent, to see the experience through the eyes of the participant.

Another situation in which connections to follow may be frustratingly out-of-reach for the ethnographer, and may require some creative jumps of imagination to pursue, is provided by smartphone apps, which, via GPS, have a connection with geographic location and potentially reshape the experience of local spaces. The experience of use is highly individualized, and an observer may find it difficult to work out what is going on, or what it means to the participant. Stempfhuber and Liegl (2012), for example, described their attempts to gain ethnographic insight into the use of the smartphone app Grindr, popular among gay men, which allows users to search for potential like-minded contacts in the local area. Whilst it is possibly to use it simply by browsing the website, the app thrives on being used while out in public, as participants switch between orientation to screen and to local surroundings, building anticipation through the potential for a face-to-face meeting with someone nearby as yet unmet. The ethnographic challenge is to understand the experience of this switching. Stempfhuber and Liegl (2012) observed practices within a bar, watching participants switching their attention between screen and bar, and building use of the app into their evening out. The researchers also conducted one-to-one interviews with users, to find out more about their experience of using the app. However, the researchers were conscious that this set of observational techniques only scratched the surface of the spatial layering and complexity that is going on as users engage with the app, and that observation from within a bar setting, or on the Grindr app itself, leaves them without a direct access into the most important aspect of the app, which is the contingent connections being forged between virtual and physical space. Autoethnography provides an alternative route into understanding such situations, as will be explored later in this chapter.

Each situation is different in the nature of the connections that it offers up for the ethnographer to follow and the moves that are easy and difficult to make. In constituting the field through following up on the connections that are available, the ethnographer can benefit from being imaginative about the form that connections might take and what they might mean, and also being sensitive to when they are moving with or against the grain of culturally sanctioned moves. Fieldwork entails following connections whilst reflecting on the circumstances and actors that bring these connections into being. The ethnographer takes on a lot of responsibility for making moves and exploring connections that help to answer strategically significant questions. This does not mean that the ethnographer has to develop a god-like overview of everything that is going on. The ethnographer also benefits greatly, in experiential terms, from being immersed in the same conditions of uncertainty. As documentary traces are often too thin to give participants themselves certainty about what is going on and who they are dealing with, it is useful for the ethnographer to learn from immersion in these same conditions of uncertainty. Nonetheless, it is important that the exploration does not focus only on the ethnographer's journey and thus neglect the experience of the various participants in the phenomenon being explored. It is useful, when finding connections to follow, to consider the extent to which the kind of following that the ethnographer is doing mirrors anything that the participants in these settings might be doing.

The idea of a connective, itinerant, or networked ethnography, divorced from a necessary connection to a specific location and open to exploring connections as they present themselves, is fundamental to conducting ethnography for an embedded Internet that may mean quite different things in different settings. The connection between online and offline space is not a once-and-for-all issue to be settled, but an ongoing question for both participants and ethnographer. The understanding of the field is built on the ethnographer's embodied experiences, reflecting on moves that are easy and difficult to make, and on the experience of following connections that mirror those that participants themselves might make. The field also encompasses both everyday and topicalized Internet, exploring the contingent connections between these two experiences of the Internet that are forged in the practices of participants and being alert to frictions that may arise between specific experiences and the universalized notion of "the Internet," as Tsing (2005) counsels. The form that the field site takes is thus highly unique to each ethnographic project, reflecting the huge variability in potential meanings and practices woven through and around the Internet.

STANDARD ETHNOGRAPHIC REPERTOIRES IN EMERGENT INTERNET FIELD SITES

Having mapped out some strategies for defining and exploring a field, and having talked in abstract terms about the ethnographer "following connections" and "reflecting on experiences," it is now time to turn to a more concrete consideration of what the ethnographer actually *does* when in the field. This section therefore focuses on exploring the role of the ethnographer in the field, discussing the transfer of conventional modes of fieldwork such as observation, making field notes, and interviewing into a non-spatially defined field site, which involves at least some mediated interaction.

As discussed earlier in this chapter, ethnographers place considerable emphasis on immersion in the setting as a means of knowledge generation. For an ethnographer in a face-to-face setting, "being there" may entail at the outset a fairly straightforward matter of physical displacement into the right place. It will also, however, depend on some more subtle but nonetheless crucial issues involving negotiating access with key gatekeepers and making oneself socially acceptable to the relevant people in the setting. "Being there," in order to maintain an effective ethnographic presence, is thus about more than simply being physically present in a setting. For the ethnographer in a virtual setting, similar issues arise: an effective presence as an ethnographer is not achieved simply by logging into whatever the setting might be. Ethnographers in virtual environments need to make themselves effectively present by getting to a point where they are accepted within that setting, and able to both observe events and interact with other participants as the features of the setting allow. The process through which this is achieved will vary between platforms. In some cases there will be official gatekeepers and a formal process of negotiating access. In other instances, becoming acceptable is a more diffuse process of building whatever form of presence the platform allows and then gradually developing connections with an array of appropriate informants. An ethnographer in Facebook, for example, will become present by signing up for a personal Facebook page, and then make choices about aspects of his identity to signal, photographs to upload, people to friend, and status updates to make. An ethnographer on Twitter will need to make choices about the name to adopt, the personal features to reveal in a profile, and the nature of any tweets and retweets they wish to make. In each case, effective presence requires some initial active choices from the ethnographer about how to portray an identity and an ongoing attention to being socially acceptable within the setting.

The choices ethnographers make about how to portray themselves and their projects in various media can be highly consequential for relationships with informants. To some extent, ethnographic presence in social media is built one medium at a time as we make choices about building profiles for each platform in turn. However, as we carry out studies that cross between different platforms, and as our informants habitually check us, and one another, out across different platforms, ethnographers also have to think about the extent to which they are building a coherent and consistent persona across various sites that participants may access. Informants may not stick to accessing only those aspects of our online presence that we have built specifically for ethnographic purposes, and so it may not be possible to maintain a strict separation between one's ethnographic persona and one's wider personal and professional life. To some extent this may always have been true: the immersive nature of ethnography means that boundaries between the ethnography and other aspects of the ethnographer's life were always potentially hard to maintain, particularly where the ethnography takes place geographically and socially close to one's home (Dyck 2000). Latterly, however, the advent of social media means that many ethnographers will have a readily accessible digital presence that far exceeds that which they have built for ethnographic purposes, and thus to some extent all ethnography potentially takes place uncomfortably close to home. Being co-present with one's research site on social media may entail giving off more information about oneself than feels comfortable. It may also be the occasion for having to give accounts of one's actions and interpretations beyond the field site to informants, as the searchability of the Internet and the increasing culture of open access in academic writing gives them the opportunity to read words produced for other audiences. Informants do not necessarily stay tidily within the field sites that we have mapped out for them, and this in itself can be a source of ethnographic insight.

Social media sites such as Facebook can become embedded into many different forms of fieldwork, as they offer a way to connect and keep up with informants even when we have defined the group not specifically because of their participation in a social media platform *per se*, but because of some other quality or connection that they share. Schneidermann (2014), for example, conducted an ethnographic study of hip hop in Uganda, which involved face-to-face participant observation in Kampala. Social media were, however, vital to the practices of the group and formed an integral part of the meaning of hip hop in their lives. It was essential, therefore, that Schneidermann (2014) also be co-present with her informants on Facebook, enabling her to participate in the interplay between social media spaces and geographic spaces and to understand the various forms of connection and mobility that resulted. The social media connection gave an ongoing sense of co-presence with the field when back at home, facilitated periodic fieldwork visits to Uganda, and helped to build an experiential understanding of a globally interconnected hip hop movement. Another example of fieldwork making use of, but not subsumed by, social media is offered by Baker (2013), who used Facebook in a research project following the literary practices of young adults in the transition from school to university. Facebook acted as a means to communicate with research participants, as a source of data on their literary practices and as a space for observation in its own right.

Facebook here facilitated a longitudinal dimension to the research through its ability to sustain a connection between researcher and participants even when the participants moved to living in a different place. The negotiation of informed consent with participants involved exploring with them the extent to which aspects of their Facebook activities could be made private from the researcher, and also the extent to which their participation in the project and some of their activities would become visible to other participants.

The Internet, and particularly social media, therefore offer means of establishing co-presence with research participants and extending a field site in time and space beyond a notion of a specific bounded online or offline site. The ethnographer's presence is achieved by learning how to use the relevant technologies, both in a technical sense and in terms of building socially acceptable profiles and behaviors within each platform. Developing appropriate presence is thus an opportunity for learning-by-doing, as the ethnographer has to engage in the same process of becoming present that any of the participants in the setting being studied will have gone through. Learning-by-doing is an important component of the ethnographer's reper-toire. When one is doing things for the first time, and particularly when being taught, aspects of everyday life that are often tacit or routine are brought into the foreground. Learning how to do something, whether that be a particular technical skill, or simply how to conform with the social etiquette of a new setting, enables the ethnographer to think about what skilled practitioners are taking for granted. By reading manuals, following instructions, conforming to guidance on what newbies should do, and taking word-of-mouth recommen-dation, the ethnographer is trying to work out both how, practically speaking, an activity is done, and how, socially speaking, it is learned, and what it means. In some settings the technical aspect may come relatively easily, and the ethnographer may need to focus more carefully on the social aspects of appropriate behavior. In other cases, a considerable acquisition of skill may be required: in order to study an online role-playing game, for example, the ethnographer may have to play for a considerable time in order to develop the necessary skill levels to be able to interact with participants and avoid getting in their way or being killed for long enough to conduct an effective observation or interview (Sveinsdottir 2008).

Whatever the balance of social and technical skill required to enter the field, and the technical and financial resources required to do so, it is important for the ethnographer to reflect on what is required in order to be effectively present in each setting, and to what extent these same factors also shape and constrain the participation of the various people encountered in the setting. This kind of reflection is an important part of interrogating and rendering visible the infrastructures that make certain kinds of interaction, and certain kinds of field site, possible, exposing the taken-for-granted every-dayness of the Internet to inquiry. At the point of first becoming accustomed to a new field experience the ethnographer may be particularly sensitized to aspects of the infrastructure that would otherwise be taken for granted.

When entering the field, and throughout the period of fieldwork, it is conventional for the ethnographer to record impressions and developing ideas as they go along, and this is as true of a multi-sited or multi-modal project as it is of a more conventionally geographically-sited study. Field notes allow the ethnographer to keep a record of what happens and how it feels, and enable the ethnographer to capture her provisional thoughts about what these observations may mean, her ideas about what to look at next, and her concerns about aspects that puzzle or frustrate her. In part a cathartic diary, the field notes also provoke reflection on meaning, and encourage an active interpretation that guards against the ethnographer slipping into a passive form of presence. This can be particularly important in online contexts, where the sheer volume of potential data can become overwhelming, and the temptation is simply to download and archive documents to review later. Similarly, the advent of cheap and effective recording technologies means that it can be all too tempting for the ethnographer to store data away rather than actively collecting it and reflecting on what it means, moment by moment. Keeping field notes encourages an active reflection on decisions about what is and is not to be counted as data, focuses the mind on the present moment of experience, and avoids deferring analysis to some solitary future moment away from the field. As Hirschauer (2006) discusses, ethnographic description aspires to a form of interpretation that puts the social into words in a way that straightforward recording cannot. We cannot see "the social" directly in any recordings we make, and so ethnographic description involves attempting to put into words something otherwise silent. The field notes are the first opportunity for the ethnographer to put this into practice.

Field notes were traditionally the ethnographer's private space, where thoughts could be recorded frankly without concern about what participants might make of them. Latterly, social media has occasioned development of some practices of communicating the ethnographer's emerging findings and interpretations during the research itself, which involves relinquishing the privacy of at least some of the field notes. Ethnographers can choose to blog about research as it goes along, tweet snippets of research insight, or post pictures to Flickr, Instagram, and the like (see, for example, Mortensen and Walker 2002; Gregg 2006; Halavais 2006; Ward 2006; Wakeford and Cohen 2008; Efimova 2009; Bukvova et al. 2010). For many of the new generation of ethnographers it is natural, indeed, to make one's activities public via social media. Ethnographers who engage in this practice have some potentially tricky decisions to make on how public to make emerging thoughts, and how far to censor the raw field notes. Kitchin et al. (2013) discuss the prospects of using social media technologies to forge connections across potential divides between academic and public, opening up new possibilities for debate. We still need, however, to be aware that there may be unanticipated outcomes, as the results of our work enter into the data circulation (Beer 2013). There is a risk of ethnographers over-sharing (Agger 2012) or excessively pre-empting in-depth analysis with half-baked thoughts: the ongoing social media version of field notes is not the ethnography in itself, but a step along the way, and it also might not depict all of the raw work of provisional interpretation going on in a more private version of the field notes.

Field notes are an important site of early interpretive work, in which the ethnographer begins actively to construct what will count as data for the study in progress. Ethnography in any environment is thus not about mere recording, even though digital environments may seduce us with easily recorded, archived, and searchable data. This having been said, ethnographers will want to record aspects of field experience for later perusal and in-depth analysis. Many discussion groups are archived for the purposes of their own members, and an ethnographer can make use of the same archives as members do to trawl through for answers to specific questions, or to carry out more systematic analysis of significant themes. The Wayback Machine (http://archive.org/web/) records past versions of websites, and offers a ready-to-hand tool that can encourage ethnographic reflection on the specificity of the present. There is a pleasing symmetry to the use of the same memory devices and practices (Bowker 2005) as are available to participants, and an ethnographer may well wish to reflect on the extent to which the analysis that he carries out may mirror or diverge from the practices of participants who are themselves attempting to understand the environment that they inhabit. There are numerous tools available for recording and analyzing social media data. I make specific recommendations with caution, because solutions in this domain may rapidly become obsolete, and because this is a heavily commercialized domain: currently, Scraperwiki and Hootsuite are popular sources of data scraped from social media, and provide some useful analytics for an online ethnographer, but by the time you read this there may be other alternatives, and free services might have turned into commercial products, or vice versa. Google Trends offers the possibility of insight, on a large scale, into what interests Internet users, and can potentially be used to infer social trends more broadly (Ellery et al. 2008), although with some serious caveats concerning the extent to which Google search data reflects wider society in any straightforward fashion. These readily available tools have a volatility that may be disconcerting for a researcher wishing to build a study around them. In addition, as Marres and Weltevrede (2013) argue, it can be problematic to repurpose such tools for social research, given their development in environments with different values and preoccupations. Marres and Welrevrede (2013) question whether the researcher may wish to adopt the values and assumptions embedded within these tools about what is interesting and significant: instead, they argue for a reflexive attention to the values that shape what counts as data, and a recognition that an understanding of these values counts as useful data in its own right.

In addition to publicly available social media analytics, there are also some activity logging tools, developed largely for use in software evaluation and research into Human Computer Interaction, that could be of use in more broadly conceived ethnographic projects. Keystroke logging software for desktop computers has existed for some time, but more recently researchers have developed means to log use of apps across multiple mobile devices (Bell et al. 2013), opening up the possibility of ethnographic projects that juxtapose participant observation and interview accounts with detailed data about the actual apps being used. As with data scraped from social media, data from automatic logging of activity will require considerable interpretation. Whilst logged data apparently represents exactly what participants did, it only portrays that particular stream of technologically mediated activity, and it may be difficult to reconstruct other non-technologically mediated activities that went on alongside the logged activities. In other words, because certain activities can be logged, they may come to dominate our sense of what counts as data. All forms of recording carry a danger of distracting the ethnographer from thinking on the spot, and encouraging them to defer analysis to some later date. Recording therefore potentially disembeds the ethnographer from the setting, when we are usually striving for quite the reverse.

If scraping of social media and logging of app use raise some problematic issues for an ethnographer in the extent to which they shape the definition of data, then aggregative approaches such as sentiment analysis will be even more troubling. Sentiment analysis (Prabowo and Thelwall 2009; Cheong and Lee 2011) automates the process of working out what is going on in social media activity, aggregating large streams of data into assessments of the "mood" relating to a particular topic. This type of analysis is a long way from what we would generally think of as an ethnographic approach, in the extent to which it strips away the rich context of data and makes assumptions about interpretation. However, there may be some merit to an ethnographer engaging with sentiment analysis: first as a tool which participants may be employing themselves, and which it is therefore important to understand; and, second, as a device to raise questions about developments and trends and to identify topics for a closer, more qualitative inspection. This latter approach to quantitative and aggregative analysis to guide and inform fieldwork has been used to good effect in mixed methods studies such as Howard's (2002) networked ethnography and the study that Dirksen et al. (2010) conducted of online communications within an organization. There is a burgeoning field of digital sociology that explores the forms of society being made in and through the Internet, and in doing so tries out the potential of various forms of social media and "born digital" data for exploring sociological questions (Marres 2012; Orton-Johnson and Prior 2013). Such approaches will prove increasingly fruitful for ethnographers seeking to explore the Internet via mixed methods research designs, but ethnographers will often be unsatisfied with any reliance on "big data" not complemented by more in-depth or small scale studies of meaning-making processes (Boyd and Crawford 2012).

It can certainly be useful for an ethnographer trying to characterize a population to develop some form of visualization which portrays locations and connections. The most obvious form of visualization in a conventional ethnography based on a single geographic location would be a map showing the spatial proximities and movements of the population, but schematic representations such as social network diagrams or kinship diagrams are also useful. These representations may be developed from data collected through systematic surveys, but they can also be generated by informants, and provide a means of talking through their own understandings of spatial and social connections. Visualizations do not speak for themselves in ethnography. They need to be situated: we need to work out what they mean, how they are produced and generated, what they leave by the wayside as they offer up a cleaned-up representation of how things are, and how they circulate. The everyday Internet offers a wide diversity of experiences and an overwhelming array of information and interaction, which is an issue for the everyday Internet user as well as a methodological challenge for the ethnographer. To some extent, the same tools that are provided to help the everyday Internet user cope with this vast and diverse information ecology, offering various forms of visualization, summary, search, and analysis, also provide ready-to-hand tools for the ethnographer, provided due attention is given to the extent to which these technologies shape experiences through hidden assumptions. Many of the existing approaches to aggregation and visualization of "big data" derived from the Internet tend to use homogeneous data drawn from a single platform. It can be useful for an ethnographer, therefore, to employ different methods and compare perspectives, using each to inter-rogate the assumptions and omissions of the other. The Internet also makes many archives of past activities available, both to ordinary participants and to ethnographers. Whilst often ethnographers will want to take part in real-time interactions in order to develop an experiential, moment-by-moment engagement with the setting, archives can also be useful, particularly to inter-rogate the present with insights into how things were in the past.

Whilst the ethnographer can get a long way in understanding by observing and participating, and by exploring interactions both in the raw and in aggre-gated and visualized summaries, it is still often very useful to ask direct questions. Ethnographers often use interviews as a means of having an in-depth one-to-one conversation about the topic that most concerns them at the time. As Spradley (1979) describes, there exists a continuum between friendly conversations and formal interview. While ethnographers learn a lot from unstructured friendly conversations, they will also often want to engage in some more formal encounters that cover a set of issues of particular interest to the ethnographer with an interviewee who has been chosen for his or her cultural competence in the field in question. The interview will be a way of delving into a specific informant's experiences and understandings. Although it may home in on a specific area of interest, an ethnographic interview is often conducted with quite an open schedule in mind, allowing for unanticipated avenues to be explored. The interview will also often be an opportunity for the ethnographer to try out their developing interpretations, as they offer informants the chance to comment on the ethnographer's version of what is going on in the setting. Ethnographic interviews often arise in the context of an ongoing relationship with an informant, rather than representing an isolated one-off encounter. This allows for a longitudinal aspect to emerge, and provides space for emerging issues to be explored, for points to be revisited, and for interpretations to be checked. Many of these aspects of the ethnographic interview transfer directly to studies involving the Internet. The notion of the ethnographic interview as situated within an ongoing relationship with an informant may, however, not be easy to achieve in more diffuse research settings. Instead, different modes of engagement emerge as useful, such as conducting several asynchronous email inter-views with different informants simultaneously, developing insights, and exploring their significance for different interviewees in parallel rather than in sequence.

In field sites that move across different media, the ethnographer will be faced with making a choice of the medium in which to conduct interviews. There is a burgeoning literature on the benefits and drawbacks of online interviews, and the practices that lead to successful online interviews (notable examples include Bampton and Cowton 2002; Kivits 2005; James and Busher 2006; McCoyd and Kerson 2006; Kazmer and Xie 2008; James and Busher 2009; Salmons 2009; Salmons 2011; Malta 2012). In an ethnographic context it may sometimes be deemed important that interviews be carried out face-to-face, particularly where the notion of embedding being explored involves aspects of material culture, domestic location, or institutional context. It may be very useful, in such circumstances, to encounter the interviewee in that context, allowing the ethnographer to observe the interviewee in that setting, and enabling the interviewee to draw aspects that they see as relevant to the ethnographer's attention. It can also be very useful for the interviewees to have objects around them that they might want to show the ethnographer to explain points. However, it may be just as natural for an interviewee responding by email to embed links to documents and refer to other materials that they want to show to the ethnographer: the relevant context that they wish to invoke might just as likely be digital as material. Any mode of interviewing needs to be chosen to be comfortable and convenient for the interviewee, to enable exploration of aspects of context that interviewee and ethnographer wish to invoke, and to enable a free-ranging and open interaction. The ethnographer also needs to be aware of the possible connotations of different choices of medium for the interview, as this may shape the responses that interviewees give. It can be very useful to draw on observation of how participants use various media to offer some insight into their expectations of the encounter in that medium. In an ethnography for the Internet, the interview medium is not just chosen according to how interviewees will respond "best," but as a component of building ethnographic understanding in itself and as a part of inhabiting the field.

In order to carry out interviews, one has first to identify potential interviewees who have the cultural competences one wants to find out about. This may not be straightforward in diffuse research settings where participants may only be partially visible to the ethnographer and to one another. Where a discussion forum is a focus of inquiry, for example, it may be difficult to recruit interviewees who fulfil the ethnographer's desire to find out what is going on as far as participants are concerned. A general appeal to the group often produces a limited number of volunteers, many of whom may be moved to respond by their own personal agenda, and thus not represent in any plausible way how "typical" members act. In these circumstances, more targeted approaches involving direct email contact with potential interviewees explaining specific reasons why their input may be helpful can be more effective than general appeals. Members who actively post to discussion forums may be much more likely that non-posting "lurkers" to respond to appeals for interviewees. To recruit these less active participants more creative means of recruitment may be needed. Chapters 4 and 5 discuss strategies that I used to recruit interviewees in circumstances where even the initial identification of potential interviewees was not straightforward. In each case, the strategies are different: whether or not interviewees are identifiable and easy to contact is itself a characteristic of the field. In an ethnographic study, the interview is an important moment of data generation, but so is the process of deciding who might be interesting to interview and finding some way to forge a connection with them.

Interviews are a useful way for the ethnographer to drill down on a specific issue in depth and focus on emergent themes. There are also circumstances in which an ethnographer aims for a breadth of understanding, and an overview of the territory. Whilst standardized research instruments are often thought to be anathema to ethnographers, the questionnaire is thus not without its uses in an ethnographic study. It can be very helpful for an ethnographer to be able to succinctly characterize a population according to variables of particular interest in the study, and a standardized questionnaire can be a very useful way to collect the necessary data. Baym (2000), for example, focused much of her ethnographic study of the rec.arts.tv.soaps newsgroup on viewers of one specific soap opera, but a wider questionnaire study allowed her to explore how far this specific group was typical of the viewers of other soaps using the discussion group. It can be useful to be able to specify exactly in what ways the few people who have participated in the in-depth aspects of the study are typical or distinctive. In some ethnographic studies, a survey of a wider population may be useful in developing analysis of the social networks or patterns of kinship across the population. However, it is often difficult to characterize a questionnaire conducted through online recruitment as representative, since the underlying population is often unknown. Even when the full subscriber list of a mailing list is known, it will often provide only scanty information, possibly confined only to email addresses which give an imperfect guide to country of origin, rarely indicate gender, and lack other kinds of demographic information. People who choose to respond to a survey may well be uncharacteristic in some way, or, as with interview volunteers, have a particular agenda relating to the declared topic of the research. Where field sites are diffuse, and distributed across different media, it can be problematic to gain a sense of how large the target population might be, let alone whether the sample who answer a questionnaire are in any way representative. Questionnaires employed by ethnographers in Internet-saturated field sites are thus rarely able to achieve a representative sample, but still the questionnaire can be a useful way of capturing a snapshot of a population and exploring how far any sample group within that overall population may be distinctive.

REFLEXIVITY, AUTOETHNOGRAPHY AND THE INDIVIDUALIZED EXPERIENCE

Whilst the ethnographer may use various strategies to produce data and record aspects of the research setting, the immersion of the ethnographer's embodied self in the setting remains a very significant part of the ethnographic approach. A reflexive dimension to ethnography is therefore widely acknowledged as an important corrective to an erroneous impression that ethnographers somehow produce objective accounts of pre-existing reality. The "representational crisis" in ethnography entailed a widespread recognition that ethnographers to some extent construct the object that they purport to represent (as notably captured by Clifford and Marcus 1986), and the subjectivity of the ethnographer is acknowledged as key in shaping relations with the field and constructing knowledge of the setting (Coffey 1999). This reflexive dimension acquires a particular significance in ethnography for the E^3 Internet. Everything that I have said about the construction of the field site, and the choices that the ethnographer has to make about how to move through the field and which connections to follow, emphasizes that the ethnographer has an agency that will be reflected in the accounts that he produces. A reflexive attention to the choices being made by the ethnographer in such circumstances is therefore key, considering the nature of the circumstances under which a particular account was produced, and exploring how it could have been otherwise. Whilst we strive to let the field speak for itself, at the same time it is important to acknowledge the agency of the ethnographer that brings that particular field into being, and the role of the ethnographer's subjectivity in shaping a relationship to the setting.

Internet ethnographers have often made a point of discussing their relationship to the field, and exploring the consequences of particular aspects of their status and positioning for the accounts that they produce. Baym (2000), for example, underwent a shift from participant in the group she studied to observer, allowing her to retain a sympathetic understanding of the setting whilst shifting to a different register of analysis and a different set of relationships with participants. Kendall (2002) took a consciously outsider status in the group that she studied, and notes the points at which her overt differences from the group, as brought into visibility by members of the group, constitute moments of ethnographic insight. Markham (1998) most notably develops a reflexive online ethnography as she dwells on considerations of her own subjectivity and relationships with participants as constituted through the medium as a core focus of her account. In each of these cases, positions shift and relationships progress throughout the study. This is all the more likely in a multi-sited and multi-modal study that passes through different settings and exploits different media for engagement with participants, involving the ethnographer in reworking an identity for each setting and bringing to light different aspects of commonality and difference in interactions with participants.

The reflexive dimension does not have an identifiable singular impact on the ethnographic account but suffuses the story. As Finlay (2002) suggests, reflexivity does not necessarily lead to clear answers, but instead provides "muddy ambiguity and multiple trails." This muddiness and ambiguity can, paradoxically, be illuminating in its symmetry with the conditions experienced by participants in the setting in question. In ethnography for the E^3 Internet, the reflexive dimension brings a helpful perspective on the conditions of knowledge and uncertainty that prevail in the diffuse and contingently connected fields of action that characterize many contemporary phenomena. Because the ethnographer, in the situations we are discussing, uses the same media as participants, and because those very media are at the same time the object of inquiry and the medium of inquiry, the ethnographer has an authentic insight into the conditions of existence as lived through those media. The difficulties of getting in touch with relevant people and uncertainties about what is really going on in their lives are practical frustrations for the ethnographer, but are also significant in so far as this is how the setting is: complex and imperfectly knowable, with absolute certainty always out of reach. There is a symmetry here, in that the frustrations that the ethnographer encounters on the way to finding out about the object of inquiry are a source of insight into the object. The ethnographer can usefully reflect on this symmetry, asking "how far do any of us know what is going on here?"

This point echoes an argument I have made previously (Hine 2000) that the ethnographer should not rush too quickly to triangulate observations from an online setting by arranging to meet up with participants face-to-face, where this is something that participants would not normally do. The urge to triangulate risks jeopardizing the development of a reflexive insight into the conditions of knowledge that prevail within the situation. The ethnographer can usefully draw on their own experiences as a source of insight into the unresolvable uncertainties and tensions that can be a part of the Internet experience. It is important to embrace the same kind of uncertainty that participants experience, since, as Falzon (2009a: 9) points out, "understanding the shallow may itself be a form of depth." Falzon links this point with Bloch's (1991) discussion of the kind of deep ethnographic understanding that is developed by immersion within a setting and that evades linguistic expression. A deeper understanding of uncertainty comes from immersion within these conditions of knowledge, beyond the second-hand accounts participants may give of their experiences. This links also with Hirschauer's (2006) observations about the silence of the social: ethnographers are putting into words what was previously unspoken, and their reflexive insights into what they themselves can know become an important part of accounting what is distinctive about that setting.

When we acknowledge the agency of the ethnographer in constructing the field and finding ways to navigate contingent connections we imply that the experience is to some extent unique to that ethnographer. The ethnographer aims for an authentic account of a reality, which to some extent pre-exists their engagement with it, in that they identify common threads and patterns, explore prevailing discourses, and analyze emergent structures, but these are navigated according to a highly individual, embodied agenda. In fact, the experience of a contemporary media-saturated world is potentially to be characterized as an increasingly individualized terrain (Wellman 2001), as each subject constructs a networked reality out of diverse sources of connection and influence. At this point an autoethnographic (Reed-Danahay 1997a; Ellis 2004) sensitivity may become particularly useful: because the experience of navigating the contemporary world is so individualized, an account "from the inside" of the embodied self that navigates this territory is very informative. An autoethnographic stance on ethnography for the Internet focuses on considering how connections present themselves and what choices are available for building meaning out of these diverse influences. The ethnographer as autoethnographer can attend to the generalized tropes and commonly available discourses that inform actions and shape expectations, thinking about where pressures to conform come from and how they are mediated. An autoethnography for the Internet emphasizes the embodied and emotional experience of engagement with diverse media, attending to the influences that shape and constrain the experience, and the opportunities and restrictions that emerge.

There have been concerns that autoethnographic narratives may stray into self-indulgence or narcissism, lending undue importance to the author's experience and neglecting to draw on other sources of evidence (Coffey 1999; Sparkes 2002). A universal criticism of autoethnography as self-indulgence neglects, however, a more nuanced understanding of the extent to which writing about the self always, necessarily, involves writing about relationships and contexts (Sparkes 2002). The universal rejection of autoethnography also neglects the diversity of writing which goes on under this banner: as Reed-Danahay (1997b) describes, the term autoethnography covers a diverse array of practices within an overall focus on the telling of personal experiences and emotions and in a sense all ethnographic writing is to some extent autoethnographic. It seems more reasonable then, rather than writing off all autoethnography as somehow flawed, to examine what purchase is offered in each individual instance of autoethnographic writing. In the case of ethnography for the Internet, an autoethnographic perspective allows the very individualized nature of engagement with a reality constituted through various forms of mediated and localized face-to-face interaction and material context to be explored in a far greater degree of depth than can be achieved by asking other participants for retrospective accounts alone or from simply observing what they do.

The autoethnographic approach is an answer to the concerns expressed by Crabtree et al. (2006) in their discussion of the problems attendant on carrying out ethnographic studies of ubiquitous computing "in the wild." They note that various means of logging activity and recording actions are available, producing multiple streams of data which the researcher needs to align. A log of activity may, however, give a spurious appearance of accuracy, if it records the times when messages arrived at a central server, but fails to depict when participants actually read, or were typing these messages. The researcher faces a considerable technical difficulty in aligning the various streams of data and reconstructing what the experience of participation might have been for those involved. An authoethnographic perspective offers an alternative route out of this difficulty: it loses the completeness and overview provided by the various data logs, but offered a hugely enhanced insight into how it might feel to be embedded within their emergence in real-time, making sense of the various forms of media that constitute the immersive event. Neither the autoethnographic approach nor the alignment of log file data are perfect in their portrayal of events. Each reveals a different facet of the phenomenon (Mason 2011). The autoethnographic account would not necessarily be left to stand alone, but would be interpreted alongside the accounts of other participants and the portrayal of activities as represented in log files. The autoethnographic account would be far from self-indulgent: it would, instead, be an appropriate strategic response to a very distinct gap in understanding left by the other available methods.

Whether or not self-consciously autoethnographic, ethnographic research that is carried out in and of and through mediated communications is always to some extent "insider research," since the ethnographer is using the very means of communication that are also the object of study. Being an insider presents some problems in developing an appropriate positioning and retaining the ability to question the taken-for granted: ethnographers working in familiar territories find themselves trying to balance insider positioning and stranger perspective in search of insights (Dyck 2000). It is important, however, not to over-essentialize this insider status: identifications shift over the course of a project, and attributions of insiderness are made strategically in context. Voloder (2008) suggests that it is important not to assume either strangeness or difference, but to focus instead on processes and moments of differentiation:

> I argue that the insight gained from "insider" research need not rely on assumptions of shared experiences and identifications between oneself and participants, but rather that it is in the exploration of the convergences and divergences in these experiences and identifications that the researcher's experiential self can be used as a key heuristic resource. (Voloder 2008: 28)

An ethnographer may thus be claimed by participants as "one of us" as part of accounting common experiences, but may also be "othered" as someone who can never understand. An authoethnographer may claim a commonality of experience with some wider constituency whom they claim to represent. Such identifications are, however, not stable. To draw on autoethnographic insights the goal need not be to produce an account which is wholly about the ethnographer's experience. Nor should it be to position the ethnographer as able to speak for the position of all participants, as if they could unproblematically inhabit that space. Instead, an autoethnographer ideally needs to maintain a reflexive and critical orientation to his own relationship with the constituency for whom he claims to speak.

THE PRINCIPLES OF ETHNOGRAPHY FOR THE E³ INTERNET

Having discussed specific strategies for locating field sites, positioning oneself within the field, collecting data, and developing insights, this final section of the chapter returns to some broader methodological statements, in order to summarize what, in general, might characterize the orientation of ethnography for the E³ Internet. A number of years ago, when the Internet was very different in scope and experience, I produced a set of methodological principles for a virtual ethnography that conducted its studies in, of, and through the Internet (Hine 2000). The Internet now is in many ways radically different from the territory that I navigated back then: it was restricted then to a much narrower social group of users than is now the case, and whilst newsgroups and other discussion forums gave it a participatory feel, the breadth of participation and sense of dynamism produced by social media had yet to emerge. Nonetheless, many of the strategies that I have advocated here, and the principles which underpin them, are recognizably continuous with those developed for the Internet in its prior incarnation. I have continued to stress the agency of the ethnographer in constructing the field, and the significance of a reflexive and autoethnographic insight into exploring not just what mediated communication does, but how it feels and what it enables us to know, although developments in methodological thinking more generally have offered new ways to think about conceptions of the field and the purchase offered by autoethnography. I have continued to stress the contingency of notions of the field, and the active role of the ethnographer in deciding what is to count as the field. Another continuity is the ongoing importance of consciousness of the significance of the Internet as both culture and cultural artefact, which I identified in 2000. The Internet as a place where things just simply get done exists alongside the Internet which exists in popular commentary as an agent of change and source of opportunity and risk. These complementary aspects of the Internet mutually inform one another, and thus present another level of complexity that continues to challenge the ethnographer as she navigates between Internet as culture and Internet as cultural artefact and questions how these mutually inform one another.

The key difference between the approach I advocated then and the approach I develop here stems from an increased consciousness of the diverse forms of embedding that give meaning to the Internet. As the Internet has become embedded in more aspects of everyday existence, and as the entwining of material and digital practices has deepened, so the potential form of field sites has diversified and the potential connections for the ethnographer to pursue have multiplied. As the Internet has become embedded in more devices, and taken on a new guise as a mobile technology, and as a component of intelligent devices sensing their environment and making decisions on our behalf, so fieldwork decisions have become more contingent and more consequential. The ethnographer is faced with a more complex array of potential sites and sources of data, and an increasing challenge in tying together disparate insights into the form and meaning of activities of interest. This diversification and amplification of embedding impacts upon our fieldwork strategies, emphasizing the importance of reflexive and autoethnographic strategies as it becomes apparent just how individualized the experience of the field may be, and how diverse the potential ways of understanding and illuminating what goes on there.

There is, therefore, considerable continuity with the form of virtual ethnography outlined in 2000, although I have dispensed with the epithet "virtual" as no longer helpful in the face of this multiply embedded Internet and as a distraction from the important task of understanding what this Internet, which is very real in its experience and consequences, means for our contemporary modes of existence. The epithet "virtual" was in fact always meant not to denote a study only confined to online domains, but to index that the new approaches to ethnography occasioned by the Internet were "virtually ethnography" in the old-fashioned sense, possibly not quite the real thing but good enough for the circumstances which we found ourselves facing. This proved to be misleading, and so in the current version I talk of ethnography for the Internet without giving it the epithet, although the connotations of an adaptive approach, sufficing for circumstance, remains a core concern. Some key components of this adaptive approach for an Internet which is embedded, embodied, everyday, and above all emergent, are as follows:

1 A holistic approach to ethnography need not imply that there is a pre-existing field site to be comprehensively known. Instead, the holistic approach produces the ethnographer's openness to unanticipated aspects of meaning-making, and to the emergence of forms of connection and boundary not anticipated at the outset of the study. A holistic approach entails the ethnographer taking an exploratory attitude to understanding how activities make sense to those engaged in them.

2 The field is a fluid and emergent construct. Field sites are rarely contained wholly within either online or offline space, and also build in a consciousness of what might be thought of as different scales of analysis, encompassing both "the Internet" as a notable and topical cultural object and as it is manifested in disaggregated form in specific local instances of use which might, or might not be labelled as "the Internet."

3 The Internet can be taken as multiply embedded in diverse frames of activity and meaning-making. Taking this multiple embedding seriously encourages an open approach to the identification of field sites, focused on exploring connections and discontinuities as they emerge rather than assuming the existence of boundaries, and adopting various means of visualizing and moving through the field.

4 The Internet is an embodied experience. This aspect of the Internet emphasizes the significance of reflexive and autoethnographic approaches, and

of imaginatively observing the significance of actions, making a critically reflexive use of ready-to-hand tools for recording and interpreting actions with due consciousness of the varied social textures that emerge and an awareness of the possibility of learning from all forms and stages of engagement with the field.

5 The Internet is both a mundane and a topicalized everyday experience: ethnography for the Internet can usefully consider both forms of discourse, exploring connections and disconnects between policy and practices, mass media portrayals, and everyday experiences. Ethnographers can use the everyday Internet to interrogate the topicalized Internet and vice versa, and make use of the archived past to interrogate the present, adopting a stranger perspective that considers how current conditions could be otherwise.

6 Ethnographers should expect multiplicity: there is not just one Internet, not just one experience of online phenomena. Instead, we will find diverse practices of meaning-making around a fragmented Internet which is device dependent, culturally embedded, constantly developing, and consists of multiple platforms. We will therefore need multiple ethnographies for the Internet and multiple ways of forging research objects from fragmented phenomena.

7 Ethnographers should expect uncertainty: without the prospect of a comprehensive account of a singular reality, we will be faced with constructing accounts that are not necessarily verifiable in standard terms of objectivity. Just as participants live with uncertainty about how various aspects of existence ultimately line up and inform one another, so must ethnographers.

8 Ethnographers must take responsibility for their own agency, attempting to build authentic accounts that transcend a self-indulgent reporting of a personal itinerary yet are demonstrably conscious of the extent to which the ethnographer creates an ethnography out of an array of possible cultural strands that could have been followed.

–4–

Observing and Experiencing Online/Offline Connections

This chapter is the first of three that bring the methodological principles described in previous chapters to life by exploring examples from primary research that I have undertaken in different settings. These are not presented as perfect solutions, but rather as insights into the messy reality of making decisions for the situations that I encountered as my research questions, and the strategies to explore them, were progressively developed. This chapter discusses research focused around a group of mailing lists that enable the free exchange of unwanted goods otherwise destined for landfill. The chapter evaluates a range of ethnographic strategies I have used to contribute to building an understanding of this phenomenon, including autoethnography, email interviews, face-to-face interviews, and observation of online discussions in various contexts, including both the mailing lists themselves and parallel conversations in Mumsnet and on Facebook and Twitter. The chapter will demonstrate that autoethnography is a powerful tool for exploring the ambiguities and uncertainties inherent in Internet usage and for exploring how online and offline sites are connected in contingent and flexible fashion. It also cautions against unthinking pursuit of a "complete" understanding of such a phenomenon, and counsels researchers focusing on complex online/offline phenomena to embrace the sense of uncertainty and "good enough" assumptions that permeate the experience of navigating such territory. Autoethnography is thus a powerful source of insight, but reliance on autoethnography alone provides limited perspectives on the embedding of Internet use in diverse sites of meaning-making and on different devices because it privileges the ethnographer's own positioning over that of other participants. A combination of strategies helps to develop insights into the multiple meanings of a single phenomenon, even though each of these insights contributes a facet (Mason 2011) of the phenomenon rather than adding up to a complete picture.

LOCALLY BASED ONLINE GIFTING NETWORKS: AN OVERVIEW

This chapter focuses on a phenomenon which relies upon the capacity of the Internet to connect together people who have not previously met, based on some common interests or concerns. In recent years a number of grass-roots initiatives have arisen focused on offering ways for people to locate new owners for their unwanted objects. Often these initiatives are presented as closely linked to ideals of sustainability and alternative consumption, with the overt goal of promoting re-use and keeping goods out of landfill. The best known of these initiatives is the international network Freecycle. The Freecycle network (http://www.freecycle.org) is a movement initiated in 2003, which now claims over 7 million members worldwide, divided into individual local groups each with their own online mailing lists. Users can either access their group's messages by logging into the website, or choose to receive messages singly or in digest via email. The list activity consists of messages offering items for which members no longer have a use, and which they are offering for free to other members who want them. Items sometimes have considerable commercial value, but more often have little worth in conventional commercial terms, and may even be damaged in some way. People who want the object send a message directly to the donor. The person offering the item then selects a recipient, and arranges a convenient time for the item to be collected. A successful transaction sees the recipient arrive at the prearranged place, usually the home of the original owner, and take away the item. Original owner and recipient are usually meeting one another in a face-to-face sense for the first time at the point of handover. In the U.K., another organization, Freegle, runs similar groups, with the gifting of objects organized in the same fashion. Some local areas have only a Freecycle or Freegle group, and some have both.

The Freecycle network is often described in terms of its contrast with conventional consumption. As "socially conscious consumers" (Shah et al. 2007), Freecycle members engage in alternative consumption practices (Nelson et al. 2007), and participate in a "social economy" (Seyfang 2006) linked to, but often in conscious opposition to, the mainstream economy. Freecycle networks have been described as forming a "technologically generated community" (Chayko 2007) focused around, although not confined to, online interactions. The tendency of such descriptions is to stress commonality of purpose and gloss over differences and tensions and to minimize any deviations from the top-level goal of working towards sustainability. In the spirit of Law's calls for a responsible social science methodology that attends to mess and complexity (Law 2004), and in homage to recent encouragements to recognise multiplicity (De Laet and Mol 2000), I hoped in my own study of the Freecycle phenomenon to do justice to diverse strands of meaning-making rather than reducing the group from the outset to a single straightforward description.

My study also had some foreshadowed problems that stemmed from my specific interests in the forms of relationship and social formations that arise in and through the Internet. Because Freecycle and the like have to shift from online relationships to offline relationships, if goods are ever going to be handed over, these lists seemed to offer a really interesting object to explore how in practice people navigated shifts between online and offline spaces. I was particularly interested in exploring how people embedded these mailing lists into their daily lives, and wanted to find out how participants experienced the transfer of relationships between online and offline, as objects were advertised, claimed, and handed over. How did identity performances shift between settings, and what could these exchanges tell us about material cultures and relationships with local spaces? How did notions of trust and risk play out across different settings? I also wanted to find out how people related to the underlying technology. These mailing lists offer up an infrastructure that participants populate with their own objects and their own concerns: how flexible was this infrastructure in practice, and how far did people have to sign up to a set of values connected with sustainability and the environment to participate? I was also interested to find out more about the forms of work that were needed to make these mailing lists function for participants. Was this an easy, frictionless form of relationship, or did it take effort to sustain (or to break)? From my first encounters with the list I was, overall, intrigued by the prospect that this phenomenon was a very interesting object for an Internet studies researcher to think with. There seemed to be so many stimulating avenues to explore, and so many questions to answer about how participants used the infrastructure of the mailing list and made it their own. In the rest of this chapter I will discuss the strategies that I employed in the pursuit of answers to my questions, and my dawning realization that a full understanding of the phenomenon was going to remain tantalizingly out of reach.

THE AUTOETHNOGRAPHY OF GIFTING

An ethnographic vignette ...

It is the middle of March. There are three weeks to go until Easter, when the grand family reunion will descend on our house. We're expecting four additional adults and four extra children to be staying in the house, and I don't have beds for them all. The problem of how to fit them all in has been running through my mind for days now, and I still seem to be at least one bed short. I look at the Argos catalogue, wondering what Z-beds are like these days. £90! That's a lot for something we're only going to use once in a blue moon. The paralysis continues ... what to do?

The "digest message" from the local Freecycle group arrives in my email inbox. I signed up for this list when I moved house seven years ago, and now it just keeps on coming. It's no burden, it requires no effort on my part—it's just there. Sometimes—often, in fact—I simply delete the message, unread. Sometimes I scan down the email out of idle curiosity, a kind of nosiness. I offer goods on the list every six months or so, mainly children's toys and clothes, but so far I've never actually asked for anything. Usually, I just use the list as a quick way to declutter—fill a bag of clothes on a Saturday morning, send a quick email to the list, and by Sunday evening, a few emails later, a grateful recipient will have left with the goods. It's a matter of domestic pride: I seem to be the one in our house who takes responsibility for the grand clearouts, but I'm the child of parents who grew up in wartime, and, like them, I hate throwing things away. Freecycle pleases me—it feels efficient and ethical at the same time. So usually any engagement I have with the list digest is just nosiness about what's going on. I subscribe to the list so that I can post messages about items I have to give away, but the reciprocal relationship is automatically assumed, and I receive by default the digests of messages everyone else has to offer. As I say, sometimes I delete, sometimes I take a nosy trawl through to see what everyone else is up to. This time, though, I scan down the list and the second item (Figure 4.1) leaps to my eye.

Figure 4.1   An offer message posted via Freecycle

Brilliant! Quickly, I compose an email to the donor, who is identifiable only by an enigmatic, gender-neutral nickname. I try really hard to make myself an appealing-sounding recipient, knowing that for myself I'm much more likely to give an item away to someone who seems to have a need for it, or who sounds nice. I carefully include my full name and email address so I'll sound approachable, but I don't include my mobile number, for fear that I'll seem needy or demanding, as if I'm expecting them to call:

Probably too late, I know, but this would be really useful to us if it's still available. We have a lot of family coming to stay over Easter, and this would be ideal for one of the visiting children. I'm in Guildford, and can be very flexible about collection times to suit you—daytime, evening, weekend.
Christine Hine
christine.hine@btinternet.com

A few minutes later, the reply arrives:

Hi Christine

I have just got in and had several emails but you were first in—if you can come over this evening to collect, you can have it.

Can you let me know if you can and I'll give you our address—if it is easier to call I am on Oxxxx xxxxxx and we can arrange—we are in guildford.

Kind regards

****

I feel absurdly excited—as if I somehow won the item—but also nervous. I'm usually on the other side of this transaction, giving the item away, and I'd do it differently. I would negotiate the appointment by email and then give out the address that way once we've fixed a time. Usually, as the donor, I feel quite in control even though I'm arranging for a stranger to come to my house. It feels odd to arrange things by phone, and to be the one trying to keep the donor happy. I'm also slightly on the hop because I've said I'll come any time, and in truth I have to go to a school parents' evening tonight, and I'm now under pressure to come this evening or miss out.

In the event, the phone call goes well. The donor isn't upset by the suggestion that I come on the way home from parents' evening. She gives me detailed directions to help spot her house, which turns out to be five-minute drive from my own. I pass the house several times a week on the school run. I don't recognize her name, but I wonder if we actually know each other, or more likely have children at the same schools. When I arrive, I'm nervous, turning my car in the dark on the narrow driveway, desperate not to clip a wall or get too close to their car. I ring the doorbell, and she answers quickly, standing firmly in the doorway so there's no question of me feeling that I'm being invited into the house. "It's in the garage," she says. "My husband will get it for you." I give my thanks, but I sense that this is only meant to be a brief interaction. She doesn't really want to hear the story of what I'm going to do with the bed. She doesn't leave the doorstep as her husband swings open the garage doors and wheels out the bed, so I open the car boot, load it in, and leave as quickly as possible.

Once at home, I unload my prize and wheel it into the house. I haven't even looked at it properly. Will it be useless, smelly, an embarrassment? Actually, I'm relieved—it's perfectly presentable. Someone can definitely sleep on this. I look at it and smile, feeling £90 better off.

I first encountered online gifting networks as a user. Having recently moved house, I was discussing with a colleague the problem of clutter. I was complaining that our recent house move had involved taking with us boxes of stuff that I knew had been unopened since the previous house move five years before that. Our young daughter was growing out of clothes and toys at an alarming rate, whilst accumulating new ones daily. Added to those clutter issues, we had found numerous unwanted items left by the previous residents of our new house. Attic and garage contained items I could see no potential use for, but I also had no idea how to dispose of them. The rendering of material possessions as problems, and the moral overtones of "clutter" as distinct from other categories of object, offer up rich territory for sociological analysis (Cwerner and Metcalfe 2003; Maycroft 2009). The issue of "clutter" and the constitution of my clutter as a distinct category from both rubbish and valued possession deserves further examination, and my colleague and I agreed we could have gone down this route. Instead, however, she had a practical suggestion for me: join Freecycle.

I had not at that stage heard of the Freecycle phenomenon, but from my colleague's description it sounded just what I needed. Some web searching that evening led me to the homepage of the Freecycle network and enabled me to identify a thriving local group. This group, as with all Freecycle groups, revolved around the intriguingly simple idea that we all have things we no longer want, but that might be useful to someone else. It was quickly apparent from the website that the explicit goals of the network were to promote reuse and to reduce landfill: the slogan of "changing the world one gift at a time™" clearly invoked a social and environmental aspiration. This set of values has some resonance for me, but I have to admit that I was more immediately attracted by the idea as a solution to my clutter problem, and, further than that, also attracted by its potential as a research opportunity. I view much of my everyday Internet use, from email to eBay, as a participant-observation opportunity. I like to reflect on choices and opportunities offered by different media, and Freecycle offered up some interesting chances to experience the combination of Internet communications with local settings and to explore relationships that traveled from online to face-to-face. So, without a particular concrete research goal in mind, I embarked on membership of Freecycle as an ordinary user with a fairly fuzzy ulterior motive. To begin with, my research depended solely upon autoethnographic experience, first with Freecycle and subsequently also with the similar network, Freegle, rather than any formal research practices. I did not at that stage negotiate informed consent to quote from group messages and private emails, and so I focus in this section on discussing my own experiences informed by observation of group activities and conversations with other participants, and my encounters through gifting of numerous items over a period of five years. In following sections I will describe my subsequent move into more formalized research, involving interviews and observation.

Freecycle and Freegle offer some fairly clear guidance on appropriate use of the list. General chat and discussions are discouraged. The approved way to formulate messages includes a subject line of the format:

OFFER—item name—location

or, when the item has been allocated to a recipient

TAKEN—item name—location

Members in search of a particular item are asked to use the format

WANTED—item name—location

These subject line formats are seen frequently. Rarer are messages marked "RECEIVED," where a member has obtained a wanted item, and those marked "ADMIN," sent by the moderators of the list. Appropriate content is policed by moderators who check messages before they are sent on to the group as a whole, and who may add a note of warning where a message has omitted important details, for example, leaving out the location. Moderation keeps the list free of spam and off-topic content: I have been a member of and observed many mailing lists over the years, and these are the most on-topic lists I have come across. It is hard to gain any sense of who the participants are, as the list is devoid of chit-chat and self-disclosure, beyond the choice of a nickname. Many nicknames are quite enigmatic, and do not include the user's full first name and surname.

On first joining my local Freecycle group I followed my usual practices with new Internet groups: I browsed around the website and read the Frequently Asked Questions, and I read messages over a period of days. I was able to feel confident that the list was what I thought it was, and that it suited my purposes. Also, I was able to see something of the way that members styled their messages and conducted their relationships, and to feel that I could fit in with their practices. I also was able to get a sense of the scale of object that members felt it useful to offer. It seemed that there were few limits. It was acceptable to offer a broken item that someone else might fix. There was no need for it to be a conventional consumer item: members offered surplus plants from their gardens, bathroom fittings that had been removed from their own houses, unwanted packing materials from items they had been delivered. After a period of familiarization and checking of my perceptions against the reality, finally, I was ready to send my first message.

I cannot remember now which item I first offered on Freecycle. It might have been a Dyson vacuum cleaner with a broken part that I knew we would never fix but felt that someone might—and someone did. It could have been the car radio, bought years ago for a car that was stolen before the radio was ever fitted, that was collected for a local workman's van. It could have been the rusty cast-iron fireplace we found in the garage when we moved in that was collected by a local man and his son for restoration. It might have been the collection of no-longer-working hi-fi separates that were collected by a local enthusiast, but I have a feeling that came later, when I had really begun to grasp the possibilities of Freecycle as an efficient way of finding people who wanted stuff that I did not. All of these were early items that I offered. Since then I have passed on several sacks of children's clothing, sundry baby equipment, and unwanted household items. For the most part I have posted "OFFER" messages, only once recently responding to a "WANTED" item, as described above. I rarely respond to an "OFFER" message to request an item, partly as I do not feel that there is much that I need, but also because of a personal time economy. While online gifting seems to be a quick and convenient way to get rid of items, it is not necessarily either quick or convenient as a way to acquire items. The folding bed I described above was a rare moment when opportunity and convenience aligned. More often, I see an item I might like, but it does not seem worth the time to collect it, or I reason that somebody else probably needs it more than I do. I tend, then, to use eBay for acquisitions, as being more convenient and suiting my lack of time and relative wealth. I have never posted a "WANTED" message, since I feel that I can usually afford to buy what I need quickly and conveniently elsewhere, rather than waiting for it to come up in an OFFER, and that is certainly not true of all of the people on the list. My personal circumstances shape my relationship with the list in quite specific ways, through very individual notions of time, value, desire, and responsibility.

Freecycling also participates in my family relationships and my extended kinship network in various ways. I take a certain amount of pride in being chief household de-clutterer: a moral high ground is achieved by seizing the initiative to clear the cupboard under the stairs and having the unwanted goods collected and taken away via Freecycle all within a weekend. Some goods are very easy to give away, once the decision to have a clear-out has been taken, and I am happy to see them gone without having to own the guilt of throwing them away (for I do have a quite diffuse, but nonetheless real, sense of environmental responsibility). I felt a very different set of emotions when using Freecycle to give away my recently deceased father's laptop computer, taking some time to make sure that I chose a recipient I felt happy would make use of it as he would have wished (although I chose not to disclose the circumstances to the recipient, this not being a kind of emotional exchange that Freecycle encourages). Sometimes I may be choosing a recipient on the basis of how quickly he or she can take away the object that I want to dispose of, whereas at other times the qualities of the recipient are important to me, and any email replies that simply ask for the object without explaining why it is wanted do not feel as though they offer enough for me to choose them. I navigate my Freecycle use through what makes sense to me, according to my reading of the explicit rules and implicit rules of practice of the group, my own changing circumstances and view of myself, and the object that I am giving away, and what I can glean about the other members of the group from what they say, and do not say. Most of my judgments about what is and is not appropriate on the group are made on the basis of reading between the lines.

As an autoethnographer, then, I have much to learn from my relationships with the mailing list and its participants. A deep reflection on my engagements with the list encourages me to see how my use of the list fits in with the specificity of my own circumstances and how I make the list my own. By experiencing first-hand the dilemmas of how to describe an object, how to choose a suitable recipient from among many who email to request it, and how to negotiate a safe way for the item to be picked up, I gain some significant insights into how this specific online activity becomes embedded into an offline setting, and what kinds of work it takes for that to happen. I experience as a real and present issue of personal safety the challenge of trying to work out, from a terse exchange of emails, just who I want to risk inviting to my house. I experience the rush of emotions attendant on finding out what that person is like in the flesh on the doorstep; surprise, pleasure, relief, and anxiety help to make the experience real and interesting, and keep me doing it repeatedly. I find that taking part makes me feel nicer about myself: as if I'm personally involved in something that is solidifying local community, one tiny step at a time, as we choose to give rather than discard or sell. Actually, of course, when I reflect upon it more deeply I have no way of knowing what happens to the items I give, whether they be sold on eBay or sent to the local tip. To keep on participating, as a net donor like myself, involves making the leap of faith that probably, on balance, the system works as intended—or, alternatively, that the de-cluttering was worthwhile whatever the fate of the object. As with my father's laptop, some objects seem more worth taking pains for than others. As I reflect, I learn something about the different meanings that I invest in domestic objects, and the various means of parting with them, and I discover that Freecycle makes sense for me in different ways according to the objects involved.

Autoethnographic reflection also helps me to see how engagement with the list brings into view a new perspective on my locality, and on the people who inhabit it. Thanks to use of this mailing list I have met people who live very close by to me but whom I would not have otherwise encountered. I have been struck by the role of the mailing list in bringing into view a new form of locality that connects local people in different ways and new formations, as compared to other forms of segmentation. Many of the local people I already know are immediate neighbors, or are people with children of a similar age who travel the same circuit of schools, clubs, and dance classes. These parenting networks of connection are spread across the town, tying us together according to the shared interests and ages of our children, and, if we are to be honest, according to social divisions created by our financial resources and our gender- and class-based ideas about parenting and our beliefs about the sort of activity that our children should do in their leisure time. I think I know my town, but in reality I realize that I only know one fairly socially homogeneous slice of it well. Participating in online gifting network connections show me a different side of my locality: through Freecycle I meet people who pass through the town as commuters and others who live close by but inhabit quite different networks, people who have no children, and who have children attending different schools, or have different ways of spending their leisure time. I meet people whose relationships to time and to money and the constraints upon them are quite different from mine. As a habitually nosy sociologist, I try to "read" the people who arrive on my doorstep to collect items: the experience prompts me to reflect on the categories I use, and the assumptions I draw on as I assess whether someone is like me or not, and whether he or she is like his or her online persona.

An autoethnographic insight is therefore, I would argue, very significant in developing a detailed account of how we make an infrastructure like a mailing list into something that makes sense for us. It is particularly useful in bringing to the fore the kind of emotional work that participation entails, the emotional rewards that it brings, and the altered perspectives that it provides. The complexity and shifting nature of engagement with family, with locality, and with material culture becomes apparent. Interviews with participants might have told me some of this, but by taking part, and by taking part for real, as an embodied ordinary participant interacting with other participants on my own doorstep, I experience how it feels in a visceral way that would be hard to access in an interview or observational setting.

And yet ... For all of my grand claims about my reflective insights, my analysis of feelings and connections, my insights into myself as woven into material, online, and local cultures, trying to understand Freecycle through autoethnography alone is hugely frustrating. Compared to other online settings that I have tried to study ethnographically, something seems to be missing in the qualities of Freecycle as an observable culture. Usually, I can read a mailing list and feel as though I have quite a rich sense of who the participants are, from the information that they disclose about themselves, and the way that they express themselves and interact. However, as I described earlier, the Freecycle list is the most disciplined and on-topic mailing list that I have ever taken part in. There are no public fights. There is no discussion of community goals and aspirations. There is, indeed, no community as such, just messages that tell the story of objects one might or might not want. When the personal emails from potential recipients arrive, they give tantalizing glimpses of participants, and often I will be wrong even about such basic aspects as the gender of the individual who will turn up to collect the object.

Even when people appear on the doorstep, and there is potential for engagement, the frustrations continue. Occasionally, we will have a conversation. One recipient of a bag of children's clothes chatted easily about his own sons and we talked about which of them would wear the clothes and which T-shirts he would like best, and he thrilled my own son by allowing him to sit on the seat of his motorbike as he fastened the bag of clothes to the rear carrier. He took the time to engage, and seemed not to be embarrassed or defensive. Mostly, however, the recipients are very keen to leave quickly, and there is no extended conversation. Interactions are fleeting and strained. Recipients take the bag of items quickly, thank rapidly, jump into a waiting car, and are gone. I form a quick impression of them, but have little basis on which to triangulate my initial impression, or develop a more rounded picture of the recipient as a social being. The doorstep encounter never seems quite the right moment to start a conversation about what people think of Freecycle or to begin negotiating informed consent for an interview.

When I mention this problem of the ethnographic intransigence of the Freecycle encounter to colleagues, including the person who first introduced me to the lists, I find that my own experiences of the Freecycle encounter as stilted and uninformative are not necessarily universal. She talks of people she has invited in to her home, and of extended conversations, although these experiences are in other towns, and another country, and I wonder whether the assumptions I've made about Freecycle on the basis of my own affluent town in southern England might be quite specific. This is intriguing, because it suggests that the universal framework for transactions offered by Freecycle could potentially be experienced in quite different ways. Different local cultures might adopt and adapt the standard framework in their own culturally specific fashion. My own town's experience of Freecycle might be a quite distinctive phenomenon, contextually specific in a way that I had not quite yet envisaged. However, even my knowledge of that specific local form of the Freecycle phenomenon was risking being compromised by the reticence of participants—finding out that they were reticent was one thing, but understanding the origins and consequences of that reticence was quite another. The Freecycle encounter, at least in this town, frustrates ethnographic inquiry. How will I manage to find out enough about it?

One strategy I developed to address this frustration was to explore more systematically what I knew about other members as a participant, and what they knew about me, and how this knowledge was deployed to make exchanges happen. I begin to reflect on what might constitute "enough" knowledge for a Freecycle encounter to work. Are the things that I want to know, as an ethnographer of Freecycle, different from the things that I want or need to know in order to use Freecycle as an ordinary participant? In large part, what I need to know in order to make the transaction work is only whatever is sufficient to feel that I am safe, and to feel that what has gone on makes sense in terms of how Freecycle "ought" to be. In terms of safety, I protect myself by only advertising items that I really do not want, and by making arrangements for collection without giving away details of my regular movements or when my house is empty. By these strategies of limiting disclosure, I in turn limit what I need to know about other participants. I don't need to take up references or verify identities, because I'm already protecting myself by other means. More tricky is the question of how do I know what Freecycle ought to be and how do I know whether any particular experience of it is appropriate? My expectations are strongly influenced by the publicly available presentation of the norms and values of the list, as portrayed in the official website and the instructions on use sent out to new users. My expectations are also shaped by what there is to observe of the behavior of other users, giving a sense of the kind of items to offer, and the language to use when doing so. Finally, my expectations are influenced by the expectations of other participants, to the limited extent that they are available to me.

One means through which the expectations of other participants become directly available to me, if only occasionally, is the Café. This more general discussion group is associated with the main list on which items are advertised, but is separate from it and explicitly allows advertisements, information seeking, and discussions on community matters that are not permitted on the main list. On the Café list people occasionally discuss their concerns and reservations about using Freecycle and express complaints about other users. One recurring complaint focuses on people who do not turn up at the pre-arranged time to collect an item. Another revolves around people who are suspected to be collecting items in order to sell them on, rather than for their own use. In each of these instances, inferences are being made about other participants based on incomplete knowledge and surface appearances: emails or texts seem rude, cars seem too expensive to be owned by needy recipients, goods like the ones given away are spotted at car boot sales. The Café list is only a small proportion of the users of the main mailing lists (currently the local Freecycle list has 24,844 registered members, the very similar Freegle list—of which more below—has 9,517 members, and the Café has 477 members). Nonetheless, the expression of these concerns in that forum indicates that at least some members are operating with expectations which are not, on the basis of the observable features of the interaction as they see them, giving them a sense that the interaction is as it ought to be. Very little is known for certain about other participants, but scanty clues are used to make inferences.

The discussions on the Café list indicate that gifting items is not necessarily seen as a situation where anything goes, and in which participants may be reading one another's behavior for clues as to whether the interaction has been appropriate in terms of their expectations. As an ethnographer, this thought takes me in two directions: first, that I would indeed like to drill down more intensively into how people make their judgments about whether a Freecycle encounter fits in with their expectations; second, that there appears to be some common ground between my attempts as an ethnographer, to read situations, and work out on the basis of very incomplete knowledge that might be happening there, and the attempts of participants themselves to work out what is going on. As the ethnographer I become unlike the other participants in that I am required to linger on that uncertainty to a much greater degree and to treat it as a problem to be resolved, rather than a passing matter of concern, but for ethnographer and participants alike Freecycle use depends on making inferences and reading clues in a situation of uncertainty. We all experience a certain difficulty in rendering Freecycle as a knowable object.

To add to my difficulties in rendering Freecycle as a knowable ethnographic object due to the fleeting and restricted nature of interactions, I should also add a description of the further complexity occasioned by the fragmentation of the object of interest before my eyes during the period in which I studied it. I have mentioned earlier that there was a local Freegle list, very similar to Freecycle, although not part of the same organization. The Freegle organization emerged during the period of my study of the Freecycle phenomenon, and had a somewhat complex relationship with my original object of study. In 2009 a dispute that had apparently been going on for some time between the U.S.-based originators of the Freecycle network and the U.K.-based moderators of British groups became public. In articles in the national and local press (Johnston 2009; Jones 2009; Loomes 2009) the U.S.-based Freecycle administration was accused of attempting to enforce the brand in inappropriate ways for the British culture and legal framework. In response to attempts to replace British moderators and reassert Freecycle control, these newspaper items explained that a number of the British groups were to break away from Freecycle and form a new network, Freegle. My local group was one of those that broke away from Freecycle and formed a new affiliation to Freegle. In practice, since all the groups at that time were hosted by Yahoo Groups, this could be achieved by renaming the groups, but still, crucially, leaving the membership intact. When a particular set of moderators decided to break away they could therefore take thousands of subscribers with them. In my local group the change was announced in a single email, which briefly explained the reason for the split, and gave the new name of the group. Henceforth the format of messages remained entirely unchanged. The two addresses were, in fact, remarkably similar, as my group changed from townfreecycle@yahoogroups.com to townrecycleforfree@yahoogroups.com (subsequently, most Freecycle groups have moved to a dedicated hosting site, and Yahoo Groups have continued to host Freegle, but these groups have themselves gone through changes). In common with the standard practice of the group to limit itself to OFFER, WANTED, TAKEN, RECEIVED, and ADMIN messages, there was no discussion within the group itself. A short thread of discussion on the Café (which became now associated with the Freegle group rather than the Freecycle group) explored some of the reasons for the split and offered links to further information in blogs and discussion forums.

The change of my local group from Freecycle to Freegle, for all of the grief and heartache it probably caused those most closely involved, was achieved extremely discreetly. If one were a subscriber to the list by email, were not a member of the Café, and had not paid particular attention to the single email announcing the change, it would be quite possible to miss it altogether. In fact, many of the participants did fail to notice. As a part of my ethnographic interest in online gift-giving networks, I often bring the subject into conversation with acquaintances, looking to gauge the general awareness of the concept and increase my understanding of the diverse ways that users experience it. Since the split with Freecycle, I have found that long-term users of my local group are often unaware that the change happened at all. The name Freecycle gains an immediate recognition that Freegle rarely does, and many of the people who are in fact users of the Freegle group think that they are still on Freecycle. The situation is complicated still further in that a new local Freecycle group was subsequently set up in parallel. Newer subscribers to this Freecycle group may think that they are in the same group as the older subscribers who recommend to them by word of mouth that they should join, even though the older subscribers are actually in Freegle without knowing it.

Given this complex history and the uncertain relationship of many users to the specific lists in question, I had to make some pragmatic decisions about the focus of my own inquiry. It was not practical to focus only on Freecycle as strictly defined, since for many participants the strict definition has no meaning in organizing their activities or their expectations. I am a member of both of the local groups, and I gift items through either network. I remain a member of the Café group, and I have, as I will describe later, taken on a formal role within the Freecycle group. Formally speaking, my interest is in the online gift-giving networks within a specific town in south-east England rather than Freecycle in a strict sense, but, as I will describe, this involves also taking an interest in the circulation of representations of these phenomena more widely both online and offline. The field site that evolved centered on the particular place in which I was bodily located, but ranged across a diverse set of online spaces that became meaningful along the way.

Following on from my early realizations about the tricky nature of Freecycle as an ethnographic object, I have deployed a variety of strategies to get to know the phenomenon in a more rounded, richer fashion, and to develop some triangulation on my own autoethnographic insights. The main strategies that have proved helpful are as follows:

- looking in depth at the lists themselves, using discourse analytic techniques to examine the ways in which participants make themselves and the objects that they exchange visible to one another;
- stepping outside the medium of the actual handover encounter to recruit interviewees who can give their own insights into how the phenomenon works for them;
- extending my interest from the phenomenon itself into the circulation of representations of the phenomenon, in mass media, in inter-personal interactions, and in other online spaces. This strategy, and the interviews, also involved remaining agnostic about what "the phenomenon" might be, extending my interest to Freecycle and to Freegle in so far as they were linked in public representations or participants' portrayals, without making a judgment about whether they were in fact the same under any criteria of comparison that might be invoked;
- getting involved with the running of the organization itself as a list moderator, in order to develop an insider's perspective and to understand more about the behind-the-scenes work that created the public face of the lists.

In the next four sections I will explore each of these strategies in more detail, describing why I used them, what challenges I faced, and what insights they contributed.

DISCOURSE ANALYTIC APPROACHES TO LISTS

Although, as I have said, the list messages have a very simple format that appears on the face of it too "thin" for meaningful ethnographic engagement, it is possibly a mistake to write off the list as socially uninteresting too rapidly. The list format is what it is and deserves to be examined in its own right without applying an *a priori* value judgment about its qualities as social interaction. One important strategy for developing my understanding of the list was therefore to pay close attention to the list itself, and to explore in a systematic fashion how messages were constructed. I had previously, in an autoethnographic spirit, reflected on how messages were put together in order to inform my own attempts to create appropriate messages. A more systematic examination of messages would complement this experiential understanding, by enabling me to look at what members do with the means they have at their disposal to make themselves and their objects visible to one another, and to more carefully evaluate the discursive techniques they use.

I have previously used discourse analytic techniques to explore the way in which texts on the Internet are put together. I drew on Potter's (1996) techniques for exploring how various forms of statement perform reality for us, and how we use various devices in these statements in order to render them convincing and authoritative. This discourse analytic approach does not concern itself with making judgments on the actual status of statements as facts, in terms of their correspondence with underlying reality. The discourse analysis does not ask whether the account being offered is actually true: does the object really look like that, is this person really who they say they are? Rather, the discourse analyst looks at the choices being made and the strategies being used in a text. Of all of the possible ways of describing the object, this particular way was chosen. What kind of reality does that construct: what is portrayed as important to know about objects, and for whom? I used this technique in examining online forums debating the rights and wrongs of a high-profile media case (Hine 2000). By applying discourse analytic perspectives to the messages within the group I was able to explore the artful way in which participants used social categorizations and the assumptions that went with them to present and critique claims about the case. Participants strove to make their accounts convincing to one another by invoking external sources of authority and by drawing on their own status as individuals with experience of relevant phenomena. The discourse analytic approach helped to remind that these descriptions could have been otherwise: by their contributions to the group participants made themselves textually present to one another in selective fashion, creating a social setting with its own set of values and assumptions.

Taking a discourse analytic approach is not, in itself, ethnographic, since discourse analysis relies upon an interpretation of the texts at hand without necessitating immersion in the setting or requiring the interaction with participants that characterizes ethnography as immersive and experiential. Implicitly, it may draw on the analyst's cultural competence to understand the setting, but overtly, it focuses on the text in itself. The two approaches are, however, mutually relevant (Spencer 1994), and each offers a distinctive set of advantages as a means of interrogating what is going on in a given situation. A discourse analytic approach can, for example, be a very useful component of an ethnographic approach if it is used to develop a systematic exploration of the emergent hunches and cultural competences an ethnographer has acquired through participant observation. A discourse analyst can explore how meaning is created and contested within a setting that is also understood as an ethnographic field site (Macgilchrist and Van Hout 2011). Discourse analysis can also be a strategic tool at the point at which an ethnographer feels themselves starting to take a particular practice for granted, or to be unable to see anything distinctive or ethnographically interesting about a particular practice. Discourse analysis looks closely at the mechanics of how exactly speech or writing work in a specific context, and with its starting point that any text contains choices that could have been otherwise, works as a route towards developing the ethnographer's ability to examine the taken-for-granted and make familiar experiences seem strange. When I felt myself starting to think of the Freecycle list itself as not interesting for ethnography, or as not where the proper action was, I therefore used discourse analysis of message construction to bring myself back into a sense of the list messages as artful constructions that conveyed a particular kind of meaning. My focus here is on methodological strategies, and this is therefore not the place for a full account of the outcomes of a discourse analytic approach to Freecycle messages. I therefore present only a brief account of the construction of offer messages and highlight some features which proved to be of interest for systematic exploration in order to illustrate the methodological point.

The basic message format in online gifting groups allows for few social frills. Both through advice contained in FAQ files and through the website, which offers a strictly defined template for OFFER, TAKEN, and WANTED messages, discursive possibilities are closed down. The potential donors or recipients generally confine themselves to writing about the object in question and the very specific circumstances of its anticipated collection. Within those confines, however, there is considerable potential for stories to be constructed about how items might be useful, what collection will entail, and what uses there might be for items. These stories often involve list members explicitly or implicitly thinking themselves into the role of the new owners of objects. I knew from my own autoethnographic engagements that list members know little in concrete terms about one another, and that even a successful Freecycle encounter gives few clues to the parties concerned about each other. Within this set of constraints both on the extent to which they could express themselves, and the resources available to them to judge who their audience might be, members proved to be skilled at anticipating their audiences and telling stories about themselves and their objects in a very economical fashion.

One of my early OFFER messages illustrates the kind of routine storytelling that goes on:

On offer...

A set of wall hung pine shelves. 60cm wide, 100cm high, 16cm deep, with 2 small drawers and 3 shelves. Picture available in photo albums under "Chris". Very nice, but just don't fit our décor.

A Hotpoint BH11 cooker hood, white, never used and still boxed with instructions. Bought for our previous house about 6 years ago, never fitted there and doesn't fit in this house.

Blaupunkt car radio cassette and Goodmans 3 way 60W superbass carspeaker system. About 10 years old, but still in their boxes—I have a feeling that the relevant car was stolen before they were fitted!

Technics SL-D4 linear tracking turntable—about 20 yrs old! Functioning, although long LPs may not play fully (turntable stops rotating before the end of the record). Let me know if anyone has a taste for poorly high fi separates—there are more where this came from.

All to collect from GU2, close to Guildford station.

Christine

I felt it important, having been reading OFFER messages for some time, to give a concise and carefully crafted statement of the object on offer. I was concerned to describe exactly what the item was, so that nobody should feel they had been lured into collecting them under false pretenses. Freecycle OFFERs are almost the antithesis of advertising; so careful are members to confine themselves to the precise qualities of the objects on offer. There has, however, to be a belief that the object might find a valued home. This is a slightly tricky rhetorical trick to achieve: if an item is so useful, why do I not want to keep it? Conversely, if it is so useless, why do I think someone else might want it? I wanted to avoid seeming either mean or overly bountiful, and so I felt it important to account for why I did not need the objects that I felt that someone else might want. The first three items had, I felt, a real economic value, and my account therefore gave reasons why I did not want or had not used them. The final item had a more doubtful value, and my account focuses on forensic accuracy regarding the fault, treating it as taken for granted why I did not want it myself.

My own practices were developed through immersion in the setting, working out what I needed to do in order to fit in. Taking a more systematic approach to the analysis, I observed a similar variation in presentation of

objects in many OFFER messages that I read. It seemed that many participants did find it important to offer an account of why they did not want or
need the object any more. This constructs an environment within which
continuing to own something until it has no further worth is the norm, and
thus even on Freecycle, which is all about giving items away for free, not to
keep a useful item for oneself is deemed remarkable and requires accounting
for. Sometimes, the story was an apology and a distancing from the object,
as contained in the offer of a hostess trolley that may not work and has "just
been left with me ..." The author of that message seemed to be making
sure that we do not feel that it is her fault that the trolley does not work,
nor indeed that it is her responsibility that she has one in the first place.
Items for children were often described as being "in good clean condition"
(cleanliness, we assume, being an anticipated concern of parents). Other
items were described as needing to be collected quickly, the urgency being
justified in most cases in terms of impending house moves rather than being
left unspecified, apparently for fear we might attribute it to some unrea-
sonable whim of the owner. Some donors thought themselves into the role of
collectors and described the vehicle that might be needed for a particularly
unwieldy item.

The OFFER messages construct a version of the features of the object
that are presumed relevant for new owners and also sometimes describe
the circumstances that occasion availability or prescribe prompt collection.
According to a discourse analytic perspective, these are all choices that
could have been otherwise: nothing need be said beyond a bald naming of
the object, so it seems we can take the things that people do choose to say
as being somehow important to them in making sense of circumstances. The
stories described above manifest concerns to offer objects exactly as they
are, to take appropriate degrees of responsibility (perceptions of which vary
between members) for the object one offers, and to imagine potential uses
and circumstances of collection on behalf of recipients.

TAKEN messages tend to simply note the fact of collection, without
discussing the qualities of the object or the circumstances surrounding the
offer. Implicitly, once the object has been taken, its interest to the group
is concluded. Only where there had been some concern that a recipient
had behaved inappropriately might there be a further discussion, but this
tended to take place on the Café rather than the main list. The story of
the object itself ceases with the successful collection. Often as a donor I
am left wondering whether the object really did evade landfill: did the taker
find it useless and throw it away after all? Did I pick the right recipient?
Occasionally, an item resurfaces on the list, explicitly described as having

been collected from another Freecycle member and now being passed on as no longer of potential use to the person who initially collected it. Otherwise, members have no source of reassurance of the future trajectory of items that they offer. Whilst the Freecycle list is promoted as keeping rubbish out of landfill, there is little basis for certainty about the destiny of objects, based on observation of the list alone.

A discourse analytic perspective on mailing list messages is useful to the ethnographer because it looks beneath the surface meaning of the messages to explore how they construct a moral environment of expectations and accountabilities. The analysis depends, however, on the analyst's cultural competences to understand the situation. It is also somewhat restricted as a tool for this particular ethnographic exploration, because the activities of interest are not all publicly available on the list itself. As the autoethnographic exploration demonstrated, much of the work of making the list meaningful goes on elsewhere, via email and text messages, phone calls and doorstep encounters, and in the homes of users identifying some items, and not others, as suitable to be given away. Autoethnographic engagement provided a rich picture of the embedding of the list experience in the domestic setting and an account of the emotional qualities of participation. It was, however, frustrating in the limitations of perception that follow on from closely inhabiting the conditions of knowledge and certainty attendant on list participation. There are things that list members deliberately do not know about one another, and at some point an ethnographer will want to step outside that condition of individualized ignorance and want to know more about the world of other participants. For that reason, as the next section describes, interviews became a useful, if once again frustrating, strategy.

INTERVIEWING

Having decided that I wanted to interview members of the local Freecycle and Freegle groups about their experiences of participation, I was faced with the practical question of how to recruit interviewees. I had at this point been giving items away for some time, and had retained in an email folder the messages I had received from people who wanted an item that I was offering. I was able to use this folder alongside field notes, to look at the way that these people represented themselves too me, and to recall to mind the interactions on which I based decisions about who should receive an item. I could have used these messages as the basis for a further exercise in discourse analysis looking at the techniques people used to represent themselves in the one-on-one interactions. I felt uncomfortable, however, using these private messages for analysis in this way without permission. Messages to the main list were publicly available, and thus to some extent available for analysis, but it seemed more problematic to appropriate people's private messages in this way. I reasoned, however, that it would be possible to contact these people again and negotiate retrospective consent, and at this point invite them to become part of the study and be interviewed about their experiences of using the lists. I became quite excited about this prospect: exploring with these people what they thought was going on when they arrived at the doorstep to collect the item, what experiences led them up to that point, and what happened to the object subsequently, was going to provide a fascinating complement to my autoethnographic account. I had, however, a slight suspicion that this approach might prove controversial, since it ran against that emphasis on the ephemeral nature of the Freecycle encounter that had produced my frustration in the first place. I was conscious that a wrong step could be very damaging to my chances of continuing with this study in my home town, particularly if there were to be public complaints, or I were to be reported to the moderators. Hoping to receive an endorsement that would head off any concerns, I therefore approached the moderators of the list with a description of what I wanted to do. I chose the Freegle list to approach first, because recent public discussions about the protective stance of the Freecycle organization towards its brand made me think that Freegle moderators might find it easier to act on their own judgment, and that this might dispose them more favorably towards my study. I was correct in that they were happy to exercise their judgment, but disappointed to receive an outright rejection of my request. Under no circumstances would I have their approval to re-contact any of the people I had interacted with to negotiate interviews.

I attempted to see this setback as a source of ethnographic insight. It did, after all, confirm my reading of the situation that the individual gifting/receipt encounter was intended to be ephemeral, and that the practices of the group were designed to limit ongoing interactions. The moderators' reading of the desires of the group members aligned with my own, and thus to this extent I had confirmation of the cultures of knowledge limitation that characterized group practices. However, the pleasures of having confirmed this hunch were coupled with an ongoing frustration about not being able to gain insight into how other users experienced their participation in this list. I had deepened one form of insight into the list, but at the expense of another. I therefore shifted strategies for recruitment of interviewees. If the culture demanded that interviewees could not be recruited through the medium of the lists themselves or as a direct outcome of list participation, then recruitment would have to happen via less direct channels.

Although the Freegle moderators placed an outright ban on pursuing direct contacts for interviews, they suggested that it would be appropriate to use the Café list to appeal for interviewees. I therefore posted the following message on the Café:

> I hope you won't mind me using this list to ask for your help in some research that I'm carrying out. I work at the University of Surrey in the Sociology department, and I do academic research looking at how various groups of people make use of the Internet in their everyday lives. In my current research I'm hoping to find out more about the experience of using online networks such as Freecycle and Freegle which allow people to exchange unwanted items and in particular, how people deal with the uncertainties that come with using web sites and email to describe objects and arrange exchanges with people who are otherwise strangers. I have been a long-term user myself as a local resident, mostly giving away unwanted household items and children's clothes, but I'm aware that we all use these lists in different ways and for this piece of research I need to know more about other people's experiences.
>
> I am asking you if you would be so kind as to email me at christine.hine@btinternet.com and tell me your story of giving and/or receiving objects via Freecycle, Freegle or other similar online mailing lists. This isn't a questionnaire, so feel free to tell me what you think is important about your experiences. It can be as long as you like, but even a few short thoughts would be helpful. Here are a few questions to start you thinking, but there is no need to stick to just these or to answer all of them.
>
> - Has being involved in Freecycle/Freegle etc changed your view of the place you live in, and the people who live in it? Have you met new people by being involved?
> - Do you have any worries about safety or security in relation to giving or receiving items? How do you deal with them? Do you have practical strategies you use to make encounters with other users safer? Do you give out your phone number? When do you tell people your address?
> - If you request items ... Do you request items on the spur of the moment if they sound interesting, or do you look out specifically for items you know that you need? What do you say about yourself when you're requesting an item? Have you ever posted a "WANTED" request, and if so, was it successful? Have you ever been really surprised or disappointed by an item you received?
> - If you offer items ... How do you describe items that you offer? How do you balance being honest about its faults and making it sound like something that someone would want? How do you choose who you'll give an

item to? Have you ever given away an item and wondered what happened to it? Have you ever felt really surprised or disappointed by the person who came to collect?

- Finally, can you tell me something about you in terms of age, gender, occupation, whether you have children etc., how long you've been an Internet user, and a user of this list in particular, to give me a context for understanding what you've told me? You don't need to be specific, but having this kind of background information does help in interpreting differences between people's experiences.

PLEASE respond direct to me by email at christine.hine@btinternet.com : I really don't want to clutter up the list by having all the responses here. If you respond I will promise to do all that I can to keep your identifying details confidential, and nothing that I write as a result of this research will contain your name, email address or other identifying details. I may quote from your email to illustrate a general point, but I will not identify you specifically. If you take part in the study I'll take it that you consent to this practice but you are of course free to withdraw your consent at any time. Please don't take part if you are under 16 (unlikely, I think, in this list). I will reply to all messages that I receive. Based on your initial response I may ask you some follow up questions, but, again, you can opt out of these at any time. If you wish I can send you a summary of the findings of the research once it's complete. Do let me know if you are concerned about any details of the study or if you want me to clarify any of the above. You can find out more about me at my official University site here—http://www2.surrey.ac.uk/sociology/people/christine_hine/index.htm. I did check with the moderators before using the Guildford Café list in this way but, of course, responsibility for the study lies solely with me and I'm happy to respond to any concerns you may have.

Thank you for reading all of this!

Best wishes,

Christine Hine

In creating this message I was mindful of the warnings I had received from the moderators that participants might be suspicious of researchers and wary of making extended contacts on the basis of list participation. I therefore explained the study at length, gave examples of the kind of accounts I was interested in, and gave plenty of detail to allow any interested parties to check up on me. I invited email stories, on the basis that this would allow the participants to maintain control of the interaction until trust had been built, in line with the prevailing culture of progressing relationships on from the public online setting into more private interactions in gradual steps. I would usually conduct an email interview a question or two at a time because this format allows for development of a relationship and encourages disclosure, but in this case I felt that I needed to get the whole description across in a single email, since the list rules on advertisements limited the sender to only one per month and since I was so mindful of the cautions laid upon me by the moderators. On the basis of all of these anxieties combined, I ended up with a much longer invitation to participate than I would usually use when inviting potential interviewees to volunteer. Undoubtedly, the length alone would have put some people off. As a result of the appeal, however, I received a number of contacts that resulted, ultimately, in five people sending me their own accounts of using the lists. I followed each one up with acknowledgement and further questions, engaging with what they told me and probing further into their beliefs about the lists, their practices in terms of choosing recipients and exchanging objects and trying to understand the context within which the list made sense for them. Five is a tiny number in terms of the overall list membership, but each response, in its own way, was very helpful in highlighting the specificities of my autoethnographic experience. I had in no way gained a representative overall view of the phenomenon, but had insights into some ways in which my own experiences might be contextually specific and distinctive.

These interviews were very useful as sources of insight into some people who were using the list in very different ways from myself. However, email interviews come with some frustrations of their own in the difficulty of building rapport and the constraints on developing a conversational style of interaction, and also in the lack of insight into identity and social context as compared even with the limited face-to-face encounters on the doorstep with people coming to collect objects. Being confined to how people chose to describe themselves and what they considered to be relevant to their experience of the list was frustrating, and I found myself wanting still to know more about who people were and to develop more in-depth interactions. I therefore turned to alternative means to recruit interviewees for face-to-face conversations.

Based on my emerging understandings of who was participating in list exchanges in my town, I developed two routes to recruitment for face-to-face interviews. I advertised via the Students Union website of the local university, and the newsletter of a local school. In each case, I described my interest in understanding the experiences of users of either Freecycle or Freegle. Volunteers came forward from both sites, although it proved much easier to organize appointments around the more regular schedules and stable home circumstances of the school parents rather than the students. I developed an interview schedule focused on testing out emergent themes based on autoethnographic insights, relevant to either net donors or net recipients of objects, as I was conscious that interviewees might fall into either group and would certainly not directly mirror my own ways of relating to the list. Interviews took place in domestic settings, often sitting on the sofa in the living room, in the midst of the environment which made list participation meaningful. Unlike the email conversations which tended to be somewhat stilted and focus on direct answers to questions, the face-to-face interviews developed as more wide-ranging discussions which both included generalizations and drew on specific anecdotes. I was mindful of not appearing to pry too deeply into people's private relationships, but found that interviewees often volunteered accounts of their relationships with partners, their differing perspectives on domestic labor and sustainability, and the negotiation of various pressures and constraints in the domestic setting. In telling me about how Freecycle and Freegle made sense to them, people were telling me about how their everyday lives made sense.

Across the various means of recruiting interviewees online and offline I encountered people who used the lists in quite different ways, including both those who were net donors of items and those who were net recipients. There were, however, some categories of user who were widely believed by interviewees to exist, but who did not volunteer themselves to be interviewed. Notable among these were people who were thought to be using Freecycle in ways at odds with its fundamental values (or with the implicit set of values which interviewees imposed upon it). Many interviewees, for example, were convinced that there were some users of the lists who would claim any item offered that seemed to have a financial value, with the aim of selling it on. Interviewees told me their theories about how these people operated, and gave me anecdotes that evidenced their existence, based on particular patterns of email contact, or failure to show up for collection as a "normal" user with good intentions would. I hoped to find and interview one of these non-standard users, interested in exploring this other way of experiencing the lists and resisting the dominant notion of list values. None of my methods of recruitment were successful at flushing out this category of user, however, and I was left in a similar situation to my interviewees, intuiting the existence of this category of user from indirect evidence.

The interviews that I did conduct were about much more than simply how people use Freecycle and Freegle. They helped to demonstrate how the lists were embedded in people's lives and gave people a means to articulate their identities and priorities. By illustrating the very different ways in which people related to the lists, the people who used them and the objects that were exchanged through them, the interviews also demonstrated how flexible an object Freecycle and Freegle could be, in terms of the meanings they had for users. It became clear that making the lists work was an occasion for some complex reasoning in terms of identities, responsibilities, and security. A commitment to sustainability and protecting the environment was only intermittently apparent: concerns about money and time were much more immediate. As a complement to autoethnographic insights, the interviews demonstrated the diversity of engagement with the lists and situated my own experience as quite specific to my particular domestic and professional circumstances. At the same time as emphasizing diversity and multiplicity, the interviews also confirmed some of the broader ethnographic insights into the prevalence of uncertainty in the Freecycle encounter, in that using the list meant accepting that there were many things about other participants that one would not, and according to the norms of the lists should not, know.

Interviews are therefore a powerful tool for an ethnographer, and in this study, once I had found an acceptable way of recruiting participants, they were a very useful means to contextualize and question autoethnographic insights. Interviews are, however, always doomed to be somewhat artificial, in the purposive nature of the conversation as driven by the interviewer's agenda, and in the tendency for both participants to portray themselves in an acceptable light. For an ethnographer, interviews complement but do not replace direct observation. As I have outlined, my opportunities for direct observation of others were somewhat limited in this study. It might have been possible, through building trust over a period of time, to have gained a more direct observational role in some of the activities of my interviewees, and this would have added some useful additional material to complement retrospective interview accounts and my engagements with the list. Much could be learned through conventional ethnographic approaches, including shadowing people in their activities related to giving and receiving items, talking through their email correspondence, asking them to keep diaries, and inquiring into their decision-making: this would offer a useful complement to interview accounts, and to the autoethnographic understanding of the embedded, embodied, everyday experience, rather than directly replacing either of them. Each approach offers a different facet (Mason 2011) of the phenomenon. A further facet came into view through exploration of "naturally occurring" accounts of Freecycle and Freegle, using the wider online environment beyond the lists themselves to explore how people make sense of their list participation moment-by-moment, as the next section will describe.

CIRCULATING REPRESENTATIONS OF FREECYCLE/FREEGLE

When seeking to understand the phenomena of Freecycle and Freegle, it is obvious that an ethnographer will want to engage with the lists themselves. Finding out what everyday participation in the list entails is a matter of engaging with the detail of the discursive choices within the messages, as well as using observation and interviews to explore the meanings that the people using the list derive from their participation. It is important, however, also to engage with a sense of the field that extends beyond the lists themselves in order to understand the brand each organization seeks to promote, and the extent to which the lists are publicly rendered as unique and remarkable. Each organization has a website and Facebook presence, which produce a public portrayal of the organization, create a brand, and potentially set expectations around the appropriate use of the lists. One important dimension of the ethnography is therefore to develop a critical reading of these websites, attentive to the extent to which they present normative accounts of what list participation should be, whilst mindful that actual users may well relate to the lists in quite divergent ways as they embed them into their own everyday lives. The ethnographer in such settings can follow a circulation of representations, looking at the divergent renditions of what the object means in different settings without making judgments about the accuracy or authenticity of any individual representation as a true portrayal of what the object actually is.

In addition to the core websites of Freecycle and Freegle, representations of the lists also circulate more widely, as mainstream press cover stories, such as the Freecycle/Freegle split, and describe the lists in lifestyle features. Local council websites contain descriptions of Freecycle and Freegle in their recycling and waste disposal sections, their aspirations becoming aligned by the legislated commitment on local councils to reduce landfill. Money-saving websites promote Freecycle use as a good way to get free stuff. Representations of the lists thus circulate around well beyond the confines of the lists themselves, forming paratexts (Gray 2010) that help to shape expectations of and mediate relationships with the lists themselves. Exploring these representations helps to forge an understanding of a research object that exceeds the boundaries of the mailing lists themselves and the individual instances of use, focusing on the public presence that users may draw upon in legitimizing their own experiences.

In addition to their own websites and the circulation of representations across mainstream press and various websites, Freecycle (and to a lesser extent Freegle) also have a presence in social media beyond the sites under their direct control, as users recount their everyday experiences of using the lists. Here, the paratexts come closest to the kind of insight into everyday experiences and frustrations that I felt was lacking from interviews. Interviews involved people telling quite tidy and socially desirable stories about their Freecycle use, but social media offered an insight into a more emotional, more immediate form of account. Context and interpretation might have been lacking, but sites such as Twitter and Mumsnet offered a different kind of insight—into Freecycle use in the raw.

I first began to think more deeply about exploring social media paratexts as a complement to other forms of ethnographic engagement with Freecycle when by chance I came across a thread of discussion on Mumsnet. Mumsnet (http://www.mumsnet.com) promotes itself as "By parents for parents" and hosts discussion boards on a wide array of topics that greatly exceed a direct focus on parenting matters. Discussions are notable for a frank and often abrasive style, and for the extent to which participants preserve a separation between their online and offline lives, allowing them the freedom to disclose information in the online domain that would potentially be damaging to their offline reputations. As a regular reader of active discussions and sometime researcher on the site, I was intrigued to discover that among the many lively discussions going on one day was a thread of debate around use of Freecycle. A Mumsnet user described how she had offered an item on Freecycle; then she presented the replies she had received, and asked other users how she should have responded. Other members then entered into a discussion both playful and exasperated, judging which respondent should merit the item, and recounting their own encounters with rude and demanding recipients.

After finding this one thread on Mumsnet relating to Freecycle, I carried out a search on discussions in the site's archive that contained the word Freecycle, and discovered that the term cropped up with some regularity. Members told one another their stories of outrage and frustration, of missed collections and inappropriate requests, and their concerns about whether people were who they said they were. Experiences were offered up for interpretation, as members asked one another what particular actions might mean, or what people might think they were up to. Once again, these discussions evidenced that using the Freecycle list involved reliance on a very stripped-down interaction, which to some extent was what participants desired, but which left a lot of room for interpretation, as participants brought together a sense of how an encounter should be with imperfect information about what was actually going on. These Mumsnet discussions offer up insight into everyday experiences and dilemmas of using Freecycle (although in another sense their everdayness cannot be guaranteed, since these are instances which have been deemed remarkable enough to merit reporting). These discussions offer up an alternative source of data for exploring the meaning-making that goes on around use of the list, but this is highly site-specific data conforming to the conventions of discussion in Mumsnet.

Twitter also offers an insight into the everyday experience of Freecycle, different in format and somewhat different in tone from the Mumsnet discussions. Mumsnet discussions are accessed as a threaded sequence of contributions on a single topic, allowing insight into a collective negotiation of meaning as members contribute their own interpretations in turn. The Mumsnet discussion format favors a collective interpretation of events as described by individual members. Twitter, by contrast, tends to be accessed as a set of isolated messages from individuals. While conversations may occur on Twitter as followed in real-time, when accessed via the search interface they are retrieved as isolated utterances an individual or organization felt moved to make at a moment in time. As ethnographic data, then, they are somewhat compromised by a lack of contextualization according to the particular circumstances in which they came about. As paratexts, however, they are very useful as insights into the diverse modes of interpretation of Freecycle, and the range of emotions they generate. In contrast to Mumsnet users of Freecycle, Twitter-based accounts of Freecycle are less angry. Frustrated tweets about recipients who fail to show up for appointments do happen, but there are also happy tweets about the pleasure of using a coffee maker acquired via Freecycle for a morning dose of caffeine, pictures of rooms furnished for free, and jokes about unusual items and recommendations. Twitter contains a more varied and on balance more happy vision of Freecycle, which does contain complaints about the technology and its users, but also portrays good experiences. On Twitter, the expectation is that users will make remarks about everyday life, and the threshold for something being deemed interesting enough to tweet about is relatively low. Small pleasures of life, such as receiving a good item via Freecycle, are therefore more likely to be portrayed on Twitter than on Mumsnet.

Social media portrayals of Freecycle are therefore highly site-specific accounts, produced according to the norms of a particular setting. This provides an important reminder that the nature of Freecycle is not something to be settled on once and for all. The representations of what Freecycle is will continue to recirculate and be reinterpreted in different locations. This provides some serious challenges for an ethnographer who wants to explore that phenomenon, in that one needs to make some fairly arbitrary decisions about what to include and exclude from the inquiry. I had made the decision to focus my own interest on Freecycle in one particular town, thus tying my object to a specific geographic location. However, that object being an Internet-based phenomenon meant that even a local focus had to include some online domains, and led me from the specific branded sites of the mailing lists that I was interested in into a wider array of circulating representations of those brands and to sites where they acquired another set of meanings, locally specific in a different fashion. At times I dreamed of a developing a panoptic vision in which I could come to know how my interviewees related to and connected together the various online and offline spaces in shaping their own everyday encounters of the Freecycle phenomenon. If I could only find out how other users made sense of this sea of representations, I would feel less responsibility for my own acts of making sense. As I navigated the various online spaces on my own, through search engines and tweeted links and Facebook likes, I felt sometimes as though I was tracing connections that users I imperfectly knew had forged, and at other times as though I was making the connections myself, and exerting a kind of agency in making the object of inquiry uncomfortable for an ethnographer to own. At this point an autoethnographic sensibility provides some comfort: the ethnographic object is not perfectly knowable independent of the actions of the ethnographer, because objects do not exist in the world in that way. In the end, we have to settle for a more ambiguous and less certainly delimited object, built by navigating the complexities of everyday existence in a contingently connected media-saturated landscape.

THE AUTOETHNOGRAPHY OF MODERATING

This ethnographic journey therefore traveled through multiple contingently connected sites in pursuit of the embedded, embodied, and everyday experience of Freecycle and Freegle. On the basis of my own experiences and the accounts generated by other participants in various settings, I built an understanding of the flexible and situated nature of the experience of using these lists. Inhabiting the position of the everyday user, and in that role trying to make sense of what was going on in the face of limited evidence, proved a source of considerable ethnographic insight. At each stage that I incorporated a different source of insight, moving to interviews and social media representations, I was conscious that I was potentially going to experience ethnographic loss as well as gain, as coming to know more moved me further away from the everyday experience of knowing very little that characterized Freecyle. The gains, however, seemed worthwhile in terms of producing a multi-faceted account, and as I gained more knowledge

I tried at least to reflect on the points at which the positions of ethnographer and everyday participant diverged. One last ethnographic strategy, however, appeared to make a once-and-for-all separation from my claims to inhabit the perspective of everyday user, and this was to make a more serious effort to acquire an insider perspective by finding out how the lists operated from the inside. In science and technology studies, considerable value is placed upon "opening the black box" of technologies (Latour 1987), finding out how they come to acquire the qualities we subsequently take for granted. I would not be able to join the design team and find out how the mailing list technology and websites were produced. There was, however, one highly significant insider role I could potentially inhabit, and that might allow me some very significant insights inside the black box. As I have previously described, the Freecycle and Freegle lists are some of the most on-topic that I have ever encountered. Much of this is attributable to the volunteer moderators, who take responsibility for removing inappropriate content and disciplining users who transgress site rules. Moderators, I reasoned, must have considerable insight into who users were and what they got up to. I therefore reasoned that it would be worth the once-and-for-all loss of my claims to everyday-user status to have the chance of inhabiting the panoptic moderating role.

Both Freecycle and Freegle periodically advertise for new moderators, as existing incumbents retire, move, or take on different roles. I was agnostic about which organization I would rather serve, and in the event was successful in applying to train as a Freecycle moderator. In line with an ethical commitment to openness, I declared my research interests in my application, although I made it clear that I did not intend to use the position in order to make contact with users for research purposes, and that I would negotiate informed consent for any specific materials that I intended to use for research purposes. This was accepted on the basis that I would commit not to reveal Freecycle materials about site operation that were made available only to moderators and that I would not bring the site into disrepute. It has not always been easy to determine where to draw the line on my research activities in terms of this restriction, but I have generally interpreted it as requiring me to report in only the most general terms on events that I have observed as a moderator. In practice, the most ethno-graphically insightful aspect of moderating has been reflection upon the kinds of knowledge inhabiting this position makes available, as compared to the everyday user. Had I intended a more detailed exposé of the day-to-day work of moderating, I would have needed to renegotiate the conditions of my participation and to consider quite carefully my responsibilities to the organization, to my co-moderators, and to users with whom I came into contact.

Becoming a moderator involves being accepted on the basis of an application that establishes that one has a relevant local connection, appropriate skills, and the time to commit to the job. Subsequently, a process of training involves a series of files to read and exercises to complete, which cover both the practical details of approving and rejecting posts, and the nature, aspirations, and values of the organization. Moderators are trained both as technical practitioners who keep lists functioning efficiently and advise users, and as guardians of the site ethos. Upon successfully completing my training, I discovered that I was one of only two moderators for my local list, the previous moderators having left already, and the list being temporarily in the hands of a non-local interim moderator who was holding the fort until we were trained. After a short period of oversight as we found our feet, the interim moderator signed off and left the two of us as co-moderators in charge of the list. Subsequently, we found that we were struggling to keep up with messages, particularly over the summer period when our holidays coincided, and recruited one more moderator, who has also undergone the training course.

I have built the work of moderating into my daily routine, and I feel a considerable responsibility to keep up with my duties. Much of the work of moderating consists of very small tasks, which happen in odd moments throughout the day: potentially problematic posts are flagged up by the system and appear as email alerts in the moderator's inbox. The moderator clicks to approve or reject the message and sends messages to users whose posts have been rejected because they break site rules in some way. Users who are having technical difficulty with the site, or who wish to make a complaint about another user, send messages direct to the moderator. These events require more time, and I take care to compose a message that accurately solves the technical problem, or deals sympathetically with the claims and counter-claims that users make about one another. Neither task is particularly easy: technical issues are difficult to deal with because the site is complex and because users often cannot clearly and accurately put across exactly what their problem is; social issues are tricky because one has limited sanctions available as a moderator and often cannot readily diagnose whose position is a reasonable one on the basis of the limited evidence available. Periodically, more dramatic events will occur: a scammer will try to persuade a member to send money in advance for an item, and action needs to be taken to identify and root out the scammer, send out general warnings, and tighten up the system for identifying potential rogue messages, to make them more likely to catch the scams.

I was initially somewhat shocked about the amount of responsibility for the running of the local list that I was given so readily, but I have now come to inhabit the position of moderator with more confidence. I have acquired an everyday sense of the working of the list, have internalized its rhythms, and have developed a deeper sense of the kind of problems that arise and what to do about them. I have moved away significantly from inhabiting the position of the everyday user that my autoethnographic account started out describing. In that position I described the frustrations of lack of knowledge, and the fracturing of ethnographic insight thanks to the focus on ephemeral exchange relationships. The moderator position has given me new insights into how the on-topic nature of the list is sustained, and I now see the off-topic material, the complaints about other users, the inappropriate items, and the commercial enterprises that do not make it on to the list. I have seen how the values of the site are sustained at the level of individual messages. I have not, however, acquired any kind of panoptic view as a result of this insider position. In some regards, I know as little as I ever did, and I have acquired new kinds of uncertainty that I did not possess before, as well as new kinds of knowledge. As the moderator, one still knows nothing about what happens to other list members off-list. They remain identifiable only by nickname and email address, and by the messages they choose to send. The same is true of my co-moderators: we work (virtually) alongside one another day by day, we discuss moderating dilemmas, and share the odd joke, but we have never met, and I have no notion how this activity makes sense in the context of their everyday lives. Even from this position, making Freecycle work turns out to involve a large amount of trust in the face of incomplete knowledge. Moderating Freecycle involves living with uncertainty, accepting ambiguity, and making "good-enough" judgments.

CONCLUSIONS

In describing an ethnographic focus on Freecycle I have touched on many different sources of insight and portrayed a journey that inhabits a number of different positions in relation to the object of inquiry. It remains questionable, then, to what extent this is a single ethnography and how far the different aspects of the inquiry cohere. In fact, they do not exactly cohere on a singular knowable object, but in that regard, I would suggest, this account effectively mirrors the experience of navigating through a connected world. An ethnographic field site under these circumstances is built through the agency of the ethnographer, rather than tracing out a pre-existing object in the world. The connections that we follow do not necessarily force themselves upon us and require that we take them: instead, navigating this world requires agency, and we must take responsibility for taking one step rather than another, seeing this phenomenon as accounting for that, using this thing to build our expectations of what that thing should be. Ethnography is about trying to get inside practices of meaning-making, and where these are fluid, contingent, and individualized it seems fair enough that the ethnographer's practices mirror that state of affairs. At the same time, ethnography needs to arrive at a position where it feels able to speak confidently as to the conditions it explores, and to do so it is important to retain a feel for where the agency exerted goes with the cultural tide and where it steps aside from the flow or swims against it. Even where the ethnographer accepts total responsibility for forging the object of interest, without abdicating responsibility to some pre-existing object of inquiry to be uncovered, a sensitivity needs to be retained for the ethnography as just one amongst other possible accounts, other potential ways of carving out objects that might ally with the way that particular subjects experience the world.

My ethnographic journey through the Freecycle phenomenon continually came up against contingency and uncertainty, and encountered obstacles in the way of developing deeper understanding. Whilst there is a responsibility to find out as much as possible, and to view the phenomenon from more than one restricted viewpoint, it is also important to embrace the uncertainty at the heart of the phenomenon and to acknowledge that these obstacles to understanding in themselves tell us something very significant about the phenomenon. The ethnography involves balancing a pursuit of specific verifiable insights against the purchase offered by immersion in a culture of uncertainty and incomplete knowledge for its own sake. This entails learning from the resistances that the field puts in the way of connective ethnography and recognizing that the difficulty in linking up and moving between locations is a fundamental part of the story in this instance. Autoethnography proves to carry both advantages and limits as a means to understand online interactions: in this case, it offered an immersive understanding of uncertainty, but limited engagement with the diversity and multiplicity of a very flexible phenomenon. Ethnographic positioning is very important, even when a phenomenon appears to be everywhere: there is no neutral position, all carry connotations, and have implications for the kind of vision and experience they carry. In the next section, I offer some points for reflection on the implications of some specific choices in strategies for data collection and positioning that I made in the study of Freecycle, inviting readers to reflect on their consequences and to consider whether these same strategies might transfer to other fields.

POINTS FOR REFLECTION

- Choices were made to include both Freecycle and Freegle within the study, and to focus on their use within one particular town. Were these choices justified? What consequences would these choices have for the scope of the findings?
- What research choices were made on ethical grounds? Did the decision to focus on autoethnographic accounts mean that informed consent from other participants was not needed? At what specific points would informed consent be required from other participants?
- Each method of recruiting interviewees yielded a different sample of people, with different ways of relating to the research object. Are there other ways that interviewees could have been recruited? How might these people have been different again? Is there any way to gain insights into the perspective of people who are using the mailing list in "deviant" ways, such as acquiring items to make money, given that they are unlikely to volunteer for interviews?
- Would a survey of members have been useful? How could this have been conducted, and could such a survey yield a representative sample? What might the results have contributed to the ethnography?
- What might analysis of Twitter traffic relating to Freecycle contribute to the ethnography? How would the Twitter traffic be analyzed or visualized?
- What should an ethnographer who takes on the role of moderator for the list she is studying be worried about? What are the ethnographer's ethical responsibilities?

–5–

Connective Ethnography in Complex Institutional Landscapes

This second example-based chapter describes a connective and multi-faceted ethnographic strategy developed to explore a phenomenon that was enacted in diverse sites connected in multiple and complex ways. The overall focus of this project was to explore how and why Internet-based distributed databases were being developed within a sub-discipline of biology. The outcomes of this project have been discussed at greater length elsewhere (Hine 2008, 2013), and here the account will focus specifically on methodological choices, particularly relating to the conceptualization of the field site. The study made use of ready-to-hand tools for Internet exploration as one of the means to map out the field site, supplemented by pursuit of emergent connections between different sites and sources of interpretation, and by bringing together historical materials with contemporary accounts. The choices of site and method were informed by the very particular significance of institutional structures, regulatory frameworks, and material culture as they produced systems of meaning and accountability in this field. It also became relevant to understand how high-level policy pronouncements evolved and how they were enacted in and formed a backdrop to everyday practices. The study therefore explored a complex set of mutually reinforcing dynamics between technologies as cultural artefacts and as cultural settings in their own right.

The field in question might seem a very esoteric one, and the reader might therefore reasonably have some suspicions that strategies developed in this field might not readily transfer elsewhere. In fact, the dilemmas that I faced in this project are ones any ethnographer faced with a field in which hopes are being pinned on a particular set of technical developments might face. Many of the issues that I faced, such as how to deal with the connection between policy pronouncements and everyday practice, what significance to give to online discussions about offline activities, and how to deal ethnographically with material from archives of online discussions, will face ethnographers working in quite different contemporary fields. While the precise detail of solutions is therefore specific to the circumstances of my own field, the concerns which I was facing, in a broader sense, are often recognizable across fields. In the rest of the chapter an initial introduction to the field and the foreshadowed problems that framed my approach will be followed by sections outlining key aspects of the methodological approach. As with the previous chapter, the account will conclude with some points for reflection, highlighting choices made, and inviting the reader to reflect on how these choices might apply elsewhere and how they could have been otherwise.

INTRODUCTION: BIOLOGICAL SYSTEMATICS AND THE INTERNET

The study described here focuses on the work of the people engaged in biological systematics, or taxonomy, the branch of biology concerned with the classification and naming of organisms. This field is one of the oldest established branches of science: many of the scientific names for organisms still in use today date from the work of Carl Linnaeus in the eighteenth century, and we still use the binomial system of nomenclature he employed, giving Latin names for genus and species so that, for example, the common daisy becomes *Bellis perennis*. Systematists working today have many means of analyzing organisms and classifying them into groups, different from those available to Linnaeus. DNA sequence data, for example, is now in frequent use to complement or replace the identification of features of interest by eye or by microscope. The advent of evolutionary theories in the nineteenth century lent a new meaning to the act of grouping organisms together unanticipated by Linnaeus, and subsequently led to the development of a new focus within systematics on formulating and testing hypotheses about evolutionary descent. The methods of taxonomy are increasingly technologically sophisticated. Rather than a routine work of cataloguing and assigning names, taxonomic work is seen by its practitioners as a scientific task. There are complex rules on the process for naming a new organism and publishing its description (rendering this to some extent a bureaucratic task), but the outcome, as the grouping of a set of organisms which is proposed as the best/most informative/most reflective of evolutionary descent, is considered the equivalent of a scientific hypothesis. There is therefore no formal arbitration process that decides between competing classifications or determines which set of names should be accepted. Instead, acceptance of classificatory schemes and names is left to emergent scientific consensus. Many taxonomists would defend the scientific nature of their work: in practice, however, they are also conscious of the extent to which the rest of biology depends on them to provide a stable and meaningful set of names for organisms. Whilst the methods and the scientific underpinnings have changed radically, much of the basic goal of taxonomy, focusing on providing a stable system for the naming of organisms that would express something about their similarities with one another, thus remains intact from the eighteenth century.

Current-day taxonomists face a huge task. It is hard to estimate how many species there are on earth to be described. Chapman (2009) estimates a figure of up to 12 million, while Erwin (1997) proposed 30 million. The number actually described to date is estimated by Chapman (2009) at 1.9 million. Given the scale of the remaining task, and the continuing threat to biodiversity due to loss of habitat and climate change, the taxonomic profession seems to be in serious danger of not documenting substantial portions of the global biodiversity before it disappears through extinction. Calls for increased resources for the profession, and for increased productivity and efficiency in conducting primary taxonomic work and making it available to users, are made on a regular basis (for example, in recent years Godfray 2002a, 2002b; Costello 2009; Costello et al. 2013). The significance of taxonomic work to the efforts to conserve global biodiversity has also been internationally recognized in high-profile reports: 157 countries signed the Convention on Biological Diversity at the Rio Earth Summit in 1992, committing signatories to undertake a variety of activities to safeguard the preservation of biodiversity, both in their own territories and beyond their borders by assisting developing countries. Among the priorities the Convention identified was the need to survey and document the extent of biodiversity. It was recognized that for conservation to be effective, and to be monitored effectively, information was needed on what species were there, and that this relied on the work of taxonomists to name species and give means of recognizing them.

Systematics has therefore, in recent years, acquired a political profile and received recognition of the importance of the service it provides. It faces numerous challenges, however, in the scale of the task it faces, and also in being taken seriously as a science, given its long history, and the apparent focus on routine work of cataloguing and describing rather than more spectacular forms of discovery. The twin goals of providing a useful service and conducting scientific inquiry may also not always be in harmony: insisting on the scientific nature of the classification can lead to ongoing differences of opinion on the correct name for an organism, and threaten the stability and consensus some users require from a system of names. The discipline thus faces some conflicting pressures, in terms of reputation and accountability. This situation is compounded by some complex issues relating to institutional structures and funding. Much taxonomic work is carried out not within university-based science laboratories, but in natural history museums and botanic gardens. These institutions house the massive collections of preserved specimens that taxonomists refer to when carrying out classificatory work, and are often resourced by governments through funding streams separate from those for higher education or scientific research. Specimen collections are expensive to house and maintain, and the institutions which care for them often have to balance scientific and educational roles with a significant status in terms of national heritage, retaining their funding through demonstrating worth to successive governments. Like all forms of government funding, the resourcing of systematics institutions can be politically volatile.

Systematics also faces difficulties when assessed as a science alongside others. It is common for the impact of scientific work to be evaluated according to the number of citations the work receives in subsequent scientific work. In this system, the amount of citations is used as a proxy for evaluating the extent to which the work proved to be of value to other scientists. In systematics, some work is published in scientific journal articles, but the articles reporting on primary taxonomic work (naming new species, for example) are rarely cited: instead, the work has its impact more directly through the use of the names and classifications. Some systematists therefore argue that it is difficult for systematics to hold its own within assessments of scientific impact, against other fields where citation counts give a more plausible assessment of impact (Valdecasas et al. 2000).

Contemporary systematics therefore faces tensions and challenges as well as opportunities. In the midst of this mixture of influences on the discipline, information and communications technologies have in recent years played a prominent part, both in high-level discussions around the direction and priorities of the discipline, and in the changing everyday practice of working taxonomists. The discipline has increasingly made use of computer-mediated communication, and there have also been numerous initiatives seeking to use information and communication technologies to make systematics more efficient, to increase availability of taxonomic information, and to make taxonomic resources publicly available via the Internet. Systematics has not been alone in this regard. The developments in information and communication technologies for systematics have happened at a time when the question of technological developments and priorities for science more generally has been under debate. The concept of e-science, conceived as a more productive, more ambitious, and larger-scale science enabled by intensive use of data-sharing infrastructures and high-end computation, has received significant policy attention in recent years. Funding initiatives, such as the UK's e-science program (Hey and Trefethen 2002), aimed to stimulate developments in intensive use of advanced computing facilities, in order to realize both new scientific knowledge outcomes and a new social organization for scientific practice. Inevitably such work faced challenges in designing appropriate data structures for work across disciplines, developing standards and dealing with questions of security and intellectual property, and many of these practical issues have been faced by systematists. Whilst the developments in information and communication technologies for systematics have largely occurred outside the main thrust of policy interest in e-science, there are considerable connections both in terms of practicalities, and in the more general attitude of faith in information and communication technologies to transform science for the better.

In the project described here, I set out to explore the meaning of information and communication technologies within the contemporary discipline of systematics, focusing particularly on the recent developments in distributed databases available over the Internet. Prompted by the growing policy interest in e-science, I wanted to explore why particular forms of technological solution were seen as making sense for a scientific discipline, and why others were rejected. I also wished to explore the extent to which everyday practice and institutional structures in this discipline were changing, in the face of what in high-level policy forums was being described as a need for radical change. My foreshadowed problems therefore focused particularly on the notion of change, and the various levels at which change might be envisaged, promoted, and experienced. My interest in the idea of change was also prompted, to a large extent, by a personal connection with the field. As an undergraduate in the 1980s I had for three years studied botany (before making a subsequent shift to sociology of science, and following on from that to sociology of the Internet). As a botany student at that time I managed not to use a computer for the entire duration of my studies. Many years later, I was fascinated to see the discipline that I felt I had known so well apparently transformed by the advent of computers. When I was looking for a new project that would enable me to engage with the on-the-ground reality of e-science, this starkness of contrast between systematics now and my own experiences of it as an undergraduate generated considerable curiosity to find out how this change had happened and what it meant for the field.

As a former insider within this field I had a certain amount of advantage as an ethnographer. I had a prior knowledge of the principles, practices, and values of the field that allowed me to understand terminology, and gave me an insight into why some aspects of practice and policy particularly mattered to participants. As an undergraduate student I had learned about the principles of systematics and was familiar with the university's herbarium collection of dried plant specimens and the botanic gardens' collection of living plants. I had a summer work placement one year in the university museum, labeling mineral specimens and washing fossils. Later, as an M.Sc. student studying Biological Computation, I worked at the Natural History Museum in London whilst preparing for my dissertation, reporting on the construction of a database describing British ferns. In my undergraduate work, and particularly through my museum placements, I gained a sense of the material practices of work in systematics. I learned about the significance of preserved specimens and the information associated with them, and about the way that the physical arrangement of the specimens on museum shelves was intended to portray hypotheses about the relationships between them. Subsequently, through my M.Sc., in my doctoral research and in a postdoctoral project (Hine 1995), I entered the emerging field of bioinformatics, and became aware of the existence of projects to develop databases within the field of systematics. This gave me an insider's awareness of both material practice and institutional structures in the field.

Insider knowledge is not necessarily an advantage for an ethnographer. In the pioneering laboratory ethnographies of the sociology of scientific knowledge, such as the work of Latour and Woolgar (1986) and Traweek (1988), the ethnographers took pride in treating scientists as if they were a strange "tribe." The ethnographer took the stance of a stranger, treating the beliefs of scientists as an achievement which needed to be explained, rather than a logical position to be taken for granted. These ethnographers were able to look closely at how science was done, because they did not accept the "received view" of scientific method as an adequate account for all purposes. When viewed in this light, prior insider knowledge can be a disadvantage for the ethnographer, because it may align one too closely to the beliefs of those whom one studies, and induce one to take as natural what could otherwise be seen as the upshots of specific cultural processes. Because I have some insider background within systematics, I have the advantage of a close knowledge of practices and an experiential sense of the values and priorities of participants, but I have to work extra hard not to take aspects of the field as natural givens. Being somewhat of an insider may give access to a field that an evident outsider would struggle to achieve (Aguilar 1981), but it also means losing the analytic edge that being able to treat the subjects of the ethnography as unproblematically "other" can offer (Dyck 2000).

I am not, however, simply an insider in this field. As Voloder (2008) and Aguilar (1981) describe, attributions of insider and outsider status are shifting and situated. At some points participants may claim affinity with the ethnographer, and the ethnographer may recognize a common ground, while at other points their perspectives may appear wholly divergent. At the time that I conducted the study described here, it is therefore important to recognize that, while I had some affinity and sympathy with the work of systematics, I was not actually working in that field and I was not subject to it for my professional advancement or recognition. My allegiances also shifted over time: at some points I was a very distanced observer from the field, whilst at others my engagement became almost uncomfortably too close for an ethnographer, as I was eventually invited to serve on the advisory panel for a major distributed database project of the kind that I had previously studied. As Coffey (1999) describes, sometimes I felt very closely identified with the world that I studied, and at other times I felt very distanced from it.

The problem of identifying the upshot of insider/outsider status is further compounded by the multi-sited nature of this study. I moved between institutions, discussing various projects which might, in some circumstances appear to be in competition with one another, and which brought together participants in shifting sets of alliances. I sought to maintain a sense of appropriate complicity for each situation, aiming at what Marcus (1998: 98) describes as circumstantial activism, in which I said and did what I felt ethically appropriate for each individual situation but did not aim to adopt a consistent overall stance. I was not for or against particular technical solutions or organizational arrangements, but I maintained a sense of sympathy with the tensions that participants faced and shared a sense of the importance of the tasks they were undertaking. In my writings about this project I made no attempt to erase traces of this complicity. I also sought to do justice to the high degree of reflexivity and practical sociological insight that I found amongst the systematists that I encountered. Whilst my analysis aimed to provide new insights into the dynamics of the field, I was conscious of a desire to acknowledge the people that I studied as active and reflexive agents, rather than as the victims of systems of meaning outside of their control.

The first key methodological choice that I made was therefore to choose a field that I had some knowledge of as an insider, and to use that to help me to engage with the concerns of participants. This insider knowledge helped me initially to identify locations to visit, and sensitized me to useful lines of inquiry. In the next section I will describe some of the more conventional ethnographic approaches that I used, beginning with a series of interviews with key individuals. This section takes the question of where to go fairly unproblematically, based on an understanding of the institutional hierarchy of systematics. In subsequent sections I then open up the question of how to identify key locations and how to understand their significance, first discussing the status of one particularly key online location, and then moving on to ways of navigating and visualizing interconnected online landscapes.

INTERVIEWS AND MAPPING THE FIELD

As I have described, I began this project with some prior knowledge of the institutional landscape of systematics. I had, therefore, an existing sense of the likely places I would need to go to, in order to carry out a credible study of the contemporary state of systematics. I was, however, not confident that my prior knowledge would be in any way comprehensive enough to allow me to map the field in advance, nor was this my aim. I would wish instead to be led by participants' own perceptions of key sites and significant projects in mapping the field in order to develop an insight into how it appeared from their perspective. I had to start somewhere, however, and my prior knowledge gave me some ideas as to where to begin. I planned to conduct my study in the first instance by interviewing some key individuals about their work in the field. I wanted to know what projects they were engaged in themselves and what other projects they were aware of, what were seen as the most urgent pressures on the field, what tensions it faced, and what opportunities presented themselves. I hoped to be able to find these individuals who inhabited my field of inquiry, and to begin to be able to understand how it felt to them to live in this way.

My initial mapping of the field involved identifying key institutions and progressively drilling down to identify actual individuals at those institutions whom I could approach for an interview. As I have described above, most of the systematics work in the U.K., with a few significant exceptions in universities such as Reading, Oxford, and Glasgow, is conducted in non-university institutions such as the Natural History Museum in London, the Royal Botanic Gardens in Kew and Edinburgh, and numerous smaller museums. There is no directory of all working systematists in the country, as such (although there have been some attempts to produce such a directory: http://www.gti-kontaktstelle.de/en/taxonomist), but systematists are visible to some extent to an ethnographer and to one another through institutional websites and through the publication of their work. The outputs of inquiry in systematics are published in a variety of formats, which include journal articles, but also encompass various kinds of synthesis including field guides, checklists, and atlases. Many systematists belong to organizations specific to the particular group of organisms that they study, and publish in journals dedicated to their group of interest. There are also more generic national and international scholarly societies for systematists, including the Systematics Association and the Linnean Society, both based in London. Both societies host regular meetings and events, and publish journals and special volumes. In addition, more general biological journals such as *Nature* or *Philosophical Transactions of the Royal Society B* cover high-profile topics, which have included discussions of the current state and future priorities of systematics. Because this field is a scientific discipline, and as such constituted through its literary practices as much as through the embodied work of practitioners (Swales 1998a; Swales 1998b), it is important for an ethnographer to engage with the print culture as well as interacting with practitioners face-to-face and observing their work through co-presences. Whilst I present the engagement with the literature in systematics at this point as merely an information-gathering exercise to find out who to interview, it is worth noting that this was also a form of ethnographic engagement itself, and a part of beginning to understand how the field constituted itself through its various communicative practices.

When attempting to map the field and identify key individuals there is a substantial public presence of the discipline to explore in published literature and policy documents. I developed a "hit list" of potential interviewees by trawling through these public traces, looking for mention of database projects, trying to work out who was talking publicly about technology and the future of the discipline, and who might have an interesting perspective on the field. I was also influenced by practical matters when deciding who to approach for interviews. The study was being conducted before Skype emerged as a practical proposition for interviewing. I also at this point wanted to focus my efforts on visiting people in their working context, as I was pre-disposed towards an awareness of the significance of material practice in developing digital practice. I therefore biased my list towards institutions that I could readily visit, including the Natural History Museum in London, Chelsea Physic Garden and Royal Botanic Garden, Kew in London, the Millennium Seed Bank at Wakehurst Place (the rural counterpart of the Royal Botanic Gardens, Kew), the botanic gardens and Plant Sciences department of the University of Oxford, the Musée Nationale d'Histoire Naturelle in Paris, and the Hortus Botanicus in Amsterdam.

My strategy for identifying individuals who might be useful to interview involved a certain amount of creativity and detective work. I used institutional websites to identify the people who were identified as leading strategy relating to information technology projects at each institution, and also to identify individual projects and to track down the key people in strategic roles related to them. At this point I was not focused on the everyday practice of these projects, and more interested to map out how they were seen as forming part of the landscape of the discipline and of related and inter-meshing projects. It became clear that projects in the development of databases for systematics were proliferating, and that there were complex relationships between them. Some projects were quite small-scale initiatives with clearly identifiable lead personnel, but others were multi-institutional international collaborations, or even meta-level projects aimed at promoting access to data across discrete complementary projects.

My attempts to draw up a list of individuals to approach for interview were sometimes frustrated by aspects of the field as it was manifested online. First, it was important to make sure that I identified the correct website for an institution. Public-facing institutions such as natural history museums often have website content aimed at lay visitors, but this is not particularly useful for the kind of detail that I was seeking, and I needed to find the often less immediately visible website content aimed at the research community in order to find technical information about projects and policies. The structure of the websites reflected the conflicting identities of the institutions themselves, and thus whilst the difficulty in finding out about projects was a frustration to me, in practical terms, in another way it was an instance of learning about the landscape. Similarly, it was sometimes very difficult even when I had found an interesting project to identify the actual individual I could approach for an interview, and to find their email address. Some projects adopted an impersonal style of representation on the website, largely erasing the individuals involved in the interests of creating a credible brand for the project as an independent entity. Again, this was frustrating in a practical sense, but ethnographically telling in the way that it highlighted a prevailing concern with presenting a professional and depersonalized image amongst database projects. In practical terms, I managed to get round many of the dead-ends in identifying individuals to interview by taking the names of interesting projects and conducting web searches for those projects. These searches would often turn up reports of scientific meetings at which projects had been presented. Once I had names of individuals I could go back to the institutional websites and in most cases track down further personal information, including email addresses.

That I was able to identify a list of individuals to interview in this way in itself exposes features of the emergent online culture of the discipline. The discipline, in general, clearly had a sense that the Internet was important for presenting a public identity. It proved possible to find out about institutions, projects, and individuals, but some things were much easier to find out about than others. The "public face" of institutions and the branded representation of projects were generally much more readily apparent in the first instance than the detail of the scientific work of the institutions or the names of the individuals who brought those projects into being. In some cases, the identity of individuals was very well hidden: few institutions, at this point, had publicly available comprehensive online directories of their staff members.

Having identified a starting list of potential interviewees, my strategy for approaching them was usually to send an email introducing myself and my project, and where possible to follow up with a telephone call a day or two later. This allowed me the chance to set out my stall in advance in a considered fashion in the email, but also meant that I was not left waiting hopefully for a reply to my email for long periods of time. In each case my initial approach was focused on the general goals of the project, but also made it clear why I was approaching that individual in particular, and in what capacity. I found that this approach had a good success rate: it seemed that most of the time I was approaching the right people with an appropriate pitch that made sense in terms of their view of what was topical and interesting in their field. Some individuals passed me on to other people who were, they said, more suitable to help me: whilst one may in general be suspicious, as an ethnographer, of being told that one is looking in the wrong place, in practice most of these recommendations did prove to fit in with my goals and generally reflected a staffing issue or division of expertise that simply had not been apparent from my detective work on the website.

The interviews themselves were generally extended conversations in which I explored what interviewees saw as the opportunities and pressures in their field. I aimed to listen to interviewees' own perceptions of what was important, but also took the opportunity to explore with them how they perceived the role and impact of the various high-level policy debates and initiatives that were going on in the field at the time. As interviewees spoke, they mapped out their fields of concern for me, talking about their own projects, but also situating them against other similar projects and initiatives at other institutions and in the process developing a picture of priorities and values. It proved to be very important that interviews took place within the physical institutions. I gained a sense of the physical divisions of space and working conditions in the institutions, and in museums in particular I experi-enced a sense of privileged access as we passed from the public institution into the backrooms where systematists worked. Interviewees often gave me tours of their working environments, showed me specimens that they worked with to illustrate what they were telling me about the difficulties of rendering material specimens in digital form, and brought out publications to illustrate points and to give to me for background reading.

This series of interviews enabled me to gain a rich sense of the way that institutional structures, political and financial pressures, scientific aspirations, and individual creativity played a part in shaping the current landscape of initiatives in databases for systematic. What made the interviews ethnographic, in my view, is that I was aware of the process of setting up and conducting the interviews as itself a process of moving through the field that I was investigating. The ethnographic engagement preceded the interviews, and pervaded the process of moving between online and offline as I worked out who to interview and strove to find out the necessary details in order to do so. As I conducted the interviews, I consciously navigated between the public portrayal of projects and the private experience of the individuals engaged upon them, and between grand policy pronouncements about "the discipline" and the experiences of those who inhabited and attempted to make sense of it themselves. This focus on using both the interviews in themselves, and the process of conducting them, as forms of engagement with the field, conceiving of both as a means of working out structures and systems of meaning-making, characterized these interviews as a form of ethnographic engagement, albeit within a broad field of interest rather than a specific geographically located field site.

ONLINE FORUMS AS MIRRORS OF THE DISCIPLINE

In mapping out the field for purposes of identifying interviewees, I engaged with the online landscape of the discipline as manifested in the websites of individual institutions, initiatives, and researchers. Websites, as pieces of online territory, tell us something about how the owners of that territory see their world and their place within it. These sites tell us what that institution, initiative, or individual deems it important to tell the audiences that they anticipate are interested in them. They are a form of authored space, in which the precise nature of individual authorship may be obscured behind a collective identity, but there is a clear process of purposive authorship on behalf of a single entity. It was very helpful, as an ethnographer, to navigate this network of individually authored spaces. In the next section I will discuss how I engaged in more detail with this segregated form of online space. First, however, it is important to discuss a very different form of online space which offered a more collective sense of the nature and priorities of the discipline. In this section I will discuss how I engaged with that space, a discussion list for taxonomists, and how I investigated the extent to which it could be taken as reflecting the concerns of the discipline more generally.

Throughout the research I subscribed to the mailing list Taxacom, as a way to understand the concerns of taxonomists and to find out about interesting new developments. The list had begun in 1987 as a bulletin board focused on discussing issues specifically relating to computing in systematics. Over the subsequent years it gradually became a more general forum for discussion of issues relating to the work of systematists more broadly. It was used for announcements of jobs and conferences, and for appeals for assistance to the wider taxonomic community, such as to ask colleagues' help in identifying a problematic specimen, or locating rare pieces of literature. New initiatives were often promoted on the list. There were also some heated discussions about the direction which the discipline should take, or about specific initiatives that were seen as controversial. I found myself using the list in order to gauge the reactions amongst systematists to policy initiatives and to work out what kind of concerns systematists had about the current state and future prospects of the discipline.

As well as engaging with the list in the present, reading messages as they appeared in real-time, I also engaged with list archives in order to explore how issues had changed over time and how the use of digital technologies in particular had developed. For example, when I wanted to know how far work with digital specimens and databases had become embedded in the expected work of collection curators, I was able to access job advertisements posted to the list over the years and to see how the skills and activities described as part of the curator's role were changing in this respect. When I developed an interest in the details of everyday practice with digital specimens I was able to trawl back through the archives to find out when and how the practice of identifying specimens by showing digital images became routinized. The list archive gave me a way of engaging with past practices, beyond the retrospective accounts that interviewees were giving me of how things had changed.

As an ethnographer who had initially carved out a very broad and indeterminate field of interest, the Taxacom list was a great boon, since it seemed to give me an opportunity to observe the discipline in action, complementing the in-depth but ultimately somewhat contrived situations offered by face-to-face interviews. It gave me a way of keeping in touch with developments and gaining a sense of overall disciplinary moods, or structures of feeling, in relation to contemporary situations. It was, however, also a matter of concern to me that it was rather too easy to take the list as if, unproblematically, it simply mirrored the concerns of the discipline. This was by no means to be taken for granted. In practice a relatively small number of vociferous posters dominated many of the discussions on the list, although announcements came from a wider array of individuals. The heated discussions were around issues identified as significant by a small number of participants, and there was little way to know from observing the list itself whether the majority of readers, let alone the majority of the discipline, shared their perception that the issue in question was significant and interesting. There was, it seemed, little ground for complacency in taking the list as reflective of the discipline. I felt conflicted: the list seemed so useful, as a source of ethnographic insight, but possibly I was giving it a status that it did not deserve. I therefore began to explore how the Taxacom list, as an online space, reflected and was embedded within the wider discipline.

My first route to exploring the embedding of the list within the wider discipline was to mention the list in discussions with interviewees that I met face-to-face. I found that some interviewees were enthusiastic users of the list, and that most had at least heard of it. Even non-users usually seemed to know about it, and I was told about information from the list being passed by word of mouth between colleagues at the same institution and thus spreading beyond the subscribers to the list itself. Some interviewees were quite skeptical about the list, describing it as a talking-shop, too time consuming, or dominated by particular personalities with their own agenda. It became clear that there were active ways of consuming the list and readers were questioning the value of what they were reading at the same time as they were experiencing it to some extent as a valuable source of information.

With this notion of active consumption of list content in mind, I turned back to the list itself and posted my own message, inviting users of the list to let me know how they used it. Having received permission from the list owner, I sent an initial list of questions asking participants to reflect on what the list meant to them and how it represented their discipline:

How important is this list for a practicing systematist today? Would you miss it? What would taxonomy be like without it?

How far do the kinds of issues discussed on the Taxacom list reflect the concerns of the discipline more broadly? Is there an excessive focus on particular kinds of issues? Do others get missed out?

Have you posted messages to the list, either to start a topic or respond to one? What was your experience like—did you find it helpful, enjoyable, or neither?

How many of the people who contribute to the list do you know from other contexts? Have you met many of them face-to-face?

What other lists do you belong to? How does this list differ?

I'd be particularly interested to hear from anyone who never or rarely sends messages to the list, but still finds it useful—what benefit do you get from the list? Do you know colleagues in taxonomy who don't subscribe to the list, and do they miss out?

I received responses from 25 list members in total. I replied directly to each, asking them further questions, encouraging more detail and clarification. As I had hoped, some did identify themselves as habitual lurkers, thus giving me some access into what was going on when these people, who were never publicly visible on the list itself, consumed its content.

The responses contained a wide range of opinions about the list. All, as might be expected from list members, found it useful, but some were more guarded about its value. One common theme across many responses was that respondents were using the list to gain a sense of what the discipline was up to, just as I was. However, this often involved not taking all of the issues covered in the list at face-value as "what the discipline thinks is important," but instead using selective reading practices to filter and interpret what was being read. One participant said that she stopped reading when discussions descended into "philosophical bluster," while others identified certain vocal participants as having a particular agenda that was therefore over-represented on the list as compared to the discipline as a whole. Some felt that the list had a bias towards the concerns of the U.S., while others identified a concern with the lack of vocal women on the list as compared to their knowledge of the gender distribution in the discipline as a whole. Respondents drew out strands of continuity between the representation of the discipline on the list and what they knew of the discipline from other settings, but also identified discontinuities. Whilst they felt it was a useful way of monitoring the concerns of the discipline they therefore did not treat it straightforwardly as a mirror of the overall social climate of the discipline nor of the specific concerns that it embraced.

The respondents to my inquiry on the list described how this sense of the list as a selective portrayal of the discipline shaped their own decisions about whether to actively participate. Some enjoyed participating and described it as an intellectually stimulating pursuit, whilst others were more conscious of the public nature of participation and held back from posting or responded privately via email rather than to the whole list, due to concerns about being publicly on record amongst their peers. Some saw it as a matter of duty, however, to correct the public record if what they saw as mistakes or misinformation were being left unchallenged. It was clear that many respondents did see the list as representing the public stage of the discipline and this consciousness affected their decisions about whether and how to post.

These qualitative responses gave me some reassurance in the usage I had been making of the list within my research. The respondents to my queries were seeing the list as representative of their discipline, as an important location for networking and gaining useful information, and were seeing participation in the list as consequential for one's reputation within the discipline. It was legitimate to treat it as a portrayal of the discipline, but not a straightforward mirror. Active reading and interpretation was important to participants, and as an ethnographer it would be important to understand what those active reading processes were in order to comprehend the list as an embedded part of the discipline.

In addition to the qualitative responses from a relatively small number of participants—25 out of a membership of 1,400—it was also possible to do some quantitative analysis of the extent to which the list was representative of the wider discipline, particularly focused on geographical distribution. The list owner provided me with the membership list broken down by country, and I was able to compare this with the World Taxonomist Database (http://www.eti.uva.nl/wtd.php), which was at that time available. Both sources of data had considerable imperfections, the World Taxonomist Database having incomplete and probably patchy coverage, and the list membership breakdown being based on assumptions about nationality derived from email addresses. Any conclusions could therefore only be broad approximations. It was, however, possible to explore the perception from qualitative responses that U.S. concerns were over-represented on the list. In numerical terms the U.S. subscribers were the largest national group on the list and, comparing with the World Taxonomist Database, it appeared that a higher proportion of U.S. taxonomists were on the list as compared to other nationalities.

Following on from these analyses, I continued to use the list as a form of ethnographic engagement. I still relied on the list as a way of staying in touch with the concerns of the discipline, but did so in a way consciously informed by my own active reading processes, which involved me examining how events on the list made sense in terms of other means I had of experiencing the discipline. I saw the list as embedded within the discipline and also the discipline as embedded within the list, but in neither case was there a straightforward process of reflection. This approach is generalizable for many other situations where an online setting relates to, but does not straightforwardly reflect, a corresponding offline context. Whilst for some research questions it may be sufficient for an ethnographer to look only at an online context, it is possible, and often very enlightening, to explore the embedding of a mailing list within other frames of meaning-making, and to seek to understand how participation in and consumption of the mailing list makes sense for those who engage. These frames of meaning-making happen beyond the observable confines of the list itself, and finding out about them thus requires forms of ethnographic engagement beyond the list.

VISUALIZING ONLINE LANDSCAPES

As described above, both interviews and engagement with the Taxacom list were helpful in mapping out the field for me. Interviewees told me about how they saw the different projects and institutions, and described where they saw connections and where they experienced tensions in the field and competing priorities. The Taxacom list helped me to monitor developments, and gave me an insight into some of the controversies which animated the field. Both of these ways of mapping the field were, however, quite informal and incomplete, arising in the course of conversations online or offline, and not offering a systematic overview of developments. As I sought to evaluate my emerging picture of the field, to check for omissions, and to situate the individual accounts that I was receiving, I turned to some ready-to-hand techniques for visualizing online connections. These by no means offered a definitive answer to questions about the shape and scope of the field, but offered an alternative means of depiction that proved a fruitful source of new questions to explore.

I had initially mapped out my field according to knowledge of the key institutions and then taken a snowballing approach by picking up mentions of other significant projects made by my interviewees. I had also, as I described above, done a certain amount of online detective work to track down potential interviewees and the projects that they were associated with. This online detective work had given me an experiential sense of the web geography associated with the field: I found out which institutions and initiatives figured prominently in search engine results, and explored their connections through hyperlinks, which took me from one project to another, from an initiative to its home institution, and from initiatives to individuals. I developed thus an experiential sense of the interconnections in the field through a web geography, which had emerged, of course, as a result of myriad individual decisions made by the developers of web content as they decided what to say about their projects and what additional links their readers might want to follow.

To build on this emerging experiential sense of web geography, and allow for a further interrogation of specific connections, I found a tool that visualized interconnections between websites particularly useful. There are some very impressive special purpose tools which explore web geographies and allow researchers to develop insight into the structure of web content related to specific issues (see, for example Rogers and Marres 2000; Park and Thelwall 2003; Thelwall 2004; Thelwall and Wilkinson 2004). These approaches generally involve a dedicated web crawler searching out a domain of websites specified by the researcher and subsequent visualization of the interconnections between these websites according to the hyperlinks between them. This could have been a fruitful approach for mapping out a field of inquiry. Certainly, some ethnographers have used forms of mapping and social network analysis of link and logfile data to inform strategies for ethnographic enquiry (Howard 2002; Dirksen et al. 2010). I did not, however, want to conduct a once-and-for-all link analysis which would then inform subsequent fieldwork. I was looking for a more ready-to-hand approach that I could use repeatedly to look for connections and patterns, as questions emerged from interviews and other forms of observation.

The ready-to-hand tool I turned to was provided by the Touchgraph SEO browser (formerly Touchgraph Google browser) at http://www.touchgraph. com/seo. This tool use the Google database of "related sites" to generate a visualization of networks of interconnected sites most closely related to an initial seed URL. The precise algorithm which Google uses to generate "related" sites is proprietary, but it is generally understood that it uses not only shared keywords, but also instances of co-linking, such that where a third-party site contains links to two other sites, those two other sites will be deemed to be related. For an ethnographer, this has the connotation that the Google-related sites feature offers an aggregated view of how participants actively engaged in the field and producing websites see the inter-connections between other sites. This is certainly not an objective view of the field. It should not be taken as a stable map of relationships, but rather as an aggregate view generated in real-time of how the field plays out from the perspective of some actively engaged participants.

The Touchgraph SEO browser takes a seed URL and finds the top related sites, then finds the top related sites for those in turn, and presents a visual representation of the resulting network. The format invites exploration: any of the nodes in an initial visualization can be clicked upon to generate the sites related to those nodes, allowing a progressive exploration of the web landscape. This form of exploration was very useful in discovering which initiatives clustered together, generating questions to ask of interviewees and issues to explore in policy documents. One particular issue which arose was the connection between initiatives and institutions. Some initiatives were very closely related to the institutions that hosted them, whilst others were much more evidently clustered in the web landscape with large-scale trans-institutional initiatives, or with initiatives linked by their focus on similar methodologies or the same group of organisms, and the institution which hosted them became relatively invisible in the web landscape. This prompted lines of questioning with interviewees concerning the forms of support and accountability that linked host institutions with various forms of initiative and with the aspirations of individuals.

The Touchgraph visualization also allowed exploration of the role of various standards-setting and co-ordination mechanisms. Figure 5.1 shows the visualization centered on GBIF, the Global Biodiversity Information Facility, which is an international organization focused on developing large-scale access to biodiversity information through linking interoperable databases. The visualization brings to the fore a number of other high-profile initiatives, including the standards-setting organization TDWG (Taxonomic Databases Working Group), in turn itself connected to large-scale projects such as Encyclopedia of Life and Species 2000. This peer network again focused on

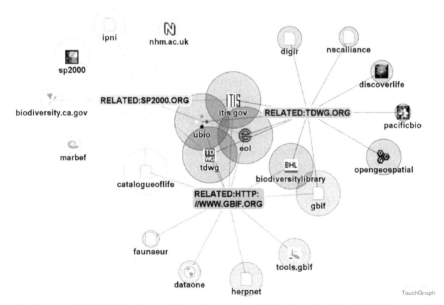

Figure 5.1   Visualization of sites related to http://www.gbif.org, site of the Global Biodiversity Information Facility, as generated by Touchgraph SEO browser (http://www.touchgraph.com/seo) from Google's database of "related sites"

trans-institutional initiatives and left invisible the role of the institutions which I knew from interviewees were so significant in enabling their work within these initiatives and yet were often the source of tensions and conflicting priorities. The web geography as portrayed in these visualizations was interesting both for the connections that were portrayed and for the connections that were absent, as compared to the accounts of interviewees.

Reflecting on the varying depiction of web connections from different perspectives and the contrast with accounts from interviewees of the tensions that they faced and the complex decisions involved in committing to various initiatives ultimately led me to develop a new set of insights into the field. I developed the term "dance of initiatives" (Hine 2008: 187) to describe the ever-shifting array of initiatives and acronyms that participants faced, and their sense of the need to participate and not be left out of significant developments whilst trying to guess which, of the many developments on the horizon, might be the successful ones. The role of institutions variously came into the foreground and receded in different accounts, reflecting a consciousness that institutions needed to support initiatives, but that large-scale participation might not be forthcoming if a particular institution were seen to be driving.

This insight did not proceed directly from the Touchgraph visualization, but was facilitated by having this exploratory tool alongside the accounts from interviews and policy documents and the individual websites. The visualization acted as a source of insights in its own right and in comparison with other accounts. It was particularly significant that the visualization was a living tool, which allowed for exploration and interrogation and did not purport to depict a final, static version of how the field was to be viewed. Visualizations can act as powerful aids to ethnographic exploration. The forms of visualization available will, of course, vary from project to project. In this particular case the open nature of the websites, and the emphasis on the public availability of biodiversity informatics in general, made this a territory readily available to Google and hence amenable to use of the Touchgraph approach. For other areas of e-science, such openness could not be assumed, and this aspect of the field is of course as much a focus of ethnographic exploration as it is a source of frustration to the ethnographic endeavor. Creative approaches to visualization and to exploring what visualization leaves unseen may be required, tailored to each individual situation.

MOVING BETWEEN POLICY AND PRACTICE

As I have mentioned in discussing interviews and mapping of the field, policy pressures were viewed as significant by participants in orienting their efforts in specific directions. Interviewees felt that there was a prevailing climate in which institutions had to be seen to be engaged in digital initiatives, whatever might be the reservations about the detail of specific projects or the diversion of resources from other efforts. Participants were in no doubt that what the major systematics institutions chose to do was a matter of public account-ability and had some visibility on an international stage, both within the discipline and in terms of international politics. It therefore proved to be of some significance to the ethnography to explore the way in which the need for database initiatives was inscribed in the policy domain and how this informed practice within the institutions concerned. Rather than treating either domain as necessarily prior to or as shaping the other, I sought to explore in detail how systematists were both represented in and represented this domain of policy, which they had described to me as informing their actions.

As a first step in exploring the policy domain it was useful to begin with the 1992 Convention on Biological Diversity, because this was a key event to which interviewees oriented themselves. The Convention on Biological Diversity was signed at the Rio Earth Summit in 1992, which was a major political event, and received significant media coverage at the time. The convention explicitly recognized that lack of taxonomic information about the organisms to be protected was a barrier to efforts to conserve biological diversity. The countries who signed up to the convention pledged to share their resources and their expertise in systematics. Interviewees involved in developing the strategic direction of systematics institutions felt that this international event propelled them onto the political stage in an unprecedented way, conferring both benefits in terms of recognition and drawbacks in terms of new pressures to perform in ways that these audiences would find acceptable. The signatories to the convention were national governments. The systematics institutions, however, played a key role at the time in informing their governments' acceptance of the convention, and subsequently became the key route through which the convention's provisions were to be achieved. A chain of accountability therefore emerged, linking the systematics institutions to a set of international respon-sibilities via commitments which their governments had entered into.

One of the overt responses to the Convention on Biological Diversity in the U.K. was an audit conducted by the House of Lords Select Committee on Science and Technology, evaluating the U.K.'s capacity to meet its obliga-tions under the convention. The report was published in 2002. It offered a significant resource for ethnographic exploration in several regards. As an explicit commentary on the state of the discipline containing a set of recommendations on what form the discipline should take in future it represented a significant intervention which interviewees oriented to as a guide to how actions that they took might be interpreted. The recommendations in the report were not treated straightforwardly as instructions on what to do. They did, however, act as a resource to portray the significance of particular initiatives in which participants were involved, and to explain why some activities should be prioritized above others.

The report was useful ethnographically as a further means of mapping out the field and identifying its priorities. The format of the Select Committee report demands that the contributors to the report are identifiable, and a record of the spoken and written evidence submitted to the committee is made publicly available. The production of the report follows on from a series of committee meetings, an open publication of invitations to submit opinions and evidence, and subsequent committee meetings in which key parties are invited for questioning by the committee. In the record it offered of the individuals who both identified themselves and were identified by the committee as competent to speak on the priorities and challenges of the discipline, the report therefore offered a useful mapping of key players. Of course, the written record is not a transparent reflection of the policy process as it happens, but the convention of openness in regard to evidence offered and examined serves a very useful purpose ethnographically speaking.

A further set of insights gleaned from the report revolved around the qualities of information and communications technologies as constructed within the policy domain. Whilst the report focused on the discipline of systematics in the U.K. in general, and its abilities to meet the requirements of the Convention on Biological Diversity in particular, it was notable that information and communications technologies featured repeatedly in the document. The executive summary to the report made a direct reference to the capacity of information and communication technologies to solve two distinct sets of problems:

> We highlight the importance of digitising the systematic biology collections, which will both increase accessibility of these data and help to update the archaic image of systematic biology. (Select Committee on Science and Technology 2002: 5)

With this statement, the report clearly identified both a practical problem in accessibility of data, and an image problem. Digitization was represented as a solution that would be seen as up-to-date, and thus improve the standing of the discipline amongst other sciences.

This portrayal of digitization as a solution to practical and reputational problems for the discipline suffused both the main body of the report and the evidence offered to the Committee. I conducted a documentary analysis of the various mentions of information and communication technologies, identifying emerging themes around the qualities invested in these technologies by participants. It became clear that systematics was participating in a form of computerization movement (Kling and Iacono 1988, 1996) in which support was being mobilized for a specific set of technological solutions in the hope of a transformation that considerably exceeded a specific set of identifiable practical benefits. In this regard, systematics was clearly not acting as a cultural island: the hopes being invested in digital technologies were symptomatic of a wider cultural current in which these technologies were seen as representing a raft of desirable qualities, and in their responses to the Committee systematists were responding to and reinforcing this cultural current.

Within this overarching positive disposition to digital technologies, the responses of systematics institutions to the report also differentiated these technologies and identified particular forms of implementation as desirable and others as inappropriate for the discipline. The report provided an opportunity also to stress some current developments which could be portrayed as aligned with the emerging desirable trend, and thus to portray the discipline as already embarked upon the direction which it was being urged to follow. Existing initiatives were presented as appropriate solutions to the pressures the discipline faced, and as carefully considered and appropriately sensitive to prevailing conditions, rather than somehow cautious or lacking in vision as critics might have argued. The spotlight cast upon systematics by the Convention on Biological Diversity offered an opportunity to put the discipline forward in a positive light. The particular form which this took is specific to systematics, but there is a more generalizable methodological point to make here, about the circulation and re-articulation of activities. Online activities, such as discussion forums or database projects, do not exist solely online, but circulate in other spaces and are re-articulated for different audiences. It is therefore important not to take descriptions by participants of the projects they are engaged in merely at face value, but to think about the values that they express, the audiences they are presented for and the work that they do in crafting the identity of the speaker.

Through discussing the report in interviews, it emerged that participants had an active process of engaging with the report. Many were aware of processes that preceded and shaped the form that the final written document took, and also used it as a resource to portray particular activities that they were engaged in as desirable, forward-looking, and in line with current priorities, as well as appropriately reflecting the heritage of the discipline. It also emerged that the report had by no means arisen as an imposition on the discipline from the outside, despite its overt status as a report by the House of Lords Select Committee about the discipline. Members of the key institutions had been actively engaged in shaping the report and supporting the Committee in developing its conclusions, and thus, to an extent, owned the conclusions as participants rather than as subjects. The very recommendations in the report can thus be taken to some extent as portraying how they wished the discipline to be seen, as much as they are practical recommendations about what it should do. In a sense, the report was no more to be seen as a direct portrayal of the discipline than the Taxacom list. Both were subject to active writing and reading processes by participants, and in both cases it was important for the ethnographer to develop a sense of those active processes in order to make appropriate use of the different sources of evidence as sites for understanding the field.

The report therefore emerged ethnographically as a live document, as much as it was a portrayal of the field and an imposition upon it. The policy debate and everyday practice proved not to be as far apart as might be imagined, for many of the participants in initiatives aimed at developing database solutions in systematics. Participants were conscious of the production of policy documents as an occasion for shaping expectations and for developing links between policy and practice. The situation described here is very specific to systematics. It is very distinctive as a scientific discipline, and in the particular combination of expectations and accountabilities placed upon it by international political developments. Nonetheless, the point about the play between policy and practice has a more general significance, and ethnographers in many fields of digital practice will want to explore how participants are held accountable, where the various accounts of what they are up to circulate, and to what effect.

It is also important, as the case study of systematic demonstrates, not to isolate a field site artificially from wider cultural currents that participants may be aware of and orient to. In particular, it is important to see which points participants see as necessary to articulate and demonstrate in detail, and which they see as taken-for-granted facts requiring no elaboration. That digital technologies represent efficiency, that they make material readily accessible, and that they are a manifestation of a forward-looking, up-to-date approach were accepted as given facts in the House of Lords Select Committee report

that I examined, and can be taken as participants' reading of the circumstances that surrounded them. These threads of meaning-making can be
followed beyond and through the specific substantive field sites that we carve
out for discrete ethnographic projects, as they inform participants' sense of
the world that they inhabit and the appropriate ways to act within it.

MATERIAL CULTURE AND DIGITAL PRACTICE

In stark contrast to many of the grand policy-level pronouncements on the
future of the discipline and the aspirations of database designers, stands the
everyday practice of working taxonomists trying to get on with their work, as
they understand it. In my interviews I had talked to key individuals because
they were immersed in specific initiatives, as I wanted to understand how that
form of work was experienced. I gained a good insight into the balance of
different forms of work they engaged in and the audiences they reached out
to as they struggled to render their projects socially, scientifically, financially,
politically, and technically feasible. I had chosen them because of the kind of
work that they did, as it contributed to the emergence of this field in which
the development of databases for biodiversity information was the natural
and inevitable solution for the demands faced by the discipline. As I explored
the work of the various initiatives and the policy climate which they both fed
on and responded to, it became clear that this work did not rely, in any direct
sense, on an understanding of user needs. Whilst the need for biodiversity
information to be openly shared was widely acknowledged, there was little
understanding of the detail of how it might be used and by whom. A rhetoric
of user needs pervaded the field, but was not accompanied by specific
insights into where, when and how these needs might be expressed, and by
whom. Contrary to many depictions of good practice in information systems
design, there was not a clear analysis of user need. Instead, database
design proceeded very often on the basis of making such data available as
could practically be achieved, on the basis that it would be found useful by
someone in due course.

As the ethnographer in this situation my role was not to set out to do the
research to fill in this gap in knowledge of who the users might be, nor to
determine whether prevailing assumptions about their needs were right or
wrong. It is not for an ethnographer to set out to provide some objective confirmation or refutation of the beliefs of participants. The insight that specific
user needs were not at this point known and did not need to be known for
the work to go ahead was in itself a significant finding that related directly to

my initial goal of finding out how a particular technical solution made sense to a specific scientific discipline. Other sets of pressures were sidelining the need for user analysis, and it was these other pressures that had produced the solution of interoperable publicly available biodiversity databases that emerged. This ethnographic finding was useful in its own right as an insight into the specific dynamics within the field. It was therefore not with the goal of questioning assumptions made by participants or overturning their beliefs that I turned to an exploration of how these databases were actually being used. It was, rather, in a spirit of finding out how the new technologies were being embedded (or not) into practice that I set out to explore the everyday work of taxonomists outside the initial narrow case of interviewees directly associated with database initiatives.

I was familiar with the material practice of systematics at the outset of the project, thanks to my earlier training in the field, and as the project progressed I sought to widen and deepen that familiarity. I visited collections of various forms of specimens, including pressed collections of plants mounted on paper in herbaria, and animals preserved in jars of alcohol. I learned about the techniques used to preserve microorganisms and fungi, and in each case explored how the characteristics of the preserved organism influenced the organization of collections and the working practices of the taxonomists who classified them. This familiarity then made it possible to explore with interviewees how collections were being manifested in digital form. Fruitful lines of discussion revolved around the qualities that digital specimens were able to maintain from the material collection and the new possibilities that digitality was seen to make available.

A series of email interviews were particularly useful in exploring how digital specimens were being embedded into everyday practice across a range of different taxonomic specialisms. I appealed once again to the Taxacom list for participants who would be willing to explore with me how they were using specimen images in their work. As before, I set out some initial questions in a message to the list, inviting participants to respond with stories from their own perspective. I received 22 initial responses, and responded to each individually as I asked clarification questions and explored practices in more depth. These email interviews could not be said to give insights into actual practice. A more direct ethnographic observation of work as it unfolded day by day would have allowed more in-depth exploration of the nuance of decisions around the sufficiency of different forms of representation for different tasks as participants co-constructed the tools available to them and the job in hand (Clarke and Fujimura 1992). However, for this project, in the time available, I had to rely on retrospective accounts.

Having a diversity of accounts available, in terms of the organisms worked on, the geographic location of the taxonomist, and the type of institutional setting (university or museum, major institution or small local outpost) offered a very clear demonstration of the highly contextual nature of the usefulness of digital specimen images. Digital specimens were becoming embedded in practice in diverse fashion, with some surprising emergent qualities. For some forms of work the digital specimen was a vital enabler of specific kinds of work, for others a practical convenience that saved time but in no way was seen to alter the nature of the task. In other instances the balance between practicality and strategic direction was more nuanced. In their descriptions interviewees often stressed the continuity of the new digitally enabled practices with previous ways of working, emphasizing that their goals were fundamentally unaltered, even though the means of achieving them might have changed. This illustrated a recurrent feature of the entire project, in that despite faith in the transformative properties of new technologies it was often important for participants to stress both that everything had changed and that everything had stayed the same. The field exhibited a strong attachment to notions of heritage and tradition, which, coupled with a desire to be seen as modern, efficient and technologically advanced, produced a complex dynamic of change and continuity.

This part of the inquiry entailed a successful use of email interviewing, even though email is often deemed not an ideal medium for developing rapport, and certainly seems a rather counter-intuitive way to explore material practice. Indeed, email interviews can be very frustrating if participants give brief answers and do not expand on their perspective at length. Some of the participants in this study were short in their answers and gave only fragmentary insights into the details of their practice. Others, however, gave lengthy descriptive answers and created a compelling picture of how, in their specific conditions of working, digital specimen images made sense. It helped that I could picture from my own explorations of online resources and digital specimen collections what kind of object they were describing, and that I understood the kind of work that they were carrying out. Of course I then risked over-projecting my own experiences on to these descriptions, which made it very important that I did share my developing interpretations with participants and check with them that my understanding seemed acceptable to them.

If the analysis was compromised to some extent by the reliance on retrospective accounts of practices rather than direct observation of those practices, then it was enhanced by the ability for participants to share links and documents with me, and thus to some extent to show me what they were describing. Where participants are embedded in a highly literate culture it will be natural for them to draw on published and web-based material in an interview, and an interview conducted via the medium of email helps them to do so. In framing follow-up questions and developing thematic interpretations I was able to go beyond the direct circumstances of the interview as the resources provided by interviewees directed me. The asynchronous nature of the email interview proved a boon as I navigated these resources and as I developed themes across the very diverse experiences of interviews conducted with several people in overlapping timeframes. Asynchronous interviewing with multiple participants simultaneously can be a very useful device for the ethnographer, offering the time to develop interpretations, which can be tested back with participants and which reflect the diverse aspects of the setting revealed by talking to different participants. A series of real-time one-to-one interviews is significantly limited by comparison, in the ability to develop and try out interpretations with a range of participants.

ETHICAL COMMITMENTS IN THE FIELD

This description of key methodological decisions will end with a note on ethical commitments in the field. This was a mobile project that involved contact with numerous participants in quite different roles at a variety of institutions, some of whom saw themselves as in direct competition or as holding incompatible perspectives with others. There were considerable ethical dilemmas in how to navigate this varied territory and to respect the different positions of participants. I needed to display knowledge of the field and interest in specific details in order to move conversations beyond bland generalizations. This meant, however, bringing up topics and perspectives that participants might disagree with, and I learned to use formulations that both distanced me from the opinions I was presenting for discussion and which avoided attributing them to any specific individuals that I might have interviewed previously. I aimed for a demeanor of discretion, in which I allowed participants to name key individuals and projects with which they might disagree rather than proposing the names myself.

Given the consciousness that individuals working in key systematics institutions have of the sensitive public role these institutions play, I have been very careful about identifying specific institutions within my writings about this project. Where it is not significant to the point being made precisely which institution an interviewee came from, I tend not to make that attribution in my writing. This is an ethnography rather than a precise historical document, and the main concern is to make a theoretically significant and insightful point about some aspect of cultural dynamics rather than to report precisely who said what when. In many cases, even while interviews have been instrumental in allowing me to arrive at an analytic point, that point can be illustrated in writing by something published on the record, rather than putting a particular individual's comments during an interview on display.

Whilst I have treated the literature of the discipline as published and on record, and therefore fair game for analysis and citation in my writings, I have not taken quite the same stance with the online forums studied. The Taxacom list is publicly available, as are its archived discussions going back many years. It might be considered, therefore, that I could with impunity quote from these public statements to illustrate points in the analysis. In practice, however, I felt that a more cautious stance was appropriate. My exploration of the significance of the Taxacom list to participants had demonstrated that many saw it as a space with reputational significance. What people said on the Taxacom list was thought to shape how others saw them as systematists, and some interviewees were very cautious about their own posting practices as a result. When I used archive material from the list to explore the history of the discipline I therefore contacted the authors of those archived postings to ask permission to quote from them in the present. It seemed quite possible that a participant could be embarrassed by my exhumation of a message buried in the archive into the present day, and I wanted to give them the opportunity not to have their past revived in this unexpected fashion. In fact, nobody refused me permission to quote from their work, and these contacts forged out of ethical duty often turned out to be interesting in their own right, as I was told more about the background to posts and about what the posters had been doing since.

Whilst I could have argued that messages to the Taxacom list were publicly available, and that I was at liberty to quote freely from them in my analysis, I was relieved that I had asked for permission when my work began to be read within the systematics community. The chapter relating specifically to the Taxacom list as a reflection of the discipline was read with interest by some members of the list, and promoted by the list owner in his message announcing the 20th anniversary of the list. The book itself was read by systematists as well as social scientists, and reviewed in biological journals (Kelly 2008; Morrison 2009). Whilst it was bruising, if inevitable, that some reviewers did not wholly agree with my framing of the issues, it was also very interesting to see my own findings entering into the very field I had been analyzing, in such a public form. It was also salutary to reflect on how important it might be for participants that I had treated them respectfully, given that that the work did take on a public status to some extent within their own field.

My ethical stance was shaped from a consciousness of my own clear affinities with the field, and my sense of complicity with it. As I outlined at the beginning of this chapter, this is a field in which I cannot be wholly outsider. This complicity shaped my sense of responsibility towards the participants in my study, such that in my writings I strove to use the sensitivities I had developed in the field in order to predict what might be embarrassing or troubling to participants and to write in ways that would alleviate the worst consequences. My work entered back into the field and became another resource that circulated amongst participants, sometimes towards ends I would not necessarily have recognized or endorsed. Ethnographers have always had to deal with unanticipated consequences when the subjects of their accounts read what they write (Brettell 1996), and it is to be expected that writings about a topical issue within a politically sensitized field will be appropriated, especially within a digital age when ethnographic writing potentially circulates more widely and more freely than the monographs of old.

CONCLUSION

The approaches that were developed to explore the field of digital technologies in systematics focused on diverse modes of embedding and re-embedding. Whilst the technologies acquired meaning through their very specific forms of embedding within the discipline, at the same time the discipline could be understood as embedded in, and enacted by, the diverse projects and practices in which its participants were engaged. The practices of systematics made sense in relation to multiple frames of meaning-making. The Taxacom list was a rich social context in its own right, embedding a depiction of the discipline, but also embedded within the discipline through the active reading practices of its subscribers. Although I was approaching the study on the level of the discipline, I found myself experiencing the discipline as constituted through practices in multiple different sites, including the online context of lists, the material reality of specimen collections, the public portrayal in policy documents, and the branded identity of major institutions and initiatives.

In exploring very different ways in which the discipline of systematics constructed and was constructed by digital technologies, I was exploring a diverse array of embodied practices and drew on my own embodied engagement with the field. I experienced different vantage points and engaged with the circulation and re-articulation of various forms of practice as they moved between everyday routine and topicalized instances of innovation and change. The methodological choices that I made took the emergence of digital technologies in the field as an embedded, embodied phenomenon, treating with symmetrical skepticism claims that these technologies were either remarkable or everyday.

The study drew on multiple forms of data, and very different forms of ethnographic engagement, including face-to-face interviews and observation, documentary analysis, online observation, archival analysis of online discussions and published literature, email interviewing, and visualization of web geographies. None of these forms of data was treated as prior to or explanatory of the others. Each in practice embedded components of the others, and each form of data offered a portrayal of the field that was selective in a different way. In navigating between these forms of data I drew on my emerging experiential knowledge of the field in order to consider what each of these different sites and forms of representation meant to those who were navigating them as part of their professional existence as systematists.

This chapter focuses on choices of ethnographic strategy and focus that were made when studying an institutionally complex, distributed set of activities, which were tied together by participants' sense that they were all part of the same scientific discipline. The contemporary world contains many instances of similar fields, which involve participants in some sense united by a common goal or identity, but also engaged in geographically distributed activities, sporadically connected by common online sites but subject to complex and divergent sets of accountabilities. The methodological choices I faced in my own study may therefore be relevant to many other contemporary settings, even though the specific circumstances and the outcomes of the choices may be otherwise. In the final section I therefore outline some points for reflection, to stress the contingent nature of ethnographic strategies, and to encourage reflection on the potential use in other settings.

POINTS FOR REFLECTION

- This chapter focuses on scientific work in particular. How far would the ethnographic strategies used here work in another setting? Would they apply, for example, in a study of the banking industry? In a study of higher education? In exploring multi-player online computer games?
- In each of these cases, what advantage would it be for the ethnographer to have some insider knowledge or status? What disadvantage would this

offer? How might the ethnographer's sense of insiderness change in the different sites of a multi-sited study, or when interacting with different participants?

- What are the dangers of using search engine results to visualize the field? How might this skew the ethnographer's perceptions? What alternative ways of visualizing the field might be possible? The web geography described here was openly available and searchable via Google, but this is not true of all settings. What data could be used to develop a visualization of other research settings, such as multi-player online gaming or banking? What data might be available for visualization if the field site were confined to a single organization?
- When an ethnographer seeks to understand a newly emerging digital practice, why might it help to understand the material practices that it replaces? Does it help the ethnography if the ethnographer learns to be able actually to do either the digital work or its material predecessors?
- How can the role of online discussion forums be understood? Can we use them to tell us about the values and perceptions of people working in the field being discussed? How can an ethnographer explore what taking part in an online discussion forum means to those involved?
- Should an ethnographer studying the details of everyday practice read what is being said about the field in policy documents and mass media? What is the significance of these "high-level" pronouncements for ethnography "on the ground"?
- Why might an ethnographer choose to use email interviews rather than face-to-face interaction with participants?

–6–

The Internet in Ethnographies of the Everyday

INTRODUCTION

In this third chapter to illustrate the application of generalized ethnographic strategies for the Internet "in the wild" through specific research examples, I discuss the use of the Internet as a methodological tool to explore mundane aspects of everyday life. I focus in particular on approaching the Internet as a form of unobtrusive method (Lee 2000: 366) for exploring the everyday, looking at research possibilities that emerge from capitalizing on the potential that the Internet provides for searching visible traces of everyday life. In previous chapters I have stressed the epistemic advantages that accrue to the ethnographer from being immersed in a setting and interacting with participants. I have emphasized the importance of entering into discussions with participants, in order to explore what is going on from their perspective, and to allow for developing hunches to be questioned or confirmed from the perspective of those most closely involved. I have tended to shun the idea that merely reading messages in an online discussion group or searching an archive could count as "doing ethnography." It therefore seems somewhat perverse that in this chapter I should turn to the virtues of unobtrusive methods. I do not claim that unobtrusive methods applied to online settings are necessarily in themselves sufficient to enable a robust ethnographic account to be constructed, and in discussing the research examples in this chapter I highlight situations where, in order to make sense of passing mentions found on the Internet, the ethnographer would need to focus in more depth, and interact with participants either online or offline in order to explore relevant frames of meaning-making. However, I would maintain that unobtrusive exploration of online landscapes can be an immersive ethnographic experience in its own right, and a particularly useful one for an ethnographer interested in those aspects of the minutiae of everyday life which participants may find it difficult to talk about retrospectively in an interview situation. Ethnographic observation is an active process of looking, interpreting, and questioning assumptions, and when viewed as such, the experience of moving through online landscapes can be an important asset in developing an ethnographic understanding that questions the taken for granted in any one place.

The examples in this chapter are drawn from research focusing on the television series *The Antiques Roadshow* (Hine 2011b). In this research I set out to develop a form of media ethnography that focused on understanding how this television text made sense to people within their everyday lives. The research utilized ready-to-hand means of searching the online landscape to find traces that people left of their engagement with the show. Rather than focusing solely on specific fan sites or discussion forums dedicated to the show, I traversed a range of forms of audience response, including producer-owned forums, comments about the show on Twitter, videos on YouTube including both recycled clips from the show, and new films made by audience members, and passing references in a wide array of discussion forums not necessarily focused on discussion of television programs at all. I therefore carried out a study that encompassed an interest in the impact of various new online platforms that encourage cross-media consumption and turn television viewing into a multi-media or two-screen experience, but also went beyond these explicitly novel aspects of television viewing to consider any engagement with television as a phenomenon that could leave interesting traces online, whether or not audience members had consciously engaged in new forms of cross-media consumption. As a result, I was able to grasp a rich sense of the diverse meanings people might make of a television program when that program became embedded in their everyday lives. This was, if not an ethnography in itself, at least a step towards a thick description of the television program *The Antiques Roadshow* and a very useful complement to other ways in which we might go about working out what media mean to audiences.

In the first section of the chapter I explore the notion of unobtrusive methods in ethnography, exploring the potential contribution that use of found data can make to the development of ethnographic understanding. I then move on to a discussion of the Internet as a mirror of the everyday and a consideration of the potential biases that are introduced by using the Internet unobtrusively as a means to explore how people go about their everyday business. The next section then goes on to discuss media ethnography in particular, introducing the strategies that I employed in order to explore the online traces of *The Antiques Roadshow*. I conclude with a consideration of the benefits and drawbacks of an unobtrusive online approach to understanding everyday life, and a reflection on other situations beyond media studies where such an approach might be beneficial. As with the other example-based chapters, I finish with some points for reflection, encouraging readers to think about applications to other research problems and the consequences of methodological choices.

UNOBTRUSIVE METHODS AND (OR INSTEAD OF) ETHNOGRAPHY?

There is a notable tradition of unobtrusive and non-reactive research methods in the social sciences, drawing on data which can be found and observed, rather than requiring active engagement from research participants. Lee (2000) has made a particularly useful summary of these approaches, building on earlier contributions by Webb et al. (1981) and by Kellehear (1993) to survey the benefits and the drawbacks, both ethically and episte-mologically, of using found data. In general, non-reactive research methods are very useful where it may be difficult for respondents to give honest or authentic answers about their behavior, possibly because answers might be seen as socially undesirable, or because it is too trivial to remember, or because the researcher's line of questioning may lead respondents to frame their comments in a particular way that they might not otherwise use. Found data has an appeal as being untainted by the researcher's hands, although of course, the decision on what counts as data in the first place is very much the product of the researcher's preconceptions. Unobtrusive methods often rely on using a form of data that can readily be collected and interpreting it as a proxy for a behavior that the researcher is interested in but cannot necessarily ask about or observe directly. Some examples are quite imagi-native: Webb et al. (1981) suggest that the noseprints that children leave on the glass of museum exhibits could be used as a proxy for the level of actual interest that people have shown in the contents. This use of traces left behind as a proxy for levels of interest is nicely symmetrical with the more recent practice of using log files of website activity to stand in for the level of interest and engagement shown by Internet users (McLaughlin et al. 1999). Such analysis of traffic to and through a website is common in commercial and institutional web activities, both in order to optimize website design and to develop marketing strategies, but it also has applications in academic research as a means to understand website audiences and infer audience interests.

The advent of social media and the participatory web (Blank and Reisdorf 2012) has dramatically increased the potential traces of behavior available to researchers (Savage and Burrows 2007), and produced such inventive studies as Thelwall's (2008) study of contemporary swearing practices using data derived from publicly available MySpace pages. A wealth of publicly available data on various forms of everyday activity can mean that traditional methods, such as interviews, seem costly and burdensome by comparison. Seale et al. (2010), for example, explore the potential for use of data from online discussion forums in health research, as an alternative to conducting interviews. They find that the data available online is often more frank and uninhibited than that produced in interviews, a finding echoed by Harvey et al. (2007) in their consideration of teenagers' discussions of sexual health. Other aspects of Internet use also leave traces that can be productive for social researchers: Ellery et al. (2008) use Google Trends data to explore changing health information-seeking behaviors, and Golder et al. (2007) use data from Facebook messaging to infer the weekly working, sleep, and socializing patters of users. Social researchers have found that the publicly available data available on the Internet permits some distinctive insight into behaviors beyond the Internet, and can be a productive way to explore some questions about everyday practices which are otherwise intractable.

Unobtrusive methods have therefore been accepted within the social sciences for the distinctive qualities that they offer, both before and after the advent of the Internet. While ethnography is largely an active pursuit that entails overt participation of an ethnographer who is visible to and known to participants in the setting, there is a tradition of unobtrusive methods within ethnography, with the unobtrusive component often entailing a process of unstructured observation rather than a more focused collection of data. I will not here be discussing face-to-face ethnographic studies that are deliberately covert from the outset, for these raise some considerable ethical concerns and very specific methodological issues. However, even where the ethnography is wholly overt in intentions, there will be times when participants relax or forget about the ethnographer's role, and the ethnographer is able to observe something very like everyday life going on around them. Ethnographers gain a lot by simply being part of the flow of everyday existence, rather than actively seeking out information and asking participants what is going on. Alternating between intellectually active but overtly passive periods of observation, and the more directed periods of focused, interactive inquiry, allows the ethnographer the opportunity to hear the field speak to her and opens up the possibility for assumptions to be overturned and new themes to emerge before deciding which directions of inquiry to pursue with active data collection. Even when not actively generating data by asking questions, the ethnographer is being active, in the sense of examining foreshadowed problems, questioning assumptions and trying to work out, in a more diffuse but still very important sense, how it *feels* to be a part of this setting. As Skinner (2008) describes, this kind of active ethnographic hanging out can happen in both online and offline settings, and can benefit from moving between them and reflecting on the emotions and memories evoked.

A form of unobtrusive method, characterized by periods of unstructured observation and a focus on experiencing the setting in whatever sense it presents itself, is therefore a part of many ethnographic projects. Ethnographers do sometimes in addition develop an interest in some specific kind of found data that has the potential to illuminate particular aspects of the setting which are of interest, and indeed Bernard's (2011) authoritative methods text for anthropologists positions such use of non-reactive traces of behavior as a standard component of anthropological fieldwork. Rodriguez (2003), for example, discusses the possibility of using a collection of traces of social action in the form of graffiti as an unobtrusive method that forms a component of building ethnographic thick description in an urban setting. Graffiti has the benefit of not being based on language and self-report generated by the ethnographer, and thus it can be taken to directly display meaning being made by participants, to some extent. Rodriguez (2003) grants that such unobtrusive methods have their drawbacks in terms of developing robust accounts of exactly what a participant might have meant by a particular piece of graffiti, but positions the collection of graffiti as a useful source of insight alongside other measures and approaches. It is in this spirit that I will be discussing the role of the Internet searching as a component in ethnographies of everyday life, not taking such unobtrusive methods as constituting ethnography in themselves, but as a component of a broader approach that seeks to understand processes of meaning-making.

Although non-reactive data does have a place in ethnography, the matter of understanding processes of meaning-making, which is fundamental to ethnography, can become highly problematic when we rely on found data and unobtrusive methods. Geertz's (1973) famous example of the wink is instructive here. From simply seeing a boy contracting an eyelid, we cannot necessarily understand whether the boy has an involuntary twitch, or is winking in order to signal a conspiracy to a friend. Geertz establishes multiple layers of complexity that could give meaning to the movement of the eyelid and give it quite different social connotations. Only by ethnographic immersion can a confident thick description be produced, which not only says what the wink is but also tells us what it does, socially speaking. An ethnographer who is present will have enough difficulties in working out these layers of complexity, but if the ethnographer is not present at the moment of the actual wink, and only sees a recording after the event, the possibilities for understanding what was going on, and what it meant to those concerned are even more restricted. Non-reactive data is therefore additionally challenging for an ethnographer in that after the event it will not always be possible to work out the various ramifications of meaning for those who were present at the time.

The problem of interpretation can arise in relation to any item of found data, such as a fragment of Internet activity. If, for example, we come across a video clip on YouTube that portrays a dog howling in time with a television theme tune, we may have to do considerable interpretive work in order to arrive at a plausible account of what that video clip might mean to the person who produced and uploaded it, and the people who watch it. For the video clip to become a component of a thick description, we could draw upon an immersive understanding of what YouTube is like, what its technical affordances might be and what its cultural conventions are, and how far this particular video uses those affordances and conforms to those conventions. We would want to situate this particular video in the context of others that the same user had uploaded, and we would read any public comments to find out what we could about the audience for the video and how it was received. This might be sufficient for us to feel that we understood how this fragment of data acquired meaning within its online context. We would, however, still be lacking other aspects of thick description that could be explored only by more active engagement: we might want to develop a relationship with the producer of the video, and find out more about the circumstances that gave rise to its production, the choices made about how to share and promote the video, and the ideas that the producer has about who the audience might be. We might want to find out how this person came to be a producer of such videos, and what this practice represented about them, to themselves, and to others around them. We might want to find out what their dog, and the television program to which the dog was responding, meant to the producer of the video. We might want to explore how the video was received, how the video producer found out about audience reception, and whether the reception met the video producer's expectations. Then we would have moved further towards something that felt like a thick description of the video as a meaningful artefact.

Individual fragments of found data may be used by an ethnographer to stimulate questioning. Collections of fragments that are similar in some way may be brought together in order to explore patterns, and to highlight similar- ities and differences which may tell us something about underlying structures and values in the contexts in which the different fragments arise. An ethno- graphic treatment of found data can permit a focus on what common forms of expression and structures of meaning are found within a population, allowing a sensitivity to what is unusual to be built up. Again, the significance of the found data can be that it avoids the contrived situation of asking people direct questions: interviews can be saved for a later stage, when patterns have begin to emerge that the people involved may not themselves be able to consciously articulate, even though they participate in them. The study of found data can therefore be one route into addressing the problem of the "silence of the social" identified by Hirschauer (2006). However, in many cases, an ethnographer will want to re-insert found data back into a more interactive setting, for example by showing the findings from a study of found data to participants in an interview, and asking them what they make of it.

It remains to consider the extent to which this use of found data, and the inference of behavior from archived traces, might be ethically defensible. In one sense there may be an ethical advantage to the use of found data, since it avoids the need to burden participants with the effort needed to produce tailored accounts according to the researcher's needs. However, there are certainly potential ethical pitfalls when the use of found data may be deemed to represent an unwarranted intrusion and people may feel they have been co-opted into the research without their consent. The collection of any data for analysis should be confined to public settings or carried out with the consent of key participants, and should be done with a sensitivity towards aspects of observation that might be deemed intrusive. The ethical considerations are not confined to data collection, but also concern analysis. It is problematic, in ethical terms, to collect observational data on people and then make inferences about those behaviors that may in some way impact on the individuals concerned without their consent. This is a strong argument for keeping interpretations of found data to a level carefully justified by the extent of evidence available and being cautious not to stray into any statements that might be deemed to be personalized diagnoses or moral judgments. This concern is all the more significant given the potential for any quoted fragments of publicly available Internet data to be connected back to the source by use of a search engine. This may be a good reason to quote sparingly and with caution from Internet data in ethnographic publications, and to devise ways of adapting quotations so that the sense comes through but direct searchability back to the source is not possible.

THE INTERNET AS A MIRROR OF THE EVERYDAY

There is no strict, principled distinction between the Internet on one hand, and everyday life on the other. Back in the early days of the mainstream

Internet, when the tendency was to talk of events on the Internet as having happened in "cyberspace," it seemed strange to think of occurrences online as having an everyday, mundane quality. Now, however, for many Internet users, much of the time, the Internet has lost its exotic edge, and both we as analysts and they as users can think about the events that happen online as a part of everyday life rather than separate from it. This is not to say that the Internet acts as a straightforward mirror of everyday life, reflecting everything that happens in face-to-face contexts without distortion. The Internet exists as a multiple and variable cultural object, which is not equally available to all, and is not interpreted in the same way by all users. Users develop a sense of what it is sensible and ordinary to do with the Internet according to a diverse array of influences (Bakardjieva 2005): we watch and learn from those around us, we receive ideas from the media about what the Internet is for, and we observe the behavior of others in the various platforms we use online, adapting our behavior to fit in with the conventions and affordances of each platform. These factors introduce biases and constraints in the kind of everyday life reflected on the Internet: to some extent it acts as a mirror of the everyday offline world, but it is a distorting mirror, which does not reflect all that is there in the offline world, and which preferentially depicts some aspects above others. The same is, of course, true of face-to-face settings. We tend to assume that face-to-face settings are natural, and that what is said and done face-to-face has some authenticity as a reflection of our deeply felt beliefs and principles. However, this "natural" interaction is just as shaped by social conventions and by the affordances of different occasions as anything that happens on the Internet. There is no principled reason to take face-to-face settings as the gold standard of unbiased interaction against which a biased Internet should be compared. Nonetheless, it is important to keep alert to the circumstances that shape the traces of everyday life available to an ethnographer both online and offline and the different sets of conventions and constraints that shape what counts as acceptable behavior in each setting.

Even though the Internet offers some distortions in the portrayal of everyday life that it offers, it offers some rich resources for an ethnographer seeking to understand mundane aspects of everyday existence. As the technical and social barriers to participation have come down, and as the participatory expectation built around social media has increased, so more and more of life's trivial mundanities have become reflected online. The Internet can therefore be used to explore a wide range of topics that may be difficult to observe in face-to-face settings, and to provide a complement to other, more directive means of exploring a topic of interest. I have made use of Internet-derived data, for example, to explore the way that parents discuss the problem of headlice in children (Hine 2014). Whilst the problem of headlice is rife amongst children of primary school age in the U.K., there still can be a stigma attached, and many parents find it difficult or embarrassing to talk about the issue in face-to-face settings. On the online parenting site Mumsnet, discussion was by contrast very frank. By convention, users of the site tend not to use their real life identity, and this detachment from real-life persona can enable frankness in talking about otherwise taboo topics. Analysis of data from Mumsnet discussions about headlice enabled me to explore representations of parenting as a particular form of effort and commitment, as juxtaposed with a set of beliefs about scientific and medical expertise. The Internet-derived data offers access to a form of talk that would not have arisen offline. It is, therefore, to some extent shaped by circumstances. It could not be said that the online data in some way expressed a set of beliefs that this group of parents held, in a stable fashion, whatever the circumstances of discussion. The data was shaped by the particular conventions of Mumsnet. However, very much the same could be said of an interview setting. If I had conducted face-to-face interviews with these parents, the views that they expressed about parenting and headlice would have been different in some regards from what they said online. The views expressed in the interview would not, however, have been straightforwardly the truth, against which a distorted version appearing on the Internet could be compared. Both could be considered to be contextually appropriate truths. A similar point is made by Orgad (2005) in her discussion of comparing online and face-to-face narratives of experiences of breast cancer. The online and offline narratives were often different, but neither medium automatically generated a more robust or truthful account.

Using the Internet in this way is akin to hanging out in a public setting, catching the prevailing cultural currents, and listening to the way that people talk about a topic when, unlike in an interview, they are not being asked to generate a formal account of their relationship with the topic. This interest in the ambient everydayness of a topic has, in the past, led to some inventive solutions for finding a suitable public place for observing cultural currents. Press and Johnson-Yale (2008), for example, explored everyday political discussions by hanging out in a hair salon and observing as the talk turned to matters of politics in response to programs on the salon television. The researchers were not interviewing people about either politics or television, or both, but were observers of the flow of conversation that moved around these topics. The talk that was observed could not necessarily be said to represent in some abstract sense the political views of those concerned, but it provided a rich insight into the interweaving of politics and media in everyday experience. The research explored politics and television as embedded phenomena, utilizing this relatively public space to bring interesting talk to light. The researchers were careful to develop a rich description of the environment in which this talk happened, contextualizing the talk that they analyzed against their understanding of the meaning which this setting had for those involved, and in particular the extent to which the owner orchestrated the environment and made particular kinds of talk desirable and possible.

In similar style, the Internet makes it possible to observe the contextual occurrence and circulation of various kinds of talk about everyday matters. Beer and Penfold-Mounce (2009), for example, explore the cultural circuits of celebrity gossip through an exploration of the generation of gossip about one particular celebrity through diverse online settings. They took an overtly imaginative stance towards generation of their insights. They explain that since they were interested in understanding, in depth and in detail, the way that those interested in celebrity gossip experienced the online landscape:

> ... we tried to emulate these practices, our method was to search for our chosen celebrity figure in the way that those interested in this gossip might do so, searching and re-searching the name on Google, then using links to locate other related sites to get the sense of how the user might move through and encounter different types of content [...] The hope is that this approach will reveal something about how interested parties might go about exercising their melodramatic imaginations in the contemporary context and what they might find. (Beer and Penfold-Mounce 2009: 2.6)

It is key to note here that Beer and Penfold-Mounce do not simply search out a dataset and immediately decontextualize it, downloading the data for subsequent analysis. Instead, they focus as much on connections and circulations as they do the data in itself, learning from the experience of searching and finding out something about the territory in which celebrity gossip arises, travels, and finds meaning.

The Internet offers some useful properties as a means of hanging out and observing chat related to a topic of interest. The searchability of the Internet confers mobility for the ethnographer wanting to pursue an object of interest across diverse locations, and in some circumstances, as with Beer and Penfold-Mounce (2009), this can offer the advantage of navigating an online territory in a way plausibly similar to the way that an ordinary user might navigate. Using ready-to-hand tools offers a means to look for common patterns of circulation, and to highlight places where options are closed off or shaped by commercial and institutional framings. It is important, for example, to consider where the juxtaposition of a discussion forum and a set of keyword-sensitive advertising that appears alongside may shape the experience and give a new meaning to the content of the user-generated discussions. Whilst using ready-to-hand tools, then, it is still important to remain sensitive to the extent to which these tools shape the experience and make some results appear more significant than others. Search engines contain biases that are not necessarily transparent to users (Wouters and Gerbec 2003; Diaz 2008; Goldman 2008; Levene 2010). If the goal were to produce an objective map of online discussions related to a particular topic, this would be a problem, but if the aim is to explore the online territory as it might present itself to an ordinary user, then a reflexively critical use of ready-to-hand tools appears an appropriate approach.

Beyond the ready-to-hand tools of search engines, which enable exploration of online fragments related to a specific topic of interest, there are other readily available ways of exploring online territory. The practice of monitoring social media, which has become commonplace across the commercial sector, and indeed in many non-commercial institutions, could also be of use in this regard. An ethnographer wanting to learn about everyday practices could make use of a wide array of commercially available tools to build an awareness of the online territory relating to that everyday practice. As discussed in Chapter 3, these tools are part of a rapidly developing commercial environment of web exploration and social media awareness monitoring, which allows for exploration of trends and temporality in social media coverage of a topic. An ethnographer could make use of these various ways of mapping, aggregating and visualizing data, just as an ethnographer would always have attempted to draw maps and explore patterns. Beer and Penfold-Mounce (2009), for example, could have used the tools available now in order extend their discussion of the circulation of celebrity gossip through real-time monitoring and visualization of social media response to offline events and appearances of the celebrity, keeping abreast of the dynamic online reflection and recreation of offline events. Visualizations offer new tools to both ethnographers and participants to conceptualize online space in new ways, and to explore different forms of connection. The key concern to keep in mind is not to be too seduced by the ability of any of these visualizations to show us something real in terms of practices of meaning-making. All are constructions, all involve multiple layers of prioritization and distortion, around what can be displayed and what is deemed appropriate to record.

These are not objective maps, but invitations to explore territory, to juxtapose, and interrogate.

These approaches suggest that fast, big data-style aggregative approaches could be complemented by a form of "slow search," which takes a more experiential approach to moving around the web (Boyd and Crawford 2012). This approach retains the embodied ethnographer at the heart of the research. The Internet allows for aggregation and juxtaposition, and collapse of scales, but it is still possible to move around slowly, to focus on movement as a form of experience, and to reflect on what shapes the expectations both of moving and of staying in one place. Big data approaches can be useful in their ability to generalize and aggregate on a large scale, but this does not substitute for the active observation of a mobile ethnographer moving across different platforms and using observations in one place to interrogate the assumptions in another. The diversity of the Internet is a major asset, since the juxtaposition of difference helps to remind us how things could be otherwise, and questions the sometimes easy assumption that any particular dataset drawn from a single Internet platform could show us something directly mirroring everyday life. Moving between different platforms is a good way to help us to remember how the technical qualities of different platforms, and the specific conventions and cultural norms that develop around them, shape what can be said.

TELEVISION AUDIENCES IN ONLINE SETTINGS

The specific research example I use to explore the purchase offered by slow movement through online space as a means of researching the everyday focuses on television consumption. The question of how to understand the way in which audiences engage with media products has preoccupied media studies researchers for many years, and produced many inventive methods for studying audiencehood (see, for example, Moores 1990; Morley 1992; Goldstein and Machor 2008). There has been an ongoing interest in how to capture the moments at which audiences are making sense of television and in turn to understand how people embed the media into the ongoing sense-making of their everyday lives. Some researchers engage with audiences at the actual time of watching, whether by setting up focus groups and showing the programs in question to them, followed by discussion, as Morley (1992) did with the Nationwide audience, or by watching alongside them in their own homes, as Skeggs et al. did (2008). Media researchers also contextualize viewing as part of a moral economy of the household

(Silverstone et al. 1992) or as a practice that acquires significance within the socio-economic, cultural, and ethnic positioning of a family (Gillespie 1995). Gillespie (1995) conducted an ethnographic study that used anthropological notions of holism, and there is a flourishing tradition of media anthropology (Rothebuhler and Coman 2005). Individual methods for study of the media are, however, often considered unsatisfying for the way in which they carve out a specific aspect of media for attention, making a cut that must to some extent be artificial. It should be noted that media studies has been criticized for its appropriation of the notion of ethnography for a far more restricted and less holistic notion of the methodology than in anthropological circles (Hirsch 1998; Murphy 1999; Schlecker and Hirsch 2001). Certainly, the notion of ethnography used in non-anthropological media studies can sometimes be focused quite narrowly on a pre-specified phenomenon, and focus on a small range of pre-determined situations to study rather than ranging around in a more open fashion. As Radway (1988) explains, media studies aspires to study "the endlessly shifting, ever-evolving kaleidoscope of daily life and the way in which the media are integrated and implicated within it" and instead often finds itself only illuminating a limited fragment of the phenomenon.

Barker (2006) reviews the extensive literature concerning audience relationships with the media, and on that basis identifies a number of "unarguable truths" about audiences, the first two of which are:

1 There is no such thing as "the audience," rather, there are a great variety of "audiences" that nonetheless display patterns and processes which bind them into researchable communities of response.

2 Being an audience for anything is never a simple or singular process. It is a process that begins *in advance* of the actual encounter, as people gather knowledge and build expectations. These prior encounters are brought to bear in different—but researchable—ways within the encounter, guiding selections ... In other words, audiences bring their social and personal histories with them. And these histories continue after the "event" as the audiencing encounter is given a place—sometimes enclosed as "that was nice/nasty/over," sometimes providing the (cognitive, affective, emotional, sensual, imaginative) resources for conceiving self and the world. (Barker 2006: 124)

Based on these truths, and the recognition they entail that our knowledge of audiences is destined to be fragile and contingent and shaped by what counts as researchable, an alternative, or additional means of exploring audiencehood offered by engagement with the traces that audiences leave on the Internet seems to offer some benefits. There is no expectation that this will be the "killer method" that ultimately allows us to know what audiencehood is all about, since Barker (2006) reminds us that any apparent unity in conceptions of the audience will only be temporary and provisional. "The audience," as such, only exists in an ephemeral contextual sense. Searching for audiencehood on the Internet may, however, allow a different conceptualization of the research object of media studies, and allow ethnographers to develop strategies to explore different forms of television engagement and provide a new way of understanding the embedding of media in everyday life.

The Internet is simultaneously an agent of fragmentation and a source of connection where audiencehood is concerned, multiplying the contexts in which audiencehood is expressed and where meaning is forged around the consumption of media projects, but at the same time making it more possible than ever for different forms of audiencehood to be juxtaposed and understood in relation to one another. The potential of Internet searching to find fragments of data relating to a phenomenon in places we could not have predicted offers a significant boon to studies of what television means to us. As Silverstone (1994) points out, a lot of our everyday engagement with television is fragmented, fleeting, and inattentive, rather than representing intense engagement or fandom. Much of the audience-related research on the Internet to date has focused on sites of fandom, looking at discussion groups in which fans congregate and exploring the entwining of the experience of the television program and the sense of membership within the group. These studies often focus on a single interpretive community of fans (for example Baym 2000; Jenkins 2006), or compare two online fan groups, in Bury's (2008) case. This choice of field site is informative if our research object is fandom itself, but is not able to capture the kind of inattentive engagement with television that Silverstone (1994) describes, which is by its nature not contained in predictable sites of intense interaction.

The phenomenon with which I will illustrate an alternative research approach is the *The Antiques Roadshow*. This show is a flagship program of the BBC, was first made in the U.K. in 1979, and has subsequently both been sold around the world and the format reproduced in a number of other countries. Each show has a very standardized format, revolving around location footage of a "roadshow" to which members of the public have brought items to be valued by antiques experts. The show largely consists of a series of individual valuation events, each involving one object or a set of objects being valued by an expert. The interaction usually begins with the owners being invited to say something of what they know of the object and how it came to them, before the antiques expert gives a narrative explaining the official stance on the object's origins, provenance, and significance. The valuation event concludes with the expert suggesting an estimated value for the object, and the owner responding with emotion (surprise and delight are common, but overt disappointment occasionally features). Much care is taken in the edited show to include an impression of the popularity of these events: long queues feature prominently, and each valuation event screened shows the owner and expert surrounded by a group of fascinated onlookers.

I chose *The Antiques Roadshow* as the object of my research because of a personal fondness for it, which had led me to reflect in some depth on the nature of the show as an embedded phenomenon. I had watched it at home as a child with my parents, lost touch with it in early adulthood, and returned to it later with pleasure. I counted myself someone who enjoyed the show, and looked forward to viewing the latest episode as a treat, something to sweeten the Sunday night task of doing the ironing. I would not have counted myself a fan, as such, but I would make a point of watching if not committed to doing something else at the time. I liked the show for aesthetic reasons, finding old things pleasing for their craftsmanship and their stories. I liked the show, too, for its human narratives. I enjoyed seeing people talking about their very different family circumstances and telling about the way that the objects they were showing had been acquired and treasured and passed down. I also took delight in watching the many ways of responding to the final valuation of the object by the expert, and enjoyed spotting the various clichés. The show featured in our family dynamics too: it was recognized by other family members as a priority for me, and time would often be made for me to watch it amongst the Sunday night family routines of tea and bedtime, as an expression of care by other family members. Changing technologies made a difference too: in fact the practice of prioritizing the show over other routines became largely a thing of the past when time-shifting technologies came along, video player was succeeded by hard drive recorder, and ultimately Wi-Fi connected television with Internet access. I have memories of this show playing a part in everyday experience going back through my childhood and through my adulthood to the present day, changing over time, and situated in particular sets of domestic and technological context. When the *Antiques Roadshow* came to a local site recently I made a point of attending, carefully assessing the item that I took for its potential to make it on to the show, and making a point of taking my daughter with me, convinced that I had read the values of the show and that a combination of a storyable object and attractive child should be a winner with the producers. In the event, we were almost but not quite successful: we were chosen as potentially appropriate for the show by our expert, but on interview by the producer we did not make the cut to have our encounter with the expert filmed. It was fascinating, however, to experience the show from the inside and to observe the remaking of my own locality through this medium, and reflect on my own skilled reading and reproduction of the show's norms.

From my own experience, then, *The Antiques Roadshow* has multiple meanings and the experience of it has changed through time and according to circumstance. This contrasts quite dramatically with the meaning often ascribed to it according to textual analysis alone, which focuses on the relations of expertise inscribed in the valuation event, and the emphasis on monetary value (for example Bishop 1999; Ytreberg 2004; Lanham 2006; McCracken 2008). Other authors offer a more complex account of the show: Clouse (2008) explores a diversity of possible readings of the show and finds a complex narrative structure that does not allow economic values alone to dominate, while Bonner (2003) discusses the existence of the show as part of a genre of "ordinary television," predictable in format and part of a popular culture that is competent to read the show on multiple levels. It is this more complex view of the television show as a multiple and embedded phenomenon which the approach that I develop here builds on and explores in new lights. By moving to exploration of what the show means to people in diverse contexts, it is possible to see not just that a single textual analysis is limited in the extent to which it tells us how actual people engage with the show, but that much of the use which people do make of the show is more like the fleeting and fragmented references Silverstone (1994) described than it is a focused act of engagement with a text.

To further explore the notion of the multiplicity of *The Antiques Roadshow*, I began with a Google search on the term "Antiques Roadshow." I visited each site on the results list in turn, finding the context in which the show was mentioned and reading around to explore associated pages and find out more about the sense in which the show was being evoked. I stored screenshots and captured pages for later review, and kept notes about emerging themes and patterns, commonly occurring forms of description and matters that struck me as unexpected, or unlike the show as portrayed in textual analysis. The number of search results was too great to explore them all, so in order not to be totally driven by the prioritization placed upon the results list by the Google algorithm, I did make a point of visiting sites a long way down the list of results as well as those at the top. The following is a non-exhaustive taxonomy of the kinds of search result that I encountered:

- BBC Antiques Roadshow website, a sub-section of the main BBC site;
- Fan forums dedicated to discussion of the show, external to the BBC site;
- Local media coverage of the show coming to the area;

- Passing mentions of "Antiques Roadshow" on other websites and discussion forums not overtly focused on the show, or indeed on television.

The last category was particularly interesting for my purposes, since it was here that the fleeting attention to television that seemed so elusive in other methods of studying media became visible. Many of the passing mentions were quite unexpected and surprising, and evoked very different aspects of the show to the standard textual analysis. To be sure, people did mention in passing a particularly high valuation for an object on a show that they had seen, but there were also mentions of the show by expats nostalgic for home making no reference to the show's contents or values at all, as if *The Antiques Roadshow* were as quintessentially British as Marmite. The show often acted as a metaphor for age: something, or someone, would be described in passing as "old enough for the Antiques Roadshow," with the expectation that readers would know what was meant without further explanation. Mentions of the show demonstrated a presumption of commonality, assuming a shared understanding, and creating a feeling of community. The theme tune featured in a number of search results, as a ringtone to download for one's phone, and as a clichéd tune to parody in different styles. The theme tune was clearly a component of a familiar domestic soundscape, and commented upon as such. *The Antiques Roadshow* was also represented by some viewers as the ultimate boring television, with "just lay around and watch Antiques Roadshow all day" being the equivalent of total inactivity, and the show being mentioned as something to put on when you're trying to do revision to make you concentrate on your work. As I moved from one search result on my list to the next, I was visiting a diverse array of sites and a very different set of interpretations of what the show was and what it meant. The juxtaposition of these varying meanings attaching to the show brought out the contingency of interpretation and emphasized the extent to which the show made sense to people according to some common themes but expressed in a form quite specific to the particular context in which they arose.

The fan forums where people engaged with the show in an intense fashion seemed familiar from other studies of interpretive communities developing around their chosen media artefact. I was surprised to find that the show occasioned a fandom that turned the antiques experts into celebrities and traded sightings and gossip about them, in addition to the groups of fans motivated more by an interest in antiques, but I was not surprised that the show offered an object of fandom. Again, moving between different versions of fandom highlighted the differing interpretations that the various fan groups made of the show and emphasized the contingency of meaning-making, such that it was clear one set of viewers were not taking the same thing from the show as others. The different groups were also not inhabiting the same online landscape, in terms of the kind of advertisements that accompanied discussions. In some discussion forums, an accompanying sidebar of keyword-sensitive advertisements promoted antiques fairs and valuation events, inviting readers to embed their understanding of the show in a commercialized territory where they too might be buyers and sellers, rather than simply viewers. Other discussion forums were devoid of advertisements, or failed to make the connection between the discussion of a television show and a commercialized antiques market.

In addition to the Google search, I also searched YouTube for "Antiques Roadshow." Here, again, I found an extensive list of search results, which I explored through viewing and reading comments, paying attention not just to the video itself, but to the placing of that video within other elements of YouTube, such as advertising and suggestions of related videos to view next. I identified commonly recurring types of video as follows:

- full episodes and notable clips uploaded by fans;
- clips featuring the person who uploaded the clip appearing on the show;
- comedy programs featuring a sketch parodying a valuation event;
- amateur video sketches parodying a valuation event;
- video of dogs howling at the theme tune.

As with the Google search results, these videos demonstrated multiple ways of engaging with the show. It became clear that *The Antiques Roadshow* represented a formulaic form of interaction, which people could both recognize when it was used to comedic effect, and could reproduce themselves. The mainstream comedy shows that parody the format tended to use the event of *The Antiques Roadshow* coming to town to bring out a weakness or failing in one of the main characters, such as greed, or stupidity, or inability to correctly read a situation. Amateurs worked in the same vein, assuming that their audiences would be skilled at diagnosing the format and able to see where an interaction deviated from what should happen between layperson and expert, with humorous effect. These amateur videos were not, on the whole, produced by committed fans of the show. Instead, they often formed part of a series of videos containing amateur comedy sketches and parodies with a variety of targets. Many of these amateur videos also evoked a sense of nostalgia relating to the show. For young adults, the show often appeared to represent the security of childhood. It was a mundane part of the ritual of Sunday night, as a boring but safe element of the routine.

The amateur comedy videos evoked *The Antiques Roadshow* as a shared cultural object that could be assumed to carry similar connotations for a broad range of viewers. Some of the videos, however, portrayed a very personal connection with the show, not necessarily directed at the broad potential audience of YouTube, but focused more narrowly on showing one's appearance on the show to friends and family. These videos brought the show into alignment with other forms of reality television, in that for some *The Antiques Roadshow* represented an opportunity to be a participant, and when this occurred it became a highly notable event in the biography of that individual. These videos tended to received very small viewing figures compared to the notable clips uploaded by fans, but the number of viewings is in itself a poor index of the significance of these occasions for those concerned.

From the diverse array of fragments generated by searching for *The Antiques Roadshow* on the Internet, a very diverse set of notions of audiencehood emerge. Whilst we have the intense fandom recognizable from many studies of fan culture online, we also have a broad array of different forms of more fleeting engagement that show people actively engaging with and making use of media as a resource in living everyday life. We find people who really enjoy and commit to the show, and others who have a more conflicted relationship with it, portraying it as not pleasurable, in fact often boring, even though they find themselves compelled to watch it. Many of these aspects of the show are not ones I would have predicted from my own domestically embedded watching experiences, nor from textual analysis of the show, or from my expectations about the various forms of fandom that would be encountered. Searching produced surprises, and these could be fuel to the ethnographic imagination, stimulating questioning of taken-for-granted ideas about how people engage with television. Each of the search results offered up a potential site to dwell in depth and work out how that fragment of engagement with the show made sense within the context both of the particular technological platform on which it appeared and the ongoing flow of events on that site, but also according to the meaning it held within the everyday life of the person who made the comment, uploaded the video, or participated in fandom. At each point, there is an opportunity to render the study properly ethnographic by exploring in depth, digging down in strategically chosen places and exploring both online and offline dimensions of meaning-making.

CONCLUSION

As Law (2004) reminds us, different research methods carve out different versions of reality, and all fail to capture in total the messy contingency of everyday life. All methods for understanding audience relationships with the media are in some sense partial: out of the tangled complexity of the interactions of diverse, uniquely situated people with an array of media in some sense shared but also in a sense personal to their own practices, predilections, and opportunities, we select out particular threads to follow and particular stories to tell, depending on what we think will be theoretically interesting or informative. Even an ethnographic approach to media audiencehood that aspires to be holistic will be in some way selective, and will begin with some initial thoughts about where might be interesting to go, and what kind of practices and connections to follow. An ethnographer interested in audiencehood might choose to dwell with a particular family, or explore the role of media as consumed within a particular neighborhood or ethnic group. It might be of interest to focus on one particular media product, or a genre, and explore how it made sense to a broader range of people in their everyday lives. These forms of study make some judgment about an interesting context, and they explore what television means in that context, and in this way they make cuts through the complexity.

The approach that I have described here is rather more agnostic about context. It takes an open approach to finding out what a particular chosen media product might mean to people or what form their engagement with it might take and where those practices of meaning-making might be found. By exploiting the potential of an Internet search engine to surprise us and to seek out traces of media engagement we might never otherwise have imagined as possible, it opens the mind of the ethnographer to context in a new way. We find surprising new contexts in which television makes sense, and can then drill down in those places to explore the varied influences that permeate them. This approach has some resonance with Marcus's (1995) exhortation to "follow the thing," allowing the carving out of field objects that are not located in a particular place that can be identified in advance, but maintain a multiple existence across an unpredictable set of locations. The Internet search engine makes the connections visible and shapes our research object, not as a neutral tool, but as an active part of shaping the territory.

This method of searching out potential contexts within which a chosen phenomenon makes sense is not, in itself, ethnographic. It could be argued, however, that no specific method of research is in itself ethnographic. Ethnography is an orientation towards the production of accounts, and it encompasses a wide range of methods, chosen for their ability to reveal some facet of a phenomenon, but always tied together, interpreted, and combined by the agency of an ethnographer making sense of the varied forms of data available. Ethnography is an adaptive approach: the ethnographer chooses methods and orientations and moves through the field according to what seems at the time to be the most useful, and the most potentially enlightening tactic. The approach that I have described has the potential to occasion new forms of ethnographic study, and to stimulate the ethnographic imagination, but simply using an Internet search engine to find traces of people talking about a particular object is in no way, in itself, inherently ethnographic. This kind of searching is, however, one of the methods of mapping out a territory for exploration that ethnography for the Internet might use, and will probably become a more common feature of ethnography in general as the Internet, as a way of carrying on our everyday lives, becomes increasingly taken-for-granted.

A form of slow searching, exploring Internet connections and dwelling on meaning-making in a diverse set of online spaces connected in some way with the phenomenon of interest has some appealing qualities for an ethnographer, and can be carried out with ethnographic sensitivity, but in order for this to happen the searching needs to be embedded in a wider project of exploring how practices make sense. To be ethnographic, this traveling will need to be accompanied by periods of dwelling in a particular place, and exploring the meaning-making that goes on there in depth and in detail. This will involve consideration of the specificities of the particular technological platform in question, developing sensitivity to the forms of connection and expression that a particular technologically mediated platform enables and closes off, and to the conventions that prevail there and considering how this might be different in another context. The strands of meaning-making that surround any individual fragment of found data relate both to a phenomenon and to the situation within which the fragment arises, co-constructing the phenomenon discussed and the setting. The ethnographer interpreting found data needs to consider diverse aspects of what any individual fragment of data means, rather than assuming that because the researcher might be treating it as data on how people interpret television it is also conceived, by the person leaving this trace, as a moment of audiencehood. What looks like "the consumption of television" to a researcher may look, to the person leaving the trace, like connecting with family, making absent strangers laugh, showing friends how clever they are, or simply passing the time.

The approach described here is certainly transferable to other issues beyond television programs. Whilst I have searched for mentions of a television program, one could instead explore mentions of a place, or a health issue, or an institution. Monitoring the online manifestations of such phenomena could become part of the hanging out that ethnographers do, developing familiarity with the territory, learning the language, identifying common discourses, and becoming sensitive to manifestations of difference. The Internet search becomes a route to understanding how a phenomenon becomes embedded in everyday life in circumstances that extend far beyond conversations which are overtly "about" that phenomenon. Passing references and casual jokes become visible and searchable on the Internet, and illuminate the phenomenon in new ways, suggesting new contexts to explore and new questions to ask. The application of this method is easier with some concepts than others, it has to be admitted, thanks to the way search engines work. It was fortuitous that the television program that I chose to research was identifiable by a phrase, "Antiques Roadshow," that could be used as an unambiguous search term that only produced results relating to that television program and gave no false positives. Where no unambiguous search term uniquely identifies the phenomenon, other search tactics may be required, following hyperlinks, exploring blogging networks, and imaginatively identifying likely discussion forums or social media groups to join. This is not a clean process of objectively identifying a data set but a messy and complex form of exploration, which draws on the researcher's reflexive insights into the factors which make some moves easy, sanctioned, and obvious and others impossible or against the grain.

POINTS FOR REFLECTION

- When should the web be treated as an immersive space in its own right? To what extent can web searching be treated as a form of fieldwork? Can a field site be constructed out of interconnected web space across different platforms?
- What are the limits to ethnographic understanding? How far can an ethnographer interpret observational data without interacting with participants? Can we term the ethnographer's presence in a web-based landscape as a form of participation, and to what extent does this fit with the principles of ethnography for the Internet outlined in Chapter 3?
- How does the technological format of YouTube, and the conventions of use which people learn, shape the kind of data that an ethnographer would find by searching for his phenomenon of interest on YouTube? Having found a video clip relating to our phenomenon, how could we find out, for example,

why it makes sense for the person who uploaded it to do so? Why would someone post a video clip of herself appearing on a television show? How could we find out what this meant to her?

· How might this approach be used in another situation, for example in relation to a health condition, or a geographic place? What might be the advantage, for example, for an ethnographer interested in cancer to spend time exploring the diverse ways that the disease is mentioned in online settings? What could that ethnographer learn that would inform subsequent fieldwork? How might an ethnographer focusing on everyday life within a particular town make use of conducting online searches for mentions of that town? What kinds of fieldwork might this search lead to?

–7–

Conclusion

The year 2014 is destined, according to business analysts and marketing gurus, to have been a big year for big data. The possibility of generating huge data sets through automated collection of digital transactional data and behavioral traces and the mining of those datasets for patterns and predictions of future behavior have been on the horizon for some time, but 2014, the analysts promise, will have seen the potential of these approaches begin to be fully realized, as behavioral modelling on the basis of big data becomes embedded more and more seamlessly into practices of commerce and governance. Expertise in the development of big data approaches is highly valued: apparently, data scientist is "the sexiest job of the 21st century" (Davenport and Patil 2012)! In the face of these developments, to focus on a methodology that argues for moving slowly through relatively small amounts of data, exploring its meanings in depth, tracing its circulation, and contextualizing its production and consumption, seems somewhat perverse. As Savage and Burrows (2007) warned, social research may appear to be an endangered species if it doggedly sticks to small-scale, laborious techniques in the face of growing belief in these large-scale insights generated without any social science input at all. However, more latterly, as Savage and Burrows hoped, scholars from the social sciences are rising to the challenge of both engaging with and critiquing the contemporary discourses of hope and hype surrounding big data. These scholars reassert the significance of traditional approaches, but suggest that we should use them alongside and as a component of a serious engagement with big data as a contemporary phenomenon that deserves attention in its own right. boyd and Crawford (2012), for example, stress that big data does not necessarily have all of the answers, and they take a critical stance on its ability to provide meaningful explanations of phenomena. Graham and Shelton (2013) argue that just as big data seems to be coming to dominate, it is all the more important to engage with big data and to understand what it can do to inform scholarly inquiry, but to do so with a view also to informing debate on the limitations of big data and the constraints that too great a faith in its explanatory powers may create.

As we find ourselves feeling overwhelmed by the Internet and the deluge of digital data that emerges from the saturation of everyday life with digital technologies, and as the whole thing becomes "too big to know"(Weinberger 2011) and apparently amenable only to big data approaches that process on an industrial scale, it becomes all the more important to tell stories about how that feels, to explore the consequences and unanticipated connections that arise, to record what is happening from both central and marginal perspectives, and to enable interventions. Even in these days of big data, the in-depth and embodied approach of the ethnographer has a lot to contribute in highlighting how we, as embodied individuals, navigate these new conditions of social existence. It is possible therefore to engage with the world of big data by sticking very closely to the purchase offered by ethnography as an immersive, experiential approach which documents activities and emotions, and retains an open-minded stance on what a phenomenon "means." Ethnography offers contemplative approaches that situate data and explore ramifications of meaning, and offer an important corrective to the tendency to treat patterns identified in big data as straightforward reflections of reality and imperatives to action. At the same time, it is important that we adapt and grow ethnographic approaches in order to enable us to engage with all forms of data, big and small, and to inhabit the changing conditions that a media-saturated, big data world produces. Digital environments provide new conditions of inquiry, and to neglect these emerging situations would leave ethnography behind as an impoverished approach that could, as Savage and Burrows (2007) suggest, find itself sidelined by a world of big data.

In this book I have explored forms of ethnography that mix methods and span different scales of inquiry, diving deep into practices of meaning-making but accepting the usefulness of aggregating, mapping, and visualizing data on a grander scale as a means of navigating territory. I have explored the necessity of moving between practices that are rapidly becoming mundane and unremarkable, and the heavily topicalized Internet that becomes the focus of our hopes and fears. I have highlighted the importance of real-time engagement with events as they happen, in order to promote an experiential sense of immersion in media-saturated and digital environments, but have also acknowledged the need to engage with archives and to explore the temporal complexities introduced by our increasing ability to preserve behavioral traces and revisit the past. I have stressed ethnography as an agile approach that evolves in the face of developing situations and is adaptive to the circumstances in which it finds itself.

In this concluding chapter I will first pull together threads from the three example-based chapters, highlighting the response that was made in each case to the circumstances offered by an embedded, embodied, everyday Internet. The next sections then move on to consider emergent ethical frameworks, and then some of the challenges faced by an ethnographer working in such territory, focusing on the skills and tools which support an ethnographic approach to the contemporary Internet, and discussing, in particular, the challenges posed by an ever-evolving, unpredictable Internet. Finally, I turn to a consideration of what lies in the future, both for ethnography and the Internet. I consider how far ethnography might transform further, in the pursuit of flexible approaches to developing informative methods for exploring the Internet, which will be agile in the face of ongoing developments both in the technology and its cultural embedding and strategic in their orientation to different forms of research question.

REVIEW: ETHNOGRAPHY FOR THE EMBEDDED, EMBODIED, EVERYDAY INTERNET

The three research case studies in Chapters 4, 5, and 6 explored research done "in the wild," carving out research objects from some very diverse circumstances. Each of them illuminated aspects of the embedded, embodied, everyday Internet that I outlined in Chapter 2, and made use of the strategies for engaging with this incarnation of the Internet as described in Chapter 3. Throughout, I strove for continuity with some recognizable principles of ethnographic knowledge production as highly personal to the individual ethnographer, involving immersion within the setting, and taking part in the same activities as participants as far as practically feasible in order to develop a deep sense of what participants do, how this feels, and what its consequences might be for the social formations that result. Being immersed in a setting is key to this form of knowledge production. However, immersion is not necessarily a straightforward matter where we deal with phenomena that are dispersed across different media and different settings, and both we as ethnographers and the participants themselves can only develop partial perspectives, constrained by the particular paths we choose to travel on and the specificities and constraints of our own positioning. For this reason, autoethnographic approaches often become central to ethnography for the Internet, allowing us to interrogate the experience of navigating mediated social territories, exposing the practices and skills of making sense and forging connections as they become available to us, and allowing us to produce rich descriptions of the emergent social territories that surround and suffuse the Internet.

Ethnographers for the Internet use some strategies that are familiar from ethnography in more conventional territory. Field notes remain a very important tool for developing the ethnographer's analysis and keeping track of emerging thoughts, although the Internet-embedded ethnographer does have some tricky decisions to make about how far field notes are to be either kept private, or publicly shared with participants through blogging, thus turning these early stages of the research more overtly into a dialogue. Interviews are as key in ethnography for the Internet as in other ethnographic settings, for exploring specific issues of concern in detail and depth with participants, and allowing them to respond to the ethnographer's tentative portrayals of his sense-making activities. Ethnographers have always surveyed and mapped, and the new possibilities offered by digital data and ready-to-hand tools of search and visualization complement and supplement these traditional approaches, offering new ways to conceive of the territory in which the ethnography takes place and stimulating thoughts about where to travel and what questions to ask. These strategies are deployed in varying ways in individual projects, depending on the circumstances found there. In some sites interviewees may be easy to identify and recruit, whilst in others they will remain frustratingly anonymous or invisible, and the ethnographer will have to work hard to find ways to supplement her own autoethnographic experiences with triangulatory perspectives from other participants. In some circumstances, archival data will be a useful resource to allow questioning of taken-for-granted assumptions about the present, and to highlight changing structures over time; other settings will be wholly ephemeral and the ethnographer will have to focus on a real-time engagement and all that this entails in developing the skills to keep up with fast-moving action, take notes, and develop analytic thoughts simultaneously. Each ethnography for the Internet deploys a unique set of strategies and faces its own set of challenges. In presenting the case studies, I hoped to explain why a particular set of strategies were chosen for each setting, and to stimulate the methodological imagination for ethnographers facing similar issues in their own research settings.

In Chapter 4 I explored the very diffuse phenomenon of Freecycle, existing in multiple incarnations online and embedded in diverse domestic circumstances. Here there were considerable challenges faced when trying to tie diverse forms of engagement together into a single, knowable research object. This occasioned some considerable soul-searching about the extent to which gaps in knowledge of the object, owing to the difficulties of recruiting interviewees and locating observable practices, compromised the account. Some gaps in knowledge remained, to the end, intransigent in the face of inventive methods, and frustrate the rendering of Freecycle as a knowable object. Navigating the phenomenon across its diverse and imperfectly connected incarnations was, however, a source of autoethnographic insight in its own right, and prompted a deeper level of reflection on the fragmented, multiple, and ineffable qualities of the phenomenon for all participants, not just the ethnographer.

The second case study, in Chapter 5, focused on the institutionally located and policy-infused domain of biodiversity databases. Here I navigated between material culture and emerging digital practice, exploring the varied influences that informed the practice of building publicly available, distributed databases of biodiversity information. I undertook research in both offline and online locations, and in particular explored the role of a popular discussion forum in constituting the discipline both for participants in the group and for my own purposes as ethnographer. This case study illustrated also the challenge of exploring connections between a policy domain where grand pronouncements were made about the future of the discipline and the desired role to be played by new technologies, and the more mundane everyday reality of participants attempting to make decisions that fitted in with their own career trajectories, institutional pressures, material constraints, and scientific aspirations.

The third case study, in Chapter 6, focused on unobtrusive methods for exploring the Internet, treating the movement of a researcher through an Internet landscape as potentially a form of immersive experience that could inform development of ethnographic thinking. The Internet preserves a myriad of traces of mundane everyday experiences, and by developing a critically reflective immersion in these traces the ethnographer is able to develop insights into both casual and passing engagements with a phenomenon of interest and more intensive and sustained forms of interaction. In each case, the fragment of data can be viewed as embedded into diverse frames of meaning-making, both online and offline. Online, a data fragment is shaped by the technological affordances of the platform on which it arises, and by the conventions of use developed by users of the site. Offline, a data fragment acquires meaning in the ongoing flow of everyday experience for its producer, both as he or she takes the decision to post, upload, or comment and as he or she subsequently receives feedback from others on these actions. An ethnographer can exploit the searchability of online traces of behavior to map out an array of potential engagements with their phenomena of interest to explore, subsequently making strategic decisions about which sites are of most theoretical or practical interest, and which frames of meaning-making might be fruitful to investigate in depth.

Each of these studies started with a phenomenon of interest but no clear prior idea about what the field site would comprise. Each study was exploratory in nature, progressively identifying useful connections to follow in order to contextualize and add meaning to understanding of significant issues. The field site that emerged from these studies was shaped by the individual agency of the ethnographer, making choices informed by personal predilection, practical constraints, and theoretical agenda. In each of these case studies, the experiential knowledge that characterizes ethnography was key in developing an understanding of the phenomenon. As an ethnographer I was able to be mobile, and to explore how phenomena gained meaning within the contexts provided by different media and how my phenomena of interest developed complex, fragmented, and multiple identities that participants were nonetheless able to navigate. It was particularly significant, in terms of developing holistic understanding, that these studies were not planned *a priori* to be contained within a particular medium or technological platform, because the world is not experienced one medium at a time. The media-infused world that we inhabit is connected in diverse and unpredictable fashion. It is often not sufficient, for many of the research questions that we wish to ask, to draw on meanings forged only within one medium, as if it offered a bounded social context. It is important to take seriously the fact that we connect interactions and events across media through our embodied experience, and that navigating this world entails making choices. These technologies that we study also, however, have a visible public presence: we aggregate them, grant them agency, and make them the topic of conversations. Ethnography for the Internet can usefully be agnostic about these public characterizations of the technologies we study, setting out to explore the nature of technologies as they acquire meaning in our beliefs and aspirations, our hope, fears, and fantasies, as well as our mundane, everyday practices.

Ethnography has a good reputation for being able to take seriously what people actually do, accepting practice on its own terms as something that makes sense for those individuals, and taking an open-minded approach to finding out just how it makes sense, and with what consequences for the social formations that result. Ethnographers also look beyond the taken for granted, enabling an exploration of assumptions that sit in the background of any social situation, making practices seem natural when in fact they could have been dramatically different. Cultural relativism enables ethnographers to take each setting as it makes sense on its own terms, whilst recognizing that what seems perfectly natural in one setting may appear totally bizarre in another. The mobility that characterizes ethnography for the Internet can be a boon in developing a cultural relativism with regard to the experience of phenomena. By tracking a phenomenon across settings, the ethnographer is able to explore the multiple existence of the phenomenon in different places. Ethnography for the Internet is not, however, about constant mobility. It is important to be reflexive about movement and stasis, considering the purchase that each offers, and sometimes resisting the urge to move in order to explore in depth the frames of meaning-making that pervade a specific place or fragment of experience. This form of ethnography gains from reflecting on how movement and connection are sanctioned from specific positions, and in what directions is it particularly easy or difficult to move. This insight into the texture of lived social experience that results relies upon an embodied, reflexive ethnographer, and cannot necessarily be gained from a distanced analysis of data harvested on large scale.

EMERGENT ETHICS FOR ADAPTIVE ETHNOGRAPHY

In conducting each of these projects I have assumed the need to maintain an ethical stance, conscious of the dignity and reputation of participants, and adapting my research practices in an attempt to preserve their welfare and treat them with respect. I take on board Marcus's (1998) warnings that one cannot predict an appropriate ethical stance in advance, but must instead adapt to the situations that one encounters as one moves through the field engaging with different participants along the way. Some ethical dilemmas that I faced were such as might be encountered by any ethnographer moving between sites and developing an emergent understanding of the field, whilst others were more specific to Internet-based field sites. There was, for example, no way to decide in advance and in principle whether material found online should be treated as public or private: instead, the decision needed to be taken on a contextual basis, as Snee (2013) describes. Quoting from online material became a practice to be undertaken very carefully, as it places the material into a new context, forging new relations of visibility, and potentially disturbing important patterns of inattention and lack of engagement. As Markham (2012) describes, our tendency to rely on direct quotations to evoke the field in qualitative research publications can be in direct tension with the need to protect informants' sensibilities. Markham (2012) thus advocates innovative strategies for qualitative reporting of such material, including fabrication of material that evokes the field without identifying participants. I have adopted this stance in some Internet-based projects that I have undertaken, adapting quotations sufficiently to prevent them being identifiable via search engines. In other cases I quote directly, but only after careful consideration with participants and based on a cautious evaluation of the potential consequences of this new form of publicity.

Rather than the ethical stance preceding the research, it therefore emerges from the engagement with the field which teaches what need to be treated as relevant aspects of context in taking ethical decisions. The field itself is also emergent in the form of ethnography that I have described, as the decisions about where to go and what to do there are taken on an ongoing basis, pursuing connections that enable sense to be made of the emergent field of inquiry. In a dual sense, therefore, it is not possible to lay out in advance exactly what steps the researcher will need to take in order to remain "ethical." Ethics becomes a constant reflexive process rather than a prior stance to be laid out in advance, and this can be particularly true in the complex conditions of connection and visibility that prevail around new information and communication technologies, as Markham (2006) argues. Viewing research ethics as an ongoing practice is, however, often at odds with the requirement of formal ethical review and approval on commencement of a project which many institutions and funding bodies define. Ethnographic research in general has found such ethical review requirements problematic in the constraints they appear to place on the flexibility of the researcher in the field and, as Librett and Perrone (2010) argue, in the emphasis they place on notions of anonymity and confidentiality, which may be problematic for ethnographers. The American Anthropological Association (2004) counsels Institutional Review Boards to understand that ethical practice in ethnographic research tends to be dynamic, and to require the researcher to be flexible throughout the project, but also notes that ethnographers should still expect their projects to come under scrutiny, and may need to expect engagement with the Institutional Review Board to occur on an ongoing basis, rather than constituting a singular moment of approval at the outset of the project. In practice, none of the research described in this book fell under the requirements for review by my own institution's ethics committee. It may be that in some institutional contexts review of the kind of project that I have described here would have required an ongoing engagement with the Institutional Review Board, based on an initial application outlining the project as a whole but then consulting and reporting at pre-agreed decision points in order to maintain a live ethical approval.

PRACTICALITIES AND CHALLENGES IN ETHNOGRAPHY FOR THE INTERNET

If ethnographer for the Internet is not the sexiest job of the twenty-first century, according to *Harvard Business Review* (Davenport and Patil 2012), it is at least a challenging one in terms of the range of skills and level of adaptability required. To some extent, the ethnographer for the Internet uses the same skills as any Internet user. There is not necessarily anything supremely complicated about these skills: the advent of social media has dramatically decreased the amount of technical skills required to be an active participant in the Internet. The problems of the ethnographer for the Internet in respect of technical skills are, however, amplified by mobility. If we choose to follow a phenomenon across different settings or platforms, we will need to develop competence in each platform in turn, and this multiple competency is often not shared by ordinary Internet users, who have their own favorite platforms that they tend to stick to. In each platform under consideration, the ethnographer needs to learn to pass as a competent user, both in technical terms and in respect of the conventions of use and polite behavior within that setting. For each new setting, then, there will be a period of familiarization, and a "newbie" phase of making embarrassing mistakes and getting things wrong, and of getting to that state where one can simply act in the setting, without too much reflection on the technicalities. To be ethnographic in Twitter, for example, one needs to know how to tweet, retweet, embed links and pictures, use hashtags, and follow in a technical sense, but one also needs to have an understanding of the kind of things that it is appropriate to tweet according to the particular social group in question. Whilst it can be a useful learning experience for an ethnographer to get things wrong and be corrected, this is a risky strategy when the thing one is getting wrong is use of the very medium one aims to study, and getting it wrong can irretrievably alienate potentially interesting contacts.

One solution to the problem of working across different platforms and sites and addressing the unique but connected issues that arise across distributed fields of inquiry can be to scale up the study by adding more ethnographers. Team ethnography is becoming more common, as we move away from the classical model of the lone ethnographer immersed in the field, and accept that we are now often interested in understanding fields that escape the perceptual limits of a single person (Erickson and Stull 1998). Team ethnography allows for a scaling up and a spreading out of ethnographic interest, multiplying the capacities of a single ethnographer to experience different perspectives on the field, and allowing the team to develop reflexive, embodied understandings of multiple aspects of a phenomenon. Where multiple platforms are involved, the team can also spread out the work of developing the appropriate skill set for each platform. New technologies have been a stimulus to team ethnography (Woods et al. 2000), and a team of ethnographers working on digital field sites certainly have some practical advantages over other ethnographic teams in the extent to which their data is digital and hence readily shareable with their colleagues. They face, however, a standard set of challenges common to many team ethnographers concerning the extent to which a level of team understanding and a sharing of embodied experience can be forged across the team members as the project proceeds (Gerstl-Pepin and Gunzenhauser 2002). Despite the best efforts of ethnographers to keep adequate field notes, so much of the ongoing interpretive work of an ethnographic project resists easy verbalization at the time, and hence becomes very difficult to share with one's team-mates. Team ethnography can be a response to the complexities of working across different digital platforms in emergent multi-sited fields, but the techno-logical advantages of digital data do not overcome all of the epistemological challenges of combining multiple embodied, embedded perspectives into a single end product.

The practicalities of working across platforms also introduce some diffi-culties for the ethnographer in terms of data storage and access. It can be challenging to find a format for keeping field notes that allows them to be cross-linked with screen-shots that might have been saved or messages collected at the same time. Keeping data can be challenging in itself: we tend to think of digital data as infinitely copyable and easily moved from place to place, but in practice proprietary formats and copying restrictions may leave the ethnographer needing to find creative solutions to producing a corpus of data. Maintaining orderly archives of field notes and data from different platforms, allowing for cross-linking between them, retrieval of connected data fragments and notes and coding of emergent themes across data formats remains one of the biggest practical challenges for an online ethnographer. Tools for Computer Aided Qualitative Data Analysis (CAQDAS), such as NVivo and Atlas-ti, are becoming good at coping with diverse data formats, but may struggle to keep up with newer incarnations of digital data. Mobility compounds the problem, as an ethnographer will often wish to move between locations and switch between devices. Cloud computing is only partially the answer to the needs of ethnographers for a flexible, accessible tool for recording and coding data, which still leaves them with control over their data and avoids being tied in to specific pieces of proprietary software.

The challenge of finding appropriate tools to capture work in progress is not just confined to fieldwork, but extends into the process of communicating the outcomes of the research. Digital media offer creative ways for ethnographers to present their studies, but using them may require considerable forward planning, and place additional demands on the ethnographer's technical skills. While conventional books still, for the time being, remain highly important as tools of academic communication, there are some very promising developments in digital ethnography, which use a variety of multimedia tools to present ethnographic projects (see, for example, projects described by Dicks et al. 2005, 2006; Underberg and Zorn 2013). In addition to developments strictly associated with ethnography, the burgeoning developments in digital humanities are also likely to prove instructive for Internet ethnographers wishing to find ways to curate, display, and explore their data.

Developments in the field of tools for ethnographers are happening apace: hopefully, by the time this book is bound, some new and more comprehensive tools will have emerged. In the meantime, ethnographers for the Internet craft their own combination of tools to meet their needs from the array available to them. Online resources such as the University of Texas Digital Ethnography Lab site (http://digitalethnography.dm.ucf. edu/), the blog of the Methodological Innovation in Digital Arts and Social Sciences project (http://midassblog.wordpress.com/), or the Ethnography Matters blog (http://ethnographymatters.net/) offer very useful spaces to explore the experiences of other ethnographers and to find out about the technical solutions they find helpful. Mailing lists can be a great resource for ethnographers searching for recommendations of a tool that works for the job at hand: for Internet ethnographers, the mailing lists of the Association of Internet Researchers (http://aoir.org/) or the EASA Media Anthropology Network (http://www.media-anthropology.net/) are likely to be useful sources of advice.

It is hard for an ethnographer to prepare for the Internet, because we rarely know comprehensively in advance what technological and social skills will turn out to be required in our emergent field site. At least in the old days we could often take a reasonable guess at the language that was used in a far-flung field site, and make some efforts to practice before we arrived. Now the ethnographer is faced with an Internet that is developing all the time, with new technologies and new platforms emerging, and others becoming obsolete, in a constantly evolving online sphere. Choosing a research site and investing in a set of tools at the beginning of a three-year doctoral study becomes a risky business, as few assurances exist that either site or tools will look quite the same by the end of the study. It is hard to acquire the skills needed to navigate the terrain in advance, when the terrain itself seems to be shifting so fast. The available techniques of collecting, mining, and visualizing data are developing all the time too, as the data scientists gain credit for being the first to do new and powerful things with data. This big data arms race can seem rather daunting to an ethnographer used to moving at a slower pace, and unequipped with the very specific skills concerned with the techniques used in this domain. The answer may lie in more creative collaborations, both between teams of differently skilled ethnographers, and between ethnographers and data scientists, developing a rapprochement between big data and rich data, and developing projects that exploit the strengths of each.

AGILE, ADAPTIVE ETHNOGRAPHY

As the Internet continues to develop apace and defeat our ability to predict, I find myself wondering what the future might be for ethnography. Promises just on the horizon include new devices in the form of wearable computing, a further entrenchment of the mobile Internet extending into a wider sector of the population and an ever-increasing set of daily activities, an expanded Internet of things embedding intelligent sensing and decision-making capacity into the objects which surround us, and an ever-expanding deployment of big data building on the capacity of digital technologies to capture traces of our everyday lives. All of these techno-social developments, in their various ways, promise to decrease the significance of any boundary that might be thought to exist between the digital and the everyday. Everyday life promises to be lived more and more through digital environments, and represented in digital format. In order to continue to narrate and interrogate the peculiar circumstances of this contemporary existence ethnographers will need to continue to follow and adapt, shaping their methods to the situations that they find and the pressing theoretical and practical issues of concern.

When I wrote *Virtual Ethnography* in 2000 I was arguing for Internet contexts to be taken seriously as cultural sites, which offered places for ethnographers to immerse themselves within and where activities of broader social significance were happening. I also, however, stressed that the Internet was a cultural artefact: in the terms I use now, I saw the Internet as a culturally embedded phenomenon, as online activities acquire meaning and significance in so far as they are interpreted within other online and offline contexts as and as accounts of what the Internet is and what it does, in general and in the particular, continually circulate through diverse online and offline contexts. At the time that *Virtual Ethnography* was written, it seemed particularly important to stress that the Internet should be taken seriously. The cultural balance has now shifted. The Internet is indeed being taken seriously, and I feel little need to argue that attention should be paid to what happens online, although I am concerned that in taking the Internet seriously we should not carve it up for attention one platform at a time, nor should we treat the online as necessarily separate from the offline. Technological boundaries should not necessarily be assumed to be cultural boundaries. Instead of arguing from first principles for taking the Internet seriously, I have focused in this text on exploring how we can engage with significant online events, and how we can explore the patterns of connection and processes of embedding through which they acquire their significance.

As I wonder what specific challenges ethnography for the Internet may face in the next incarnations of the Internet, I sometimes try out different contemporary epithets for size against ethnography: I have played with the ideas of cloud ethnography, crowd-sourced ethnography, and ambient ethnography, to use just a few contemporary buzz words. None of these quite stuck. One that has stayed with me for rather longer despite an initial instinctive rejection, however, is the idea of pop-up ethnography. The notion of the pop-up restaurant, gallery, or shop has had cultural currency for a few years now. It denotes a temporary and opportunistic development, seizing the opportunity created by a happenstance of resources such as a vacant shop, and capitalizing on a sense of immediacy, responding to a need or a cultural current which is happening just exactly now. I wondered, might there ever be a role for a pop-up ethnography? Or is this just straying too far from everything that has been said about the importance of immersion and sustained engagement that characterizes ethnography? How could a pop-up ethnography say anything useful in depth at all? As I was pondering this issue, an event happened that helped me to rethink my immediate laughing rejection of the idea.

The event was the launch weekend for a new theme park, recreating the world of a popular children's cartoon character. My family had been invited to this exclusive weekend opening thanks to my daughter's school's involvement in singing some songs on the soundtrack for the cartoon. I had no idea, in fact, what a launch event for a theme park would be like, but it was hard to turn down a free family outing, so we went along. As we arrived, we were channeled through to a marquee at the entrance, and directed to the right to collect badges and goody bags. The other channel, to the left, was much less populated. Fewer people seemed to be channeled that way. As we collected our badges, I glanced across, and thought that the person collecting a badge in the left-hand channel looked rather familiar.

As the day progressed it gradually dawned on me that the person I had recognized was a celebrity. In fact, the different-colored badges denoted different categories of visitor. We were marked out by our blue badges as guests invited because of some association with the show, or the companies associated with producing and promoting it. Other colors denoted press, and celebrity guests. All of the guests were ostensibly there on family outings, but some were clearly there in a different capacity from others and had different statuses. As we, the relatively ordinary guests, simply milled around, trying out of the rides and enjoying the small queues, some of the guests in other categories were interviewing or being interviewed, having their impressions captured on tape and film. We tried to look as if we mingled with celebrities all the time, and resolved not to point or stare.

Up to this point this was a fun family day, mildly enlightening as an insight into the way that PR works, but definitely not a research experience as far as I was concerned. Suddenly, however, the focus shifted. As we sat at tables eating lunch I overheard another visitor (blue-badged, like ourselves) saying to his family: "David Baddiel is here. He's tweeted about this." My research interest was piqued. I immediately wanted to know more about the collision of contexts that was created when two people present at an event, one of them a celebrity, became momentarily connected by the fact that one had tweeted about an event that the other was simultaneously attending, and that other had read the tweet and had his perception of the event shifted by it. I had for some time now been puzzled by the problem of working out what Twitter meant, and how it made sense to people as a means of communication. When I first signed up I could not work out what on earth people thought they were up to when they were tweeting. Just from looking at a Twitter feed, it was hard to see what those tweets meant to the people concerned. Here, in this pop-up moment, I had some fascinating fuel to think with.

I call this a pop-up ethnographic moment, because it occurred in the midst of a long process of ethnographic enquiry about the Internet. I have spent considerable time over the last two decades trying to work out what people think they are up to when using the Internet. This moment seemed to capture something that was thought-provoking and insightful about the contemporary Internet, in particular the relationship between Twitter and events. The moment passed, and I did not at the time drill down any further with the two participants concerned. The middle of a family outing is hardly the time to develop an in-depth inquiry. I did, however, store away the event, note it down as soon as I was able, and follow up subsequently by exploring the Twitter presence of the event. By doing that I came to understand much more about the practices of PR and the role of celebrities in promoting events like this, finally comprehending that the celebrity's attendance is not significant only in itself, but as a generator of tweets that their followers will see and possibly in turn pass on. The event, by being tweeted about by the celebrities who attend, acquires a growing Twitter presence that hopefully for the PR team turns into real-world approval and more paying visitors. The pop-up moment generated a growing understanding of one specific way in which Twitter makes sense. Exploring the Twitter presence of the event also shifted my own perceptions of the event that I had attended: in fact, the event grew in significance as I discovered through Twitter that far more celebrities had been in attendance than I had actually recognized on the day.

In describing this pop-up ethnographic moment, it is important to stress two things: first, that it occurred as part of an ongoing inquiry, which caused me to notice it in the first place; second, that it would have been very difficult for me to go out searching for this moment. If someone had described it to me in an interview after the event, in context of discussing how they used Twitter, it would have lost its raw immediacy, and the additional level of ethnographic understanding that came from it being embedded in my experience of that event as it happened. This brings to light a very important aspect of ethnography for the Internet: so important that it is where I choose to close this book. Much of everyday life is still not digital. It therefore lacks those magical digital qualities of searchability and replicability. It is hard to find things in a non-digital world, especially when we are interested in the pop-up moments when worlds collide, and when two hitherto separate things suddenly connect with one another. And yet, it is in these everyday non-digital moments that we make sense of the digital.

Paradoxically, then, I feel that one of the key contemporary challenges in ethnography for the Internet is to learn how to continue to take the real world seriously as a place where the Internet is interpreted and makes sense in diverse and unexpected ways. Online environments offer so much in terms of the ability to search out relevant fragments of data, to copy and archive, to mine, to map, and to recombine, that the everyday non-digital world risks being left out because it is, by contrast, so intransigent. Ethnography for the Internet makes demands of our technical skills, but it is in many ways easier to conduct a study online than it is to do the hard work of finding out how online issues matter in the offline world. We cannot search a real-time offline world, nor is there any archive or data repository to turn to in order to find out what happened when we were not there. At the same time, our interests are often not in a single offline place that we can spend extended periods of time in, hanging out, waiting for events that will relate to our research topic to happen. The real world that we study is not predictably contained in such places any more, and we have to be more inventive about capitalizing on fragments of insight whenever they occur, even if we weren't quite ready for them or we did not even realize we were going to be doing fieldwork at the time. Pop-up ethnographic moments seem to take us a long way from the sustained indwelling ethnographers held dear, but they may be an appropriate strategy to adopt if they help us to continue to take seriously the most burning questions of ethnography for the Internet, which are the real-world, feet-on-the-ground issues of how and why the Internet matters in people's lives.

References

Abbate, J. (2000), *Inventing the Internet*. Cambridge MA: MIT Press.

Agger, B. (2012), *Oversharing: Presentations of Self in the Internet Age*. New York: Routledge.

Aguilar, J. L. (1981), "Insider research: an ethnography of a debate," in D. A. Messerschmidt (ed.) *Anthropologists at Home in North America: Methods and Issues in the Study of One's Own Society*. Cambridge: Cambridge University Press: 15–26.

American Anthropological Association (2004), American Anthropological Association statement on ethnography and Institutional Review Boards. Available from, http://www.aaanet.org/stmts/irb.htm (accessed May 1, 2014).

Amit, V. (ed.) (1999), *Constructing the Field*. London: Routledge.

Anand, N. (2011), "Pressure: the politechnics of water supply in Mumbai." *Cultural Anthropology* 26(4): 542–64.

Aouragh, M. (2011), "Confined offline: traversing online Palestinian mobility through the prism of the Internet." *Mobilities* 6(3): 375–97.

Argyle, K. and Shields, R. (1996), "Is there a body in the net?" in R. Shields, *Cultures of Internet: Virtual Spaces, Real Histories, Living Bodies*.London: Sage: 58–69.

Arora, P. (2012), "Typology of Web 2.0 spheres: understanding the cultural dimensions of social media spaces." *Current Sociology* 60(5): 599–618.

Bakardjieva, M. (2005), *Internet Society: The Internet in Everyday Life*. London: Sage.

Baker, S. (2013), "Conceptualising the use of Facebook in ethnographic research: as tool, as data and as context." *Ethnography & Education* 8(2): 131–45.

Bampton, R. and Cowton, C. (2002), "The e-interview." *Forum Qualitative Sozialforschung/Forum: Qualitative Social Research* 3(2). http://www.qualitative-research.net/index.php/fqs/article/viewArticle/848 (accessed August 22, 2014).

Barker, M. (2006), "I have seen the future and it is not here yet …: or, on being ambitious for audience research." *The Communication Review* 9(2): 123–41.

Baym, N. (1995), "The emergence of community in computer-mediated communication," in S. Jones (ed.), *Cybersociety*. Thousand Oaks CA: Sage: 138–63.

—(2000), *Tune in, Log on: Soaps, Fandom and Online Community*. Thousand Oaks CA: Sage.

—(2005) "Introduction: Internet research as it isn't, is, could be, and should be." *The Information Society* 21(4): 229–32.

Beaulieu, A. (2005), "Sociable hyperlinks: an ethnographic approach to connectivity," in C. Hine (ed.), *Virtual Methods: Issues in Social Research on the Internet*. Oxford: Berg: 183–98.

—(2010), "Research note: from co-location to co-presence: shifts in the use of ethnography for the study of knowledge." *Social Studies of Science* 40(3): 453–70.

Beaulieu, A. and Simakova, E. (2006), "Textured connectivity: an ethnographic approach to understanding the timescape of hyperlinks." *Cybermetrics: International Journal of Scientometrics, Informetrics and Bibliometrics* 10. http://cybermetrics.cindoc.csic.es/articles/v10i1p5.html (accessed August 22, 2014).

Beer, D. (2013a), *Popular Culture and New Media: The Politics of Circulation*. Basingstoke: Palgrave Macmillan.

—(2013b), "Public geography and the politics of circulation." *Dialogues in Human Geography* 3(1): 92–5.

Beer, D. and Penfold-Mounce, R. (2009), "Celebrity gossip and the new melodramatic imagination." *Sociological Research Online* 14(2): 2. http://www.socresonline.org.uk/14/2/2.html (accessed August 22, 2014).

Bell, D. (2001), *An Introduction to Cybercultures*. London: Routledge.

Bell, M., Chalmers, M., Fontaine, L., Higgs, M., Morrison, A., Rooksby, J., Rost, M., and Sherwood, S. (2013), Experiences in Logging Everyday App Use. DE2013—Open Digital, Fourth RCUK All Hands Digital Economy Conference, Salford, U.K.

Bernard, H. R. (2011) *Research Methods in Anthropology: Qualitative and Quantitative Approaches*, 5th ed. Lanham MD: AltaMira Press.

Bijker, W. E. and Pinch T. J. (1987), "The Social Construction of Facts and Artefacts: Or how the Sociology of Science and the Sociology of Technology might Benefit each Other," in W. E. Bijker, T. P. Hughes, and T. J. Pinch (eds), *The Social Construction of Technological Systems: New Directions in the Sociology and History of Technology*. Cambridge MA: MIT Press: 17–50.

Bishop, R. (1999), "What price history? Functions of narrative in television collectibles shows." *Journal of Popular Culture* 33(3): 1–27.

Blank, G. and Reisdorf, B. C. (2012), "The participatory web." *Information, Communication & Society* 15(4): 537–54.

Bloch, M. (1991), "Language, anthropology and cognitive science." *Man* 26(2): 183–98.

—(2008), *How We Think They Think: Anthropological Approaches to Cognition, Memory, and Literacy*. Boulder CO: Westview Press.

Boellstorff, T. (2008), *Coming of Age in Second Life: An Anthropologist Explores the Virtually Human*. Princeton NJ: Princeton University Press.

—(2010), "A typology of ethnographic scales for virtual worlds," In W. S. Bainbridge (ed.), *Online Worlds: Convergence of the Real and the Virtual*. London: Springer: 123–33.

Boellstorff, T., Nardi, B., Pearce, C., and Taylor, T. L. (2012), *Ethnography and Virtual Worlds: A Handbook of Method*. Princeton NJ: Princeton University Press.

Bolter, J. and Grusin, R. (2000), *Remediation: Understanding New Media*. Cambridge MA: MIT Press.

Bonner, F. (2003), *Ordinary Television: Analyzing Popular TV*. London: Sage.

Bowker, G. (2000), "Biodiversity datadiversity." *Social Studies of Science* 30(5): 643–84.

—(2005), *Memory Practices in the Sciences*. Cambridge MA: MIT Press.

Bowker, G. C. and Star, S. L. (1999), *Sorting Things Out: Classification and its Consequences*. Cambridge MA: MIT Press.

boyd, D. and Crawford, K. (2012), "Critical questions for big data: provocations for a cultural, technological, and scholarly phenomenon." *Information, Communication & Society* 15(5): 662–79.

Brettell, C. B. (1996), *When They Read What We Write: The Politics of Ethnography*. Westport CT: Bergin & Garvey.

Bukvova, H., Kalb, H., and Schoop, E. (2010), "What we blog: a qualitative analysis of research blogs." Publishing in the Networked World: Transforming the Nature of Communication, 14th International Conference on Electronic Publishing, June 16–18, 2010. https://helda.helsinki.fi/bitstream/handle/10227/599/978-952-232-086-5.pdf (accessed August 22, 2014).

Burrell, J. (2009), "The field site as a network: a strategy for locating ethnographic research." *Field Methods* 21(2): 181–99.

Bury, R. (2008), "Textual poaching or gamekeeping?: A comparative study of two Internet fan forums," in P. Goldstein and J. L. Machor (eds), *New Directions in American Reception Study*. New York: Oxford University Press: 289–305.

Buscher, M. and J. Urry (2009), "Mobile methods and the empirical." *European Journal of Social Theory* 12(1): 99–116.

Candea, M. (2007), "Arbitrary locations: in defence of the bounded field-site." *Journal of the Royal Anthropological Institute* 13(1): 167–84.

Chapman, A. D. (2009), "Numbers of living species in Australia and the world" (2nd ed.). Canberra: Australian Biological Resources Study. http://www.environment.gov.au/node/13865 (accessed August 22, 2014).

Chayko, M. (2007), "The portable community: envisioning and examining mobile social connectedness." *International Journal of Web Based Communities* 3(4): 373–85.

Cheong, M. and Lee, V. (2011), "A microblogging-based approach to terrorism informatics: exploration and chronicling civilian sentiment and response to terrorism events via Twitter." *Information Systems Frontiers* 13(1): 45–59.

Clarke, A. E. and Fujimura, J. H. (1992), "What tools? Which jobs? Why right?" in A. E. Clarke and J. H. Fujimura (eds), *The Right Tools for the Job: At Work in Twentieth-Century Life Sciences*. Princeton NJ: Princeton University Press: 3–44.

Clifford, J. and Marcus, G. E. (eds), (1986), *Writing Culture: The Poetics and Politics of Ethnography*. Berkeley CA: University of California Press.

Clouse, A. (2008), "Narratives of value and the *Antiques Roadshow*: a game of recognitions." *Journal of Popular Culture* 41(1): 3–20.

Coffey, A. (1999), *The Ethnographic Self: Fieldwork and the Representation of Identity*. London: Sage.

Cohen, A. P. (1985), *Symbolic Construction of Community*. Chichester: Ellis Horwood.

Cook, J., Laidlaw, J. and Mair, J. (2009), "What if there is no elephant? Towards a conception of an un-sited field," in M. A. Falzon (ed.), *Multi-sited Ethnography: Theory, Praxis and Locality in Contemporary Research*. Farnham: Ashgate: 47–72.

Costello, M. J. (2009), "Motivating online publication of data." *BioScience* 59(5): 418–27.

Costello, M. J., May, R. M., and Stork, N. E. (2013), "Can we name Earth's species before they go extinct?" *Science* 339(6118): 413–16.

Courtois, C., Mechant, P., Paulussen, S., and De Marez, L. (2012), "The triple articulation of media technologies in teenage media consumption." *New Media & Society* 14(3): 401–20.

Crabtree, A., Benford, S., Greenhalgh, C., Tennent, P., Chalmers, M., and Brown, B. (2006), Supporting Ethnographic Studies of Ubiquitous Computing in the Wild. ACM Symposium on Designing Interactive Systems, June 26–28, 2006, University Park, PA.

Cwerner, S. B. and Metcalfe, A. (2003), "Storage and clutter: discourses and practices of order in the domestic world." *Journal of Design History* 16(3): 229–39.

Davenport, T. H. and Patil, D. J. (2012), "Data scientist: the sexiest job of the 21st century." *Harvard Business Review* 2012 (October): 70–6.

Davies, C. A. (2012), *Reflexive Ethnography: A Guide to Researching Selves and Others*. London: Routledge.

De Laet, M. and Mol, A. (2000), "The Zimbabwe bush pump: mechanics of a fluid technology." *Social Studies of Science* 30(2): 225–64.

Diaz, A. (2008), "Through the Google goggles: sociopolitical bias in search engine design," in A. Spink and M. Zimmer (eds), *Web Search: Multidisciplinary Perspectives—Springer Series in Information Science and Knowledge Management 14*. Heidelberg: Springer: 11–34.

Dibbell, J. (1999) *My Tiny Life*. New York: Henry Holt.

Dicks, B., Mason, B., Coffey, A., and Atkinson, P. (2005), *Qualitative Research and Hypermedia: Ethnography for the Digital Age*. London: Sage.

Dicks, B., Soyinka, B., and Coffey, A. (2006), "Multimodal ethnography." *Qualitative Research* 6(1): 77–96.

Dirksen, V., Huizing, A., and Smit, B. (2010), "'Piling on layers of understanding': the use of connective ethnography for the study of (online) work practices." *New Media & Society* 12(7): 1045–63.

Downey, G. L. and Dumit, J. (eds) (1997), *Cyborgs and Citadels: Anthropological Interventions in Emerging Sciences and Technologies*. Santa Fe: School of American Research Press.

Downey, G. L., Dumit, J., and Williams, S. (1995) "Cyborg anthropology." *Cultural Anthropology* 10(2): 264–69.

Dutton, W. H. and G. Blank (2011), *Next Generation Users: The Internet in Britain 2011*. Oxford: Oxford Internet Institute, University of Oxford.

Dutton, W. H., Blank, G., and Groselj, D. (2013), *Cultures of the Internet: The Internet in Britain*. Oxford: Oxford Internet Institute, University of Oxford.

Dyck, N. (2000), "Home field advantage," in V. Amit (ed.), *Constructing the Field: Ethnographic Fieldwork in the Contemporary World*. London: Routledge: 32–53.

Efimova, L. A. (2009), "Passion at work: blogging practices of knowledge workers." Doctoral thesis submitted to Novay PhD Research Series Vol. 24 (2009), http://igitur-archive.library.uu.nl/dissertations/2009-0626-200434/UUindex.html (accessed August 22, 2014).

Ellery, P., Vaughn, W., Ellery, J., Bott, J., Ritchey, K., and Byers, L. (2008), "Understanding internet health search patterns: an early exploration into the usefulness of Google trends." *Journal of Communications in Healthcare* 1(4): 441–56.

Ellis, C. (2004), *The Ethnographic I: A Methodological Novel about Autoethnography*. Walnut Creek CA: Alta Mira.

Erickson, K. C. and Stull, D. D. (1998), *Doing Team Ethnography: Warnings and Advice*. Thousand Oaks, CA: Sage

Erwin, T. L. (1997), "Biodiversity at its utmost: tropical forest beetles," in M. L. Reaka-Kudla, D. E. Wilson, and E. O. Wilson (eds), *Biodiversity II*. Washington DC: Joseph Henry Press: 27–40.

Eysenbach, G. (2008a), "Credibility of health information and digital media: new perspectives and implications for youth," in M. J. Metzger and A. J. Flanagin (eds), *Digital Media, Youth, and Credibility: The John D. and Catherine T. MacArthur Foundation Series on Digital Media and Learning*. Cambridge, MA: MIT Press: 123–54.

—(2008b), "Medicine 2.0: social networking, collaboration, participation, apomediation, and openness." *Journal of Medical Internet Research* 10(3): e22. http://www.pubmedcentral.nih.gov/articlerender.fcgi?artid=2626430 (accessed August 22, 2014).

Falzon, M. A. (2009a), "Introduction: multi-sited ethnography: theory, praxis and locality in contemporary research," in M. A. Falzon (ed.), *Multi-sited Ethnography: Theory, Praxis and Locality in Contemporary Research*. Farnham: Ashgate: 1–23.

—(2009b), *Multi-sited Ethnography: Theory, Praxis and Locality in Contemporary Research*. Farnham: Ashgate.

Farnsworth, J. and Austrin, T. (2010), "The ethnography of new media worlds?: Following the case of global poker." *New Media & Society* 12(7): 1120–36.

Fields, D. and Kafai, Y. (2009), "A connective ethnography of peer knowledge sharing and diffusion in a tween virtual world." *International Journal of Computer-Supported Collaborative Learning* 4(1): 47–68.

Finlay, L. (2002), "Negotiating the swamp: the opportunity and challenge of reflexivity in research practice." *Qualitative Research* 2(2): 209–30.

Garton, L., Haythornthwaite, C., and Wellman, B. (1997), "Studying online social networks." *Journal of Computer Mediated Communication* 3(1). http://onlinelibrary.wiley.com/doi/10.1111/j.1083-6101.1997.tb00062.x/abstract (accessed August 22, 2014).

Geertz, C. (1973), *The Interpretation of Cultures: Selected Essays*. New York: Basic Books.

—(1993), *Local Knowledge: Further Essays in Interpretive Anthropology*. London: Fontana Press.

Geiger, R. S. and Ribes, D. (2011), Trace ethnography: following coordination through documentary practices. *Proceedings of the 2011 44th Hawaii International Conference on System Sciences*, IEEE Computer Society 1–10.

Gershenfeld, N., Krikorian, R., and Cohen, D. (2004), "The Internet of things." *Scientific American* 291(4): 76–81.

Gerstl-Pepin, C. I. and Gunzenhauser, M. G. (2002), "Collaborative team ethnography and the paradoxes of interpretation." *International Journal of Qualitative Studies in Education* 15(2): 137–54.

Gibson, W. (1984), *Neuromancer*. New York: Ace.

Gies, L. (2008), "How material are cyberbodies? Broadband Internet and embodied subjectivity." *Crime, Media, Culture* 4(3): 311–30.

Gillespie, M. (1995), *Television, Ethnicity and Cultural Change*. London: Routledge.

Godfray, H. C. J. (2002a), "Challenges for taxonomy: the discipline will have to reinvent itself if it is to survive and flourish." *Nature* 417(6884): 17–19.

—(2002b), "Towards taxonomy's 'glorious revolution.'" *Nature* 420(6915): 461.

Golder, S. A., Wilkinson, D., and Huberman, B. A. (2007), *Rhythms of Social Interaction: Messaging within a Massive Online Network*. 3rd International Conference on Communities and Technologies (CT2007). June 28–30, 2007, East Lansing MI. http://www.hpl.hp.com/research/idl/papers/facebook/ (accessed August 22, 2014).

Goldman, E. (2008), "Search engine bias and the demise of search engine utopianism," in A. Spink and M. Zimmer (eds), *Web Search: Springer Series in Information Science and Knowledge Management 14*. Berlin: Springer-Verlag: 121–33.

Goldstein, P. and Machor, J. L. (2008). "Introduction: reception study: achievements and new directions," in P. Goldstein and J. L. Machor (eds), *New Directions in American Reception Study*. New York: Oxford University Press: xi–xxviii.

Graham, M. and Shelton, T. (2013), "Geography and the future of big data, big data and the future of geography." *Dialogues in Human Geography* 3(3): 255–61.

Graham, S. (2004), "Beyond the 'dazzling light': from dreams of transcendence to the 'remediation' of urban life: a research manifesto." *New Media & Society* 6(1): 16–25.

Gray, J. (2010), *Show Sold Separately: Promos, Spoilers, and Other Media Paratexts*. New York: New York University Press.

Gregg, M. (2006), "Feeling ordinary: blogging as conversational scholarship." *Continuum: Journal of Media & Culture Studies* 20(2): 147–60.

Gupta, A. and Ferguson, J. (1997a), *Anthropological Locations: Boundaries and Grounds of a Field Science*. Berkeley, CA: University of California Press.

—(1997b) Discipline and practice: 'the field" as site, method and location in anthropology," in A. Gupta and J. Ferguson (eds), *Anthropological Locations: Boundaries and Grounds of a Field Science*. Berkeley CA: University of California Press: 1–46.

Halavais, A. (2006), "Scholarly blogging: moving toward the visible college," in A. Bruns and J. Jacobs (eds), *Uses of Blogs*. New York: Peter Lang: 117–26.

Hannerz, U. (2003), "Being there ... and there ... and there!: reflections on multi-site ethnography." *Ethnography* 4(2): 201–16.

Haraway, D. J. (1991), *Simians, Cyborgs, and Women: The Reinvention of Nature*. New York: Routledge.

Hargittai, E. (2008), "The digital reproduction of inequality," in D. Grusky (ed.), *Social Stratification*. Boulder, CO: Westview Press: 936–44.

Harvey, K. J., Brown, B., Crawford, P. Macfarlane, A., and McPherson, A. (2007), "'Am I normal?': teenagers, sexual health and the internet." *Social Science & Medicine* 65(4): 771–81.

Hey, T. and Trefethen, A. E. (2002), "The UK e-Science core programme and the Grid." *Future Generation Computing Systems* 18(8): 1017–31.

Hine, C. (1995a), "Information technology as an instrument of genetics." *Genetic Engineer & Biotechnologist* 15(2–3): 113–24.

—(1995b), "Representations of information technology in disciplinary development: disappearing plants and invisible networks." *Science Technology & Human Values* 20(1): 65–85.

—(2000), *Virtual Ethnography*. London: Sage.

—(2002), "Cyberscience and social boundaries: the implications of laboratory talk on the Internet." *Sociological Research Online* 7(2). http://www.socresonline.org.uk/7/2/hine.html (accessed August 22, 2014).

—(2005), "Internet research and the sociology of cyber-social-scientific knowledge." *The Information Society* 21(4): 239–48.

—(2007), "Connective ethnography for the exploration of e-science." *Journal of Computer Mediated Communication* 12(2). http://onlinelibrary.wiley.com/doi/10.1111/j.1083-6101.2007.00341.x/abstract (accessed August 22, 2014).

—(2008), *Systematics as Cyberscience: Computers, Change and Continuity in Science*. Cambridge MA: MIT Press.

—(2011a), "Internet research and unobtrusive methods." *Surrey Research Update* 61. http://sru.soc.surrey.ac.uk/SRU61.pdf (accessed August 22, 2014).

—(2011b), "Towards ethnography of television on the internet: a mobile strategy for exploring mundane interpretive activities." *Media Culture & Society* 33(4): 581–96.

—(2013), "The emergent qualities of digital specimen images in biology." *Information, Communication & Society* 16(7): 1157–75.

—(2014), "Headlice eradication as everyday engagement with science: an analysis of online parenting discussions," *Public Understanding of Science* 23(5): 574–91.

Hirsch, E. (1998), "Bound and unbound entities: reflections on the ethnographic perspectives of anthropology vis-à-vis Media and Cultural studies," In F. Hughes-Freeland, ed., *Ritual, Performance, Media*. London: Routledge: 208–29.

Hirschauer, S. (2006), "Puttings things into words: ethnographic description and the silence of the social." *Human Studies* 29(4): 413–41.

Howard, P. N. (2002), "Network ethnography and the hypermedia organization: new organizations, new media, new methods." *New Media & Society* 4(4): 551–75.

—(2004), "Embedded media: who we know, what we know, and society online," in P. N. Howard and S. Jones (eds), *Society Online: The Internet in Context*. Thousand Oaks CA: Sage: 1–27.

Intel (2009), Rise of the embedded Internet. White Paper, Intel embedded processors. Intel Corporation. http://download.intel.com/newsroom/kits/embedded/pdfs/ECG_WhitePaper.pdf (accessed August 22, 2014).

International Telecommunications Union (2012) Measuring the Information Society 2012. Geneva, Switzerland: International Telecommunications Union.

James, N. and Busher, H. (2006), "Credibility, authenticity and voice: dilemmas in online interviewing." *Qualitative Research* 6(3): 403–20.

—(2009), *Online Interviewing*. London: Sage.

Jenkins, H. (2006), *Fans, Bloggers, and Gamers: Exploring Participatory Culture*. New York: New York University Press.

Johnston, I. (2009), "Freecycle in bitter transatlantic split." http://www.telegraph.co.uk/technology/news/6208589/Freecycle-in-bitter-transatlantic-split.html (accessed August 14, 2010).

Jones, S. (2009), "Accusations of very tight control split UK recycling network from US parent." http://www.guardian.co.uk/environment/2009/oct/12/freecycle-freegle-recycling-networks-groups (accessed August 14, 2010).

Jones, S. G. (ed.) (1995), *Cybersociety*. Newbury Park CA: Sage.

—(1997), *Virtual Culture*. London: Sage.

—(1998), *Cybersociety 2.0: Revisiting Computer-Mediated Communication and Community*. Newbury Park CA: Sage.

Kazmer, M. M. and Xie, B. (2008), Qualitative interviewing in Internet studies: playing with the media, playing with the method. *Information, Communication & Society* 11(2): 257–78.

Kellehear, A. (1993), *The Unobtrusive Researcher: A Guide to Methods*. St Leonards, NSW: Allen & Unwin.

Kelly, K. (2008), "Technological twist on taxonomy." *Nature* 452(7190): 939.

Kendall, L. (2002), *Hanging Out in the Virtual Pub: Masculinities and Relationships Online*. Berkeley CA: University of California Press.

Kitchin, R., Linehan, D., O'Callaghan, C., and Lawton, P. (2013), "Public geographies through social media." *Dialogues in Human Geography* 3(1): 56–72.

Kivits, J. (2005), Online interviewing and the research relationship," in C. Hine (ed.), *Virtual Methods: Issues in Social Research on the Internet*. Oxford: Berg: 35–50.

Kling, R. and Iacono, S. (1988), "The mobilization of support for computerization: the role of computerization movements." *Social Problems* 35(3): 226–43.

—(1996), "Computerization movements and tales of technological utopianism," In R. Kling (ed.), *Computerization and Controversy: Value Conflicts and Social Choices*. San Diego: Academic Press: 85–105.

Kozinets, R. V. (2009), *Netnography: Doing Ethnographic Research Online*. London: Sage.

Lanham, R. A. (2006), *The Economics of Attention: Style and Substance in the Age of Information*. Chicago: University of Chicago Press.

Larsen, J. (2008), "Practices and flows of digital photography: an ethnographic framework." *Mobilities* 3(1): 141–60.

Latour, B. (1987), *Science in Action: How to Follow Engineers and Scientists Through Society*. Cambridge MA: Harvard University Press.

Latour, B. and Woolgar, S. (1986), *Laboratory Life: The Construction of Scientific Facts* (2nd ed.). Princeton NJ: Princeton University Press.

Law, J. (2004), *After Method: Mess in Social Science Research*. London: Routledge.

Law, J. and Lien, M. E. (2013), "Slippery: field notes in empirical ontology." *Social Studies of Science* 43(3): 363–78.

Leander, K. M. and McKim, K. K. (2003), "Tracing the everyday 'sitings' of adolescents on the Internet: a strategic adaptation of ethnography across online and offline spaces." *Education, Communication & Information* 3(2): 211–40.

Lee, R. M. (2000), *Unobtrusive Methods in Social Research*. Buckingham: Open University Press.

Levene, M. (2010), *An Introduction to Search Engines and Web Navigation* (2nd edn). Hoboken NJ: Wiley.

Librett, M. and Perrone, D. (2010), "Apples and oranges: ethnography and the IRB." *Qualitative Research* 10(6): 729–47.

Lin, Y.-W. (2011), "A qualitative enquiry into OpenStreetMap making." *New Review of Hypermedia & Multimedia* 17(1): 53–71.

Loomes, N. (2009), "Brighton Freecycle leaders go solo. http://www.theargus. co.uk/news/4625650.Brighton_Freecycle_leaders_go_solo/ (accessed August 14, 2010).

Lupton, D. (1995), "The embodied computer/user," in M. Featherstone and R. Burrows (eds), *Cyberspace/Cyberbodies/Cyberpunk: Cultures of Technological Embodiment*. London: Sage: 97–112.

Lynch, M. (1985), *Art and Artifact in Laboratory Science: A Study of Shop Work and Shop Talk in a Research Laboratory*. London: Routledge and Kegan Paul.

Macgilchrist, F. and Van Hout, T. (2011), "Ethnographic discourse analysis and social science." *Forum Qualitative Sozialforschung/Forum: Qualitative Social Research* 12(1). http://www.qualitative-research.net/index.php/fqs/article/viewArticle/1600 (accessed August 22, 2014).

Mackenzie, A. (2005) Untangling the unwired: Wi-Fi and the cultural inversion of infrastructure. *Space & Culture* 8(3): 269–285.

—(2006), *Cutting Code: Software and Sociality*. New York: Peter Lang.

Malta, S. (2012), "Using online methods to interview older adults about their romantic and sexual relationships," in M. Leontowisch (ed.), *Researching Later Life and Ageing: Expanding Qualitative Research Horizons*. Basingstoke: Palgrave Macmillan: 146–72.

Marcus, G. E. (1989), "Imagining the whole." *Critique of Anthropology* 9(3): 7–30.

—(1995), "Ethnography in/of the world system: the emergence of multi-sited ethnography." *Annual Review of Anthropology* 24: 95–117.

—(1998), *Ethnography Through Thick and Thin*. Princeton: NJ Princeton University Press.

—(2012), "Multi-sited ethnography: five or six things I know about it now," in S. Coleman and P. von Hellermann (eds), *Multi-sited Ethnography: Problems and Possibilities in the Translocation of Research Methods*. London: Routledge, 16–33.

Markham, A. (1998), *Life Online: Researching Real Experience in Virtual Space*. Walnut Creek CA: AltaMira.

—(2006), "Ethic as method, method as ethic: a case for reflexivity in qualitative ICT research." *Journal of Information Ethics* 15(2): 37–54.

—(2012), "Fabrication as ethical practice: qualitative inquiry in ambiguous Internet contexts." *Information, Communication & Society* 15(3): 334–53.

Marres, N. (2012), "The redistribution of methods: on intervention in digital social research, broadly conceived." *The Sociological Review* 60: 139–65.

Marres, N. and Weltevrede, E. (2013), "Scraping the social?: issues in live social research." *Journal of Cultural Economy* 6(3): 313–35.

Mason, J. (2011), "Facet methodology: the case for an inventive research orientation." *Methodological Innovations Online* 6(3): 75–92. http://www.methodologicalinnovations.org.uk/wp-content/uploads/2013/11/MIO63Paper31.pdf (accessed August 22, 2014).

Maycroft, N. (2009), "Not moving things along: hoarding, clutter and other ambiguous matter." *Journal of Consumer Behaviour* 8(6): 354–64.

McCoyd, J. L. M. and Kerson, T. S. (2006), "Conducting intensive interviews using email." *Qualitative Social Work* 5(3): 389–406.

McCracken, G. D. (2008), *Transformations: Identity Construction in Contemporary Culture*. Bloomington and Indianapolis: Indiana University Press.

McLaughlin, M., Goldberg, S. B., Ellison, N., and Lucas, J. (1999), "Measuring internet audiences: patrons of an on-line art museum," in S. Jones (ed.), *Doing*

Internet Research: Critical Issues and Methods for Examining the Net. Thousand Oaks, CA: Sage: 163–78.

Miller, D. (2011), *Tales from Facebook*. Cambridge: Polity.

Miller, D. and Horst, H. A. (2012), "The digital and the human: a prospectus for digital anthropology," in H. A. Horst and D. Miller (eds), *Digital Anthropology*. London: Berg: 3–38.

Miller, D. and Slater, D. (2000), *The Internet: An Ethnographic Approach*. Oxford: Berg.

Mol, A. (2002), *The Body Multiple: Ontology in Medical Practice*. Durham NC: Duke University Press.

Moores, S. (1990), "Texts, readers and contexts of reading: developments in the study of media audiences." *Media Culture & Society* 12(1): 9–29.

Morley, D. (1992), *Television, Audiences and Cultural Studies*. London: Routledge.

Morrison, D. A. (2009), "Review of systematics as cyberscience: computers, change, and continuity in science. *Systematic Biology* 58 (2): 277–9.

Mortensen, T. and Walker, J. (2002), "Blogging thoughts: personal publication as an online research tool," in A. Morrison (ed.), *Researching ICTs in Context*. Oslo: InterMedia Report: 249–79.

Murphy, P. D. (1999), "Media cultural studies' uncomfortable embrace of ethnography." *Journal of Communication Inquiry* 23(3): 205–21.

Nardi, B. A. (2010), *My Life as a Night Elf Priest: An Anthropological Account of World of Warcraft*. Ann Arbor, MI: University of Michigan Press.

Nelson, M. R., Rademacher, M. A., and Paek, H.-J. (2007), "Downshifting consumer = upshifting citizen? An examination of a local Freecycle community." *The ANNALS of the American Academy of Political and Social Science* 611(1): 141–56.

O'Reilly, T. (2005), "What is Web 2.0? Design patterns and business models for the next generation of software." http://oreilly.com/web2/archive/what-is-web-20.html (accessed February 10, 2011).

Oftel (2000) "Consumers' use of Internet: summary of Oftel residential survey Q2." August 2000 London: Oftel. http://www.ofcom.org.uk/static/archive/oftel/publications/research/int1000.htm (accessed August 22, 2014).

Olwig, K. F. (2003), "'Transnational' socio-cultural systems and ethnographic research: views from an extended field site." *International Migration Review* 37(3): 787–811.

Orgad, S. S. (2005), "From online to offline and back: moving from online to offline relationships with research informants," in C. Hine (ed.), *Virtual Methods: Issues in Social Research on the Internet*. Oxford: Berg: 51–65.

Orton-Johnson, K. and Prior, N. (eds) (2013), *Digital Sociology: Critical Perspectives*. Basingstoke: Palgrave Macmillan.

Park, H. W. and Thelwall, M. (2003), "Hyperlink analyses of the World Wide Web: a review." *Journal of Computer-Mediated Communication* 8(4). http://onlinelibrary.wiley.com/doi/10.1111/j.1083-6101.2003.tb00223.x/abstract (accessed August 22, 2014).

Perry Barlow, J. (1996), "Declaration of independence of cyberspace." https://projects.eff.org/~barlow/Declaration-Final.html (accessed October 8, 2013).

Pink, S. (2009), *Doing Sensory Ethnography*. London: Sage.

Plantin, L. and Daneback, K. (2009), "Parenthood, information and support on the Internet: a literature review of research on parents and professionals online." *BMC Family Practice* 10(1): 34.

Poster, M. (1995), *The Second Media Age*. Cambridge: Polity.

Postill, J. (2008), "Localizing the internet beyond communities and networks." *New Media & Society* 10(3): 413–31.

Potter, J. (1996), *Representing Reality*. London: Sage.

Prabowo, R. and Thelwall M. (2009), "Sentiment analysis: a combined approach." *Journal of Informetrics* 3(2): 143–57.

Press, A. and Johnson-Yale, C. (2008), "Political talk and the flow of ambient television: women watching Oprah in an African American hair salon," in P. Goldstein and J. L. Machor (eds), *New Directions in American Reception Study*. New York: Oxford University Press: 307–25.

Radway, J. (1988), "Reception study: ethnography and the problems of dispersed audiences and nomadic subjects." *Cultural Studies* 2(3): 359–76.

Rainie, H., Rainie, L., and Wellman, B. (2012), *Networked: The New Social Operating System*. Cambridge MA: MIT Press.

Reed-Danahay, D., ed. (1997a), *Auto/ethnography: Rewriting the Self and the Social*. Oxford: Berg.

—(1997b), "Introduction," in D. Reed-Danahay (ed.), *Auto/ethnography: Rewriting the Self and the Social*. Oxford: Berg: 1–18.

Rheingold, H. (1993), *The Virtual Community: Homesteading on the Electronic Frontier*. Reading MA: Addison-Wesley.

Robinson, L. and Schulz, J. (2009), "New avenues for sociological inquiry: evolving forms of ethnographic practice." *Sociology* 43(4): 685–98.

Rodriguez, A. (2003), "Sense-making artifacts on the margins of cultural spaces," in R. P. Clair, *Expressions of Ethnography: Novel Approaches to Qualitative Methods*. Albany: State University of New York Press: 231–40.

Rogers, R. (2013), *Digital Methods*. Cambridge, MA: MIT Press

Rogers, R. and Marres, N. (2000), "Landscaping climate change: a mapping technique for understanding science and technology debates on the World Wide Web." *Public Understanding of Science* 9(2): 141–63.

Rothebuhler, E. W. and Coman, M. (eds), (2005), *Media Anthropology*. Thousand Oaks CA: Sage.

Ruppert, E., Law, J., and Savage, M. (2013), "Reassembling social science methods: the challenge of digital devices." *Theory, Culture & Society* 30(4): 22–46.

Salmons, J. (2009), *Online Interviews in Real Time*. Thousand Oaks, CA: Sage.

—(2011) *Cases in Online Interview Research*. Thousand Oaks, CA: Sage.

Savage, M. and Burrows R. (2007), "The coming crisis of empirical Sociology." *Sociology* 41(5): 885–99.

Schaap, F. (2002), *The Words that Took Us There: Ethnography in a Virtual Reality*. Amsterdam: Aksant Academic Publishers.

Schatzman, L. and Strauss, A. L. (1973), *Field Research: Strategies for a Natural sociology*. Englewood Cliffs NJ: Prentice-Hall.

Schlecker, M. and Hirsch, E. (2001), "Incomplete knowledge: ethnography and the crisis of context in studies of media, science and technology." *History of the Human Sciences* 14(1): 69–87.

Schneidermann, N. (2014), "'Mic power': 'public' connections through the hip hop nation in Kampala." *Ethnography* 15(1): 88–105.

Seale, C., Charteris-Black, J., MacFarlane, A., and McPherson, A. (2010), "Interviews and Internet forums: a comparison of two sources of qualitative data." *Qualitative Health Research* 20(5): 595–606.

Select Committee on Science and Technology (2002), "What on Earth?: the threat to the science underpinning conservation." London: House of Lords.

Seyfang, G. (2006), "Harnessing the potential of the social economy? time banks and UK public policy." *International Journal of Sociology and Social Policy* 26(9/10): 430–43.

Shah, D. V., McLeod, D. M., Friedland, L., and Nelson, M. R. (2007), "The politics of consumption/the consumption of politics." *The ANNALS of the American Academy of Political and Social Science* 611(1): 6–15.

Silver, D. (2000), "Looking backwards, looking forwards: cyberculture studies, 1990–2000," in D. Gauntlett (ed.), *Web.Studies: Rewiring Media Studies for the Digital Age*. London: Arnold: 19–30.

Silverstone, R. (1994), *Television and Everyday Life*. London: Routledge.

Silverstone, R., Hirsch, E., and Morley, D. (1992), "The moral economy of the household," in R. Silverstone and E. Hirsch (eds), *Consuming Technologies: Media and Information in Domestic Spaces*. London: Routledge: 15–31.

Skeggs, B., Thumin, N., and Wood, H. (2008), "'Oh goodness, I am watching reality TV' How methods make class in audience research." *European Journal of Cultural Studies* 11(1): 5–24.

Skinner, J. (2008), "At the electronic evergreen: a computer-mediated ethnography of tribalism in a newsgroup from Montserrat and afar," in T. L. Adams and S. A. Smith (eds), *Electronic Tribes: The Virtual Worlds of Geeks, Gamers, Shamans, and Scammers*. Austin, TX: University of Texas Press: 124–40.

Snee, H. (2013), "Making ethical decisions in an online context: reflections on using blogs to explore narratives of experience." *Methodological Innovations Online* 8(2): 52–67. http://www.methodologicalinnovations.org.uk/wp-content/uploads/2013/12/4.-Snee.pdf (accessed August 22, 2014).

Sparkes, A. C. (2002) Autoethnography: self-indulgence or something more?" in A. P. Bochner and C. Ellis (eds), *Ethnographically Speaking: Autoethnography, Literature, and Aesthetics*. Walnut Creek, CA: AltaMira: 209–32.

Spencer, J. W. (1994), "Mutual relevance of ethnography and discourse." *Journal of Contemporary Ethnography* 23(3): 267–79.

Spradley, J. P. (1979), *The Ethnographic Interview*. New York: Holt, Rinehart and Winston.

Star, S. L. (1991), "Power, technologies and the phenomenology of standards: on being allergic to onions," in J. Law (ed.), *A Sociology of Monsters? Power, Technology and the Modern World: Sociological Review Monograph No. 38*. Oxford: Basil Blackwell: 27—57.

—(1999), "The ethnography of infrastructure." *American Behavioral Scientist* 43(3): 377–91.

—(2002), "Infrastructure and ethnographic practice: working on the fringes." *Scandinavian Journal of Information Systems* 14(2): 107–22.

Stempfhuber, M. and Liegl, M. (2012), "Grindr: empirical observations on some contemporary mediations of the pick-up-line." Paper presented at the Society for Social Studies of Science annual conference, Copenhagen Business School, Frederiksberg, Denmark.

Sterne, J. (2006), "The historiography of cyberculture," in D. Silver and A. Massanari (eds), *Critical Cyberculture Studies*. New York: New York University Press: 17–28.

Stone, A. R. (1992), "Will the real body please stand up? Boundary stories about virtual cultures," M. Benedikt (ed.), *Cyberspace: First Steps*. Cambridge MA: MIT Press: 81–118.

—(1996), *The War of Desire and Technology at the Close of the Mechanical Age*. Cambridge MA: MIT Press.

Sveinsdottir, T. (2008), "Virtual identity as practice: exploring the relationship between role-players and their characters in the massively multiplayer online game *Star Wars Galaxies*." Doctoral thesis submitted to Department of Sociology, University of Surrey. http://epubs.surrey.ac.uk/2112/1/492978.pdf (accessed August 22, 2014).

Swales, J. M. (1998a), *Other Floors, Other Voices: A Textography of a Small University Building*. Mahwah NJ: Lawrence Erlbaum.

— (1998b), "Textography: toward a contextualization of written academic discourse." *Research on Language & Social Interaction* 31(1): 109–21.

Takhteyev, Y. (2012), *Coding Places: Software Practice in a South American City*. Cambridge MA: MIT Press.

Taylor, T. L. (2003), "Intentional bodies: virtual environments and the designers who shape them." *International Journal of Engineering Education* 19(1): 25–34.

—(2006), *Play Between Worlds: Exploring Online Game Culture*. Cambridge, MA: MIT Press.

Thelwall, M. (2004), *Link Analysis: An Information Science Approach*. Amsterdam: Elsevier Academic Press.

—(2008), "Fk yea I swear: cursing and gender in MySpace." *Corpora* 3(1): 83–107.

—(2009), *Introduction to Webometrics: Quantitative Web Research for the Social Sciences*. San Rafael CA: Morgan and Claypool.

Thelwall, M. and Wilkinson, D. (2004), "Finding similar academic web sites with links, bibliometric couplings and colinks." *Information Processing & Management* 40(3): 515–26.

Traweek, S. (1988), *Beamtimes and Lifetimes: The World of High Energy Physicists*. Cambridge MA: Harvard University Press.

Tsing, A. L. (2005), *Friction: An Ethnography of Global Connection*. Princeton, NJ: Princeton University Press.

Turkle, S. (1995), *Life on the Screen: Identity in the Age of the Internet*. New York: Simon and Schuster.

Turner, B. S. (1991), Review article: "Missing bodies: towards a sociology of embodiment." *Sociology of Health & Illness* 13(2): 265–73.

Underberg, N. and Zorn, E. (2013), *Digital Ethnography: Anthropology, Narrative, and New Media*. Austin: University of Texas Press.

Valdecasas, A. G., Castroviejo, S., and Marcus, L. F (2000), "Reliance on the citation index undermines the study of biodiversity." *Nature* 403(6771): 698.

Voilmy, D., Smoreda Z., and Ziemlicki, C. (2008), "Geolocation and video ethnography: capturing mobile Internet used by a commuter." *Mobilities* 3(2): 201–22.

Voloder, L. (2008), "Autoethnographic challenges: confronting self, field and home." *The Australian Journal of Anthropology* 19(1): 27–40.

Wakeford, N. and Cohen, K. (2008), "Fieldnotes in public: using blogs for research," in N. Fielding, R. M. Lee, and G. Blank (eds), *The SAGE Handbook of Online Research Methods*. London: Sage: 307–26.

Ward, M.-H. (2006), Thoughts on Blogging as an Ethnographic Tool. The 23rd Annual Conference of the Australasian Society for Computers in Learning in Tertiary Education, University of Sydney, Sydney University Press. http://ascilite.org.au/conferences/sydney06/proceeding/pdf_papers/p164.pdf (accessed August 22, 2014).

Webb, E. J., Campbell D. T., Schwartz, R. D., Sechrest, L. and Grove, J. B. (1981), *Nonreactive Measures in the Social Sciences* (2nd edn). Dallas TX: Houghton Mifflin.

Weinberger, D. (2011), *Too Big to Know*. New York: Basic Books.

Wellman, B. (2001), "The rise of networked individualism," in L. Keeble and B. Loader (eds), *Community Informatics*. London: Routledge: 17–42.

Williams, M. (2007), "Avatar watching: participant observation in graphical online environments." *Qualitative Research* 7(1): 5–24.

Woods, P., Boyle, M., Jeffrey, B., and Troman, G. (2000), "A research team in ethnography." *International Journal of Qualitative Studies in Education* 13(1): 85–98.

Wouters, P. and Gerbec, D. (2003), "Interactive Internet? Studying mediated interaction with publicly available search engines." *Journal of Computer-Mediated Communication* 8(4): 0-0. http://onlinelibrary.wiley.com/doi/10.1111/j.1083-6101.2003.tb00221.x/abstract (accessed August 22, 2014).

Ybema, S. and Kamsteeg, F. H. (2009), "Making the familiar strange: a case for disengaged organizational ethnography," in S. Ybema, D. Yanow, H. Vels, and F. H. Kamsteeg (eds), *Organizational Ethnography: Studying the Complexity of Everyday Life*. London: Sage: 101–19.

Ytreberg, E. (2004), "Formatting participation within broadcast media production". *Media Culture & Society* 26(5): 677–92.

Index

Milton Keynes UK
Ingram Content Group UK Ltd.
UKHW031148141024
449569UK00024B/975